Groundwork of Christian Ethics

Groundwork of Christian Ethics

Richard G. Jones

EPWORTH PRESS

ISBN 7162 0399 5
First published 1984
by Epworth Press, Room 195,
1 Central Buildings,
Westminster,
London SW1-9NR
Second impression 1987

Photoset at The Spartan Press Ltd,
Lymington, Hants
and printed in Great Britain by
The Camelot Press Limited, Southampton

Contents

Preface

THIS book has been written to provide an introduction to the study of Christian ethics that will be useful to ministers and theological students, teachers and preachers, and all involved in the leadership of the local church. It takes its place alongside others in a series initially designed for preachers, but also to serve the wider needs of adult Christian education. It does not penetrate far into the field of moral philosophy in general; there are several good introductions which serve that purpose. It is more concerned to outline the work in ethics which the churches have undertaken, based upon the biblical traditions and other resources, and especially to bring that up-to-date with regard to recent work on contemporary issues.

I am particularly grateful to Mrs Isobel Manktelow and Mrs Anita Ingham who have worked hard to type the manuscript, to the Revd Dr John Harrod for invaluable advice, and to my daughter, the Revd Nichola Jones, who prepared the Index. SCM Press Ltd has kindly given permission for an extensive quotation. The biblical text used has been that of the Revised Standard Version.

Norwich   Richard G. Jones
December 1983

Chapter 1

Christian Ethics – The Close Scrutiny of Christian Behaviour

ETHICS is the study of how we ought to behave in big and small matters. Moral philosophy is the study of the various mental systems and frameworks underlying our understandings of ethics. This means that in practice there is precious little difference between the two terms – ethics and moral philosophy –and that they are virtually interchangeable. In the past, moral philosophy was the most honoured term, and when discussed within Christianity in general it was called 'moral theology'. This term has slowly been slipping out of use nowadays. There are hardly any modern textbooks on the subject. 'Christian ethics' is the favoured term. It is regarded as a study which is of immense practical and immediate use, especially since modern living seems to throw up more and more difficult moral problems.

Everybody lives by some sort of moral code or system, some set of principles or values or rules which enable decisions to be taken and aims pursued. Many of these principles, values and rules are so deeply engrained in us, or patterned into our personality structures, that we are unaware of them. Only occasionally do we bring them up into our minds for reflection, usually when we are deeply worried or under criticism. Otherwise they remain in our sub-conscious.

Sometimes Christians talk as if they alone have such a moral system or code, and can be heard saying things like 'Of course, we all know that Communists have no morals.' That is both arrogant and false. Communists have a very clear moral system; they have to, otherwise they, like everyone else, would have to stop making even the most trivial decisions about life – they would have to stop living. In many important ways their ethics overlap with those of most Christians; in some other important matters there are sharp differences. The question whether or not their system is better than that by which most Christians live depends, of course, upon what we regard as most important for any ethical system, and that depends upon our basic attitudes towards life, upon our faith.

One can notice these differences in ethical systems not only between believers in different faiths, such as Christians in contrast to Hindus or Moslems, but also between those who adhere to different ideologies, such as Christians in contrast to communists or fascists. Further, there are obvious differences between Christians of different traditions. One can also notice contrasts between members of different sub-cultures, even in a deeply Christianized society like that of modern England. For example, a pleasant and alert young man, brought up in a typical English middle-class Christian home, trained to become a Probation Officer. Early in his course he was obliged to listen very attentively to young prisoners. He thought that they had 'no ethics' because they had no time for many authority figures, for telling the truth, for values like self-sufficiency, self-discipline or respect for others' property. He was disgusted. He was told to listen more carefully, and then began to discover a different sort of moral code from that with which he had been brought up. This laid much more stress on group loyalty, on not letting your mates down, with a strong streak of generosity within it. He began to revise his initial judgments. The prisoners were not 'immoral'. Instead, here was a different set of values, some being more healthy than those of his own which he had uncritically assumed all his life.

Not only is ethics the study of everyday behaviour, and so a study to which everyone can supply many of the necessary items out of normal experience; it is intensely interesting. The most profound discussions that most people have, and some of the most earnest arguments, are about ethics, about right and wrong behaviour and attitudes. Consider an imaginary scene one evening when a Christian family shares a meal together. Mother works as a nurse, father as a senior clerk in local government, the son has just completed an apprenticeship in an engineering trade, the daughter is training to be a secretary.

The father looks tired and slightly harrassed. He explains that he has been caught up in lengthy negotiations for his union with a committee representing the management. They have told him that if he presses for better pay and conditions they will be obliged to sack some of the workers. Father says glumly that whatever he does, it can't possibly be right. As a Christian, he can't go on with the claims and yet, as a Christian, he believes that they are just and should be pressed. His daughter says that he must make it a matter of prayer and God will give him the assurance that what he does is right. The mother says it isn't as easy as that, since God doesn't often give any sort of assurance either way and you have to live with uncertainty. The son says that, as far as he can see, everyone engaged in modern industry or organizations is always having to compromise some principle or other. He is. He has found that he often tells white lies to the boss or the foreman, so as to show solidarity with his mates. His sister is appalled. No Christian can ever compromise God's will, she says. He replies that their father should 'play the power game as it is', without too many scruples.

Then mother remarks that she nearly made a major compromise today. She was asked to help in the theatre where some abortion operations were taking place. It was the first time that had happened. She demurred, and someone else did it, but she knows that she will be asked again. What should she do? Her daughter says that the Bible will tell her, but the father says that there is no such help in the Bible over that problem, or over his problem. Her son says that she should be willing to help, since otherwise she will only be pushing a nasty job over on to other people. Father says she should be guided by her conscience. Mother seems unhappy, saying that it is almost the same as murder, since she would be helping to take away a human life. Son protests; it is not a 'human life', but a bundle of tissues. Daughter gets very cross at this, saying that it is a 'human soul'.

Mother says she simply can't square abortion with Christ. He wouldn't do that operation. Daughter asks father what the church teaches about it, but he is not quite sure. He knows that the Roman Catholics oppose it, but imagines that most Protestants don't. Son says that in that case the Bible and church aren't much use to us. He says, for example, that he has never yet heard a helpful sermon on the issues of nuclear war and our country possessing the nuclear deterrent. In his view it is the biggest moral question of our time. Mother doesn't quite agree. She thinks that every problem boils down to doing the most loving thing. Daughter sides with her, and says that there is lots about love in the Bible and in many church services. Father is not sure. How, he says, does that help him with his problem at work? How

can he expect the clerks to be all-loving towards the management, or the management towards them? Son echoes those
doubts. He can't see how Britain can be expected to be 'loving'
towards Russia, or Russia towards Britain. He doesn't think it is
a matter of love at all, but of courage, firmness and honesty.
Father says we need a strong world government.

The conversation goes on. Nobody seems satisfied, and they
cannot wholly agree about anything. When father tries to finish
it all by saying, 'Well, I suppose we must just follow our
consciences,' the others say that that isn't enough. Mother
openly wonders whether her conscience is always 'pure and good
enough to do its job'. Son says that one's motives are what
matter, they should be 'pure', but in any case we should use our
common sense and our wits. Daughter says that we all need a
much better set of everyday rules, clearly taught us by the church
and based upon the Bible. The real problem is that this is a
permissive age which won't help people to listen to God's word.
But father shakes his head. He is convinced that that is precisely
what the Bible does not offer, and anyway, the Bible writers
knew nothing about many of the problems which so bother us
today. Son agrees there. He says that he thinks that you get the
most help, in the end, from being in a family that will talk
honestly through problems. Mother adds, somewhat wistfully,
how she wishes they could live real Christian lives in a real
Christian community, something like an extension of their own
family. The daughter nods vigorously. There the discussion
ends.

Some current debates

The imaginary discussion above introduces a large number of
the problems encountered today in trying to sort out the nature
of Christian ethics. Many of these problems are present in other
ethical systems as well, but for the moment let us concentrate on
the ethics of Christians. There is the problem of the obvious
disagreements between the four people on the manner in which
one does Christian ethics – or, put in another way, on the nature
of Christian ethics, the sort of expectations one should have,
methods one should utilize, and terms that should be employed.
The differences are not necessarily a weakness. Today there is a
wide range of disagreement within most congregations on how
to practise theology, leading to similar disagreements about the

actual content of Christian belief. It is inevitable, then, that there will be disagreements about ethics, which is the application of our theology to practical living. This is not inherently a weakness, but a sign of the considerable range of beliefs and approaches that one can expect to encounter within any group of Christians. It is a sign that Christians do not live closed up within a strait-jacket of belief imposed by authority. If, however, it leads to such confusion that nobody knows even loosely what most Christians actually or officially believe, so that no common judgments can be made and no teaching offered within the Christian community, then of course Christian ethics has become a chaos and a grave source of weakness in the Christian witness. It is the basic conviction of this book that that is not the case today, that there is sufficient cohesion about our theology and ethics to provide adequate guidance to Christians, and that Christian ethics is in a fairly healthy condition. We shall note, however, those writers and bodies of Christian opinion that disagree with this general attitude, sometimes sharply.

Reverting to the imaginary family conversation, there is a straightforward problem about 'the right'. The father says that in his situation it is impossible. One gets the feeling that this is because he assumes that the 'right' course must always be one that can plainly be identified with a moral principle like 'justice' (e.g. in a wage demand). Or a generally accepted 'good thing' like maximum numbers being employed. If there is an inevitable conflict between such concepts he suspects that he cannot possibly do 'the right'. Should he assume that? If, for example, Christians see 'the right' as another way of talking about the will of God for us, should we always assume that it is bound to be plainly related to a simple, clear-cut moral principle? In many complex situations this would appear to be extremely naive.

That leads us on to the issue of compromise. It has usually been assumed within Christian circles that compromise is generally a bad thing. But there are two quite different types of action being considered here. First, there is that sort of compromise in which a person knows what is right to do, but has not the courage to do it because it would involve unpopularity, or sacrifice, or some other undesirable personal outcome. That is the compromise of moral weakness. Second, there is the compromise of some one moral principle (e.g. justice in wage levels, as in the case above) because several other equally valid moral principles are also involved. In such complex situations some sort of compromise is essential or no decision could be taken at all. The first sort of compromise is deplorable, the second is inevitable and has to be made clearly and bravely.

Consider these two examples. A person makes a verbal promise to lend a friend £200 to buy a car. Then another way of utilizing that spare £200 arises. It is spent, let us say, on new clothes. The friend buys the new car, asks for the money, and is then told that the obligation doesn't really exist, that it was only a vague promise, that it wasn't seriously meant. The intending borrower has every right to feel let down by someone who hadn't the moral integrity to keep an obligation. The first person has become 'compromised'.

Now consider a famous incident that roused much debate at the time. The Chancellor of the Exchequer in the late 1940s was a deeply sincere person who made no secret whatever of his Christian commitments, Sir Stafford Cripps. He was widely respected both in this country and abroad. The British economy was in an extremely difficult condition in the aftermath of war, and many observers suspected that the Chancellor would be obliged to devalue the pound. Sir Stafford Cripps was repeatedly asked if he was going to do so. He adamantly insisted that he was not. Then, suddenly and without warning, he did. His detractors immediately accused him of lying. He replied that if he had given previous notice of his intention there would have been a wholesale scramble on the world's financial markets to sell pounds, and that it would have led to a severe loss of British money. He claimed that he had spoken as he did because he had a first loyalty to protect the economy and that that was what he was appointed to do in office as Chancellor. He had, then, had to compromise between honesty in public utterance and loyalty to the economy. Who is in a position to say that, as a Christian, he was wrong? Politics and public life are especially areas within which such 'compromise' is quite inevitable. Perhaps, in the end, only God could decree whether or not Sir Stafford was justified; it behoves other Christians to avoid judgment, especially those who have never been Chancellors of the Exchequer.

Other terms cropped up in that sample discussion, and caused trouble. 'Soul', for example. What does it mean? It is rarely used in everyday conversation nowadays, rarely used in the Bible and very difficult to define. How can one declaim that a foetus or embryo has a 'soul' if one does not quite know what such a word refers to? Or the word 'conscience'. That is much more common and has a long history of Christian usage behind it. The father at one point said that one had to follow it, as if that solved our problems, but the mother wasn't sure that hers was good enough. In Christian history the term has had a range of meanings, so that sometimes it has meant the after-effects of reflecting on something wrong ('I have a conscience about that act of mine yesterday'), but sometimes it has meant the faculty of moral discernment. In the former usage a 'bad conscience' would be the later regret felt about a moral misdemeanour, in the latter usage it would mean an inadequacy in being able to make moral judgments. Here we should note in passing that there has been a tendency for Catholics to stress the competence of conscience, and for Protestants to stress its inherent sinfulness along with every other aspect of our human make-up. To make matters more complicated some psychologists (e.g. Freud) use the term to describe the repressed super-ego, or the way in which society's expectations smother our deep desires and act as an inbuilt moral watchdog, always keeping us under review. The term hardly appears in the Bible, except in connection with the 'wrath of God' which is also a difficult concept. We shall look again at this term in a later chapter.

The term 'motive' cropped up. Is it true that every act can be assessed by the motive or motives of the actor or actors? Supposing that an ambulance driver careers at break-neck speed through a busy street with the motive of rushing to a seriously ill patient, and in doing so knocks someone over. Does his laudable motive excuse his actions? Suppose someone withholds a painful truth from someone else with the laudable motive of not causing them great pain, does that in itself justify the lack of truth? Or, putting another problem, does an otherwise good act become morally bad because it was done with a bad or defective motive? Someone might give a large sum of money to the poor with the motive of avoiding tax, or of satisfying a nagging doubt about the activities that earned them the money in the first place, or desiring to appear honourable to others, or indeed to placate God. Do such motives render the giver immoral or blameworthy? Again, if motive is what renders an act morally acceptable or unacceptable, are we ever likely to be clear about what our motives are? According to the psychologists much of our motivation takes place in the sub-conscious, where we cannot have ready access to it. According to many theologians we must always beware of the infinite capacity of the human self to deceive itself. So we will never get a realistic view of our own motivations. 'Motives' are thus very tricky to assess.

Importantly, there is a deep difference about the nature of moral judgments. The daughter believes that they must be determined by a series of rules which the Bible provides, or of which one can become aware by some profound insight granted by God. The others, on the whole, disagree. The mother wonders whether somehow 'love' is the key here. In all these matters, do the most 'loving' thing. The two men are not persuaded by that notion at all, and tend to suggest that such talk is inappropriate for some areas of moral decision-making (e.g. weapon deployment between Russia and Britain). At this point the discussion was verging on a debate which has waged hotly during the late 1960s and the 1970s. It has been dubbed 'the situation-ethic debate'. It erupted in 1963 after an American ethicist named Joseph Fletcher wrote a book entitled *Situation Ethics*[1] in which he asserted that nothing else is 'good' except 'love' and that this means willing the neighbour's good whether we like the neighbour or not, and using our reason to calculate out in every situation what that 'good' will be. He deliberately repudiated every attempt by Christians to live by moral rules, or codes, or laws. In this country John Robinson appeared to argue on the same lines.[2] The dust of the controversies over this has not yet quite subsided, as we shall see, but it has left many Christians with the vague feeling that morality is mainly a matter of being 'loving'.

There are important differences about the value of the Bible in helping Christians, and when the question is asked about the church's teaching on a vital contemporary issue (abortion), nobody is quite sure what it is. The son thinks that that is because the preaching in the churches has been too irrelevant to the crucial moral problems of today. But the prior problem is that of the Bible. Does it offer us clear rules for all time, or not?

There is the suspicion that we are living in a 'permissive' age, and that therefore moral standards are sliding. The word 'permissive' is one which moral philosophers avoid. It is too vague for an adequate moral discussion. After all, most Christians have always held that there are many moral matters which can never be covered fully by rules or laws and that therefore the believer is 'permitted' to evaluate for himself. However, the term has been popularly used to denote a more open and flexible attitude towards sexual morality, a matter on which Christians ought to be profoundly concerned. It will be more fully discussed later. For the moment we should be aware that underlying the scathing references to the permissive society there often lurks the conviction that modern society is somehow much more 'immoral' than that of Edwardian or Victorian times. It would be more accurate and helpful to start with the assumption that moral values are always subtly changing as society changes, and as the patterns of living change. Changes are not necessarily for the worse, or the better. They usually introduce new opportunities both for the good and the bad, involving both moral gain and loss.

Several attempts have been made recently to produce a sketch-map of the different sorts of Christian ethics, showing which thinkers or traditions or denominations take up the various positions and which considerations they stress. None of these efforts to put our different styles and forms of doing ethics into some neat 'positions' or pigeon-holes has been entirely successful, but an American writer – Edward LeRoy Long, Jr – has suggested a fairly simple system of understanding this complex and often muddled matter. In a book called *A Survey of Christian Ethics*,[3] he tried to sort out the various ethical approaches into two sets of three possible alternatives. To that sketch-map we now turn.

A sketch-map of Christian approaches

LeRoy Long makes much use of the word 'motif', which seems to be a shorthand term for the dominant theme or notion. Then he makes a basic distinction between the standards, or goals, or norms, or objectives which we aim to fulfil or meet or attain in our ethics, and then the ways in which we go about the necessary decisions and justify one method of effecting one desired objective rather than another. It is the same distinction that exists between means and ends. If a young person is determined to meet suitable persons of the opposite sex, the 'end' could be that of seeking a marriage partner as quickly as possible, or of appearing to be as normal a young person as possible, or of pleasing the parents, or of living up to the general expectations of the peer group, or sexual satisfaction, or escape from a miserable loneliness, or curiosity about the other sex, or a combination of several of these. The 'means' could be going to lots of local dances and discos, putting an advert in a young persons' magazine, hanging about in coffee bars to talk to others, ingratiating oneself with any other group with which one is in contact, taking up all sorts of interests by joining all sorts of clubs, or several of these. But both the 'ends' and 'means' are subject to ethical evaluation. Some will be presumed 'better' than others.

In the first grouping, when considering ends, Long suggests that Christians tend to emphasize either the deliberative, or the prescriptive, or the relational motif. The first of these is one in which reason is especially stressed, which will usually mean that the end is one which will be readily acceptable to one of the dominant schools of philosophy. It may mean that a widely-accepted general idea of the 'good' becomes used as the principal motif likewise in the Christian framework of under-standing. Thus, if a general notion of 'justice' becomes widely acceptable in contemporary life, Christians might also find themselves claiming that this is the end which they too must seek, and might also be found justifying this by extensive references to the Bible and the Christian tradition. This may be linked with a clear understanding of a 'natural law' which runs right through all human communities and to which every human being knowingly owes allegiance.

In the Christian tradition this position was most fully and powerfully developed by Thomas Aquinas in the thirteenth century. He made extensive use of the classical Greek moral philosophy of Aristotle and believed that it had a great deal of common ground with Christian thought, but that the latter supplemented it by virtue of the revelation given to Christians. Thus Thomas regarded it as self-evident that every person in a right mind will feel an obligation to preserve the self, for example, or will accept the command 'Do not cause injury to others' as obligatory, whether or not the person is a Christian. The Thomist position has been completely dominant within Roman Catholicism until recently, so that Catholic ethics could legitimately be labelled 'deliberative'.

Many other ethicists have stressed the role of reason, and have often done so in order to stress the amount of common ground between Christians and others and thus to ensure that Christians can readily side with others in the pursuit of desirable objectives (e.g. as is done in such diverse bodies as Alcoholics Anonymous, Amnesty International or Friends of the Earth). Long cites several Protestant writers utilizing this motif, including Paul

Tillich, Paul Ramsey and Reinhold Niebuhr. In the family discussion, the son appeals most clearly to 'common sense', using one's wits.

The second, the prescriptive, is that in which it is presumed that the end is prescribed for us by God. It is set out for us in the Bible, or the teaching of the church, and so the responsible Christian becomes someone who tries hard to discover the whole range of these commands, and then to keep them. The Christian life is primarily a matter of learning the rules, laws, command-ments, and then of obedience. Again and again there have been movements within Christianity to emphasize this motif. Amongst Protestants it has been most obvious when appeal is made to the moral teaching in the Bible which is to be obeyed because it is God's direct word, and amongst Catholics when appeal is made to the magisterium, the teaching office of the church, and the believer has been expected to obey because 'the church says so'. Especially has this motif been welcomed when the times appeared to be most bewildering, general moral standards to be in flux, or many urgent issues to be incredibly complex. Inevitably then we want to have some clear and authoritative guidance from somewhere, since ethical judg-ments seem to be so intensely difficult. It is of course another matter whether or not the Bible is constructed to provide that sort of guidance, or whether the church is so ordered that it can do so; judgments on those basic issues lie, strictly speaking, outside the scope of this book but, as we shall see, we keep returning to them.

Especially when the prescriptive motif is dominant, Christians become involved in the practice known technically as casuistry. In general use this has acquired a somewhat sinister flavour, but it is a neutral term to describe a process with which all Christians are familiar, the application of a general command to more specific circumstances. Thus, there is a command that one should keep the Sabbath holy, but in itself it does not define what is holy and what is not, nor does it say what cannot be done on Sunday. When one applies the general command to the specific issues of Christians living in place A and deduces that it means that one should go to church twice, not purchase anything from the local shops, and only do such essential work as will provide basic needs in the home and for the animals, one is engaging in casuistry. Thus if Christian ethics is in any sense a matter of seeking ends which have been prescribed for us by God, casuistry must be practised or we cannot translate these ends into our immediate situations.

In the family discussion the daughter obviously favoured this motif. She wanted clear and direct instruction from the Bible and, perhaps, the church. She wanted right conduct to be *prescribed* for her (the word means, literally, 'previously written').

The third motif, the relational, is that in which the Christian sees the end as in some fitting response to an encounter with its source, that is, to God. One must lead a life of overwhelming gratitude to, or excitement at, God's gracious coming to us in Christ. Or the Christian may be completely fascinated with Jesus. Long has no difficulty in referring to many eminent theologians who write like this (Augustine, Luther, Barth, Bultmann, Lehmann, and so on). He has no difficulty either in pointing out how the biblical traditions often present ethics as a matter of glad response to what God has done, or promised, or instigated. When this motif is dominant one will hear much more about the Christian's freedom than about the commands or laws by which Christian life is determined. Initiative, discovery, allegiance to Christ, the experience of grace, these are the notes which tend to dominate, rather than faithfulness, obedience, resolution, as with those who are dominated by the prescriptive. One tends also to hear a little bit more about the worried conscience from the previous group, a little bit more about devotion to Christ and waiting upon his will from the latter. In the family discussion, one hears echoes of this in the mother's remarks.

In the second grouping, Long suggests that Christians tend, when considering means, to be using a motif which is mainly institutional, or operational, or intentional. The institutional motif is dominant when Christians stress the need to control power, to support firm and strong social structures like the state, its laws, the family, the principles by which family life should be conducted, and in which these 'orders' are seen as being created by God. These social forms may be called orders, or mandates, and be invested with deep respect; those who serve in leading positions are given extra respect, with a stress on their special roles and the way in which they must act perhaps differently in their role than they would in personal life. The example already cited of Sir Stafford Cripps would appeal especially to Christians who see the strong ordering of social life as the primary means for effecting God's will in this fallen world. They would also stress the wildness and viciousness of human sin, and the need for human society to build protective dykes and walls to control it and prevent too much harm being done by its dreadful ever-present vitality.

Traditionally, many of the greatest Christian thinkers have appeared to be using the institutional motif. The great Augustine of Hippo, the first major Christian thinker to attempt to construct an over-all understanding of the place of the Christian within the world of competing nations, traumatic historical developments, war, trade and rebellion, was clearly thinking in these terms. Much Roman Catholic theology and ethics has followed suit, through Thomas Aquinas and up to Pope John XXIII. But so too has Protestant theology, and Luther and Calvin both express this motif powerfully. Luther's doctrine of 'the two kingdoms' (to be discussed later) is a classic instance. Coming to this century, some of the most persuasive Christians have undoubtedly shared this attitude, as can be seen in Karl Barth and Dietrich Bonhoeffer (who coined the term 'mandates') and, in this country, in the teaching of William Temple (the first avowed Socialist ever to become Archbishop of Canterbury). A version of it is also noticeable in the movement that was known as the 'social gospel'.

Those adopting this motif have been regularly and sometimes violently criticized for being essentially conservative. They seem to want to keep the existing social order intact, for fear that if it is in any way dismantled then human sin will make the next state worse than the first. They dread anarchy; they prefer even an unjust order to a feeble one, since in feeble structures sin has a special chance to play havoc and get its own way and hurt other human beings. If they are members of an established church they will often defend the collusion between church and state on grounds that reflect this motif. They often overstate what social order can achieve for the welfare of human beings. In the family discussion this sometimes appeared in the father's comments. He pined for a world government and presumably believed that this would solve many problems. But would it?

The operational motif is dominant when Christians are much more aware of where power and influence rest, and are mainly concerned to see that they are able to be involved in exercising it. If they are, they believe that it will then be channelled into better acts and better ends. We should always be attempting to create a 'sea of influence' over a whole range of matters, and to be seen to be bringing that influence to bear upon those who are in positions of power. This means using all the normal means whereby power is exercised within the human community, from pressure groups and campaigns to the formation of political parties or the committing of an established party to the position being advocated. Here again there are elements in Augustine's thought which sound as if he advocated this motif. The most persuasive Christian voice in recent times has been Reinhold Niebuhr, who seemed to see it almost as his life's work to make Christians aware of the way power actually works in our human societies, how it can be influenced, and how all human powers need to be held in check by other human powers, otherwise they will become demonic.

This motif is also apparent in many Christians who would not share Niebuhr's profound sense of the sinfulness and tragic element within all human nature, and the way in which all human communities and societies are structured to promote the self-interest of the group concerned. Many more theologically conservative thinkers may tend to this motif, as do those who advocate non-violence as an effective social strategy to produce a more just society. Thus Martin Luther King is to be included, together with many Christians very active in a considerable range of current campaigns and causes. In the family discussion, the son's remark that 'one should play the power game as it is without too many scruples' aligns him with this position.

Finally, the intentional motif is dominant in those Christians who see their task as primarily the establishment of a small group, or society, in which the gospel obligations and style of life can be practised almost completely, despite the surrounding sea of sin and compromise which characterizes the world at large. This motif is obvious in the case of monasticism and the attempt of monks and nuns to withdraw from the largely wicked world and live in peace and prayer together. It is equally obvious in the case of the holiness sect teaching its members to be indifferent to the world and to concentrate upon the internal life of the sect in which sanctification may be experienced.

But it has always been present in most periods of Christian history and most Christian traditions. It may not have embraced the rigours of some forms of monasticism, or a total withdrawal from the world, but it will always have stressed the contrast between the Christian way of life and that in the community as a whole. It will have wanted to emphasize the distinctiveness of the Christian way. Even if Christians have to be normálly involved in worldly affairs, nevertheless there must be a small group or circle to which they can withdraw in which 'real' Christian living, sharing and supporting takes place. John Wesley's class meetings, and the modern proliferation of cell groups, small communities, retreat houses, house churches, are all signs of this motif. In the family discussion the last wistful remarks of the mother and daughter could reflect this motif.

LeRoy Long does not claim that his sketch-map is perfect. Sometimes the distinctions between one motif and another seem somewhat artificial; sometimes it is difficult to say whether or not a particular group or thinker belongs to one or the other or maybe to two (as with Augustine). Nevertheless his distinctions are useful in giving us one fairly simple way of charting the very different styles, methods and objectives which one encounters in Christian ethics. The three motifs found in the pursuit of ends – the deliberative, prescriptive and relational – and the three noticed in the choices of means – the institutional, operational and intentional – will be noticed again and again in the course of the outlines with which this book is concerned.

Questions for Discussion

(a) What moral decisions do you think that you have had to make recently? As an individual? Within the family? Within the group you work with? Which were the most difficult? Why?

(b) What advantages or disadvantages might there be if Christians were expected to agree on the decisions taken on such moral issues?

Chapter 2

Ethics in the Bible

The Old Testament

IN many a parish church or village chapel one can still see tablets on which important elements in Christian teaching are inscribed. These will often feature the Lord's Prayer, the Beatitudes, the Creed, or the Ten Commandments. The last one is the most common, reflecting the widespread notion that the highest point of the ethical teaching in the Old Testament is to be found in the Ten Commandments (or 'Decalogue', meaning 'ten words'), and that this is the most permanent element there, which ought therefore to be widely taught in modern society.

There are many problems with this notion. The first and obvious one is that the Decalogue is hardly ever referred to in the Old Testament itself, with the possible exception of Jer. 7.9, where five of the ten laws may be cited. It is hardly ever referred to in the New Testament either, with the possible exception of Mark 10.19, where six commandments are cited (but reduced to five in the parallel passage in Luke 18.20, and reported as a slightly different six in Matt. 19.18–19). Moreover it is largely negative, telling us what we must *not* do and giving few hints as to what right conduct involves. Further, it stresses conduct, and only one commandment refers to motivation, namely, the last (you shall not covet).

We must begin a glance at the Old Testament ethical traditions by noting, then, that the Decalogue should not be assumed to be the major teaching there. The most important feature of the Old Testament witness may be that which is quietly assumed throughout, that God, Yahweh, the God of Abraham and Isaac and Jacob, is in himself the source of all that is right. What is morally good is what is willed by him. He steadily reveals this to us, for he is a revealing God who does not hide his will in inscrutable darkness, but makes it plain to us. He is a God who 'speaks', and who guides man by his 'word'. Nowhere are these tremendous assumptions argued about; there is no moral philosophy to assess these claims and to investigate their cogency. The Old Testament writers present their witness to them, not their philosophical defences of them. There is a 'take it or leave it' feel about that witness. Or, expressed more accurately, there is a flavour of, 'This is good and right, because God says so. Live it out for yourself. Taste and see.'

There are three broad strands of tradition suggesting how this 'word' can be determined. The three correspond roughly to the three components into which the Jews divided the Old Testament literature: the Law, the Prophets and the Writings.

1. The Law

One very noticeable strand of Old Testament tradition asserts that God reveals his will through *torah* (law), through clear and unambiguous commandments. The life of the good man is one in which he both learns what the commands are, and then obeys them. Morality is a matter of listening (or learning) and obedience. There are probably six different sets of such commandments to be discerned in the literature, coming from different periods in Israel's life. Scholars differ slightly in their assessment of these six sets, and of precisely what constituted them. They are:

1. The 'Ritual Decalogue'
2. The Decalogue
3. The book of the Covenant
4. Deuteronomy
5. The Law of Holiness
6. The 'Priestly Code'

The so-called 'Ritual Decalogue' is in Ex. 34.14–28. It consists of twelve laws in all, almost all of them relating to the ways in which Israel's worship should be conducted. One of them is decidedly quaint (do not seethe a kid in its mother's milk); none of them describes conduct between one human being and another; all of them appear to reflect a primitive agricultural community. Some scholars hold that this is the earliest known pattern of law, and may derive from the life of the Kenite tribes who lived in areas south of Jerusalem long before the sojourn in

Egypt and the times of Moses. Others place it later, during the early period of the settlement in Canaan, and wonder whether Deut. 27.15–26 may not represent the earliest laws (the 'Shechemite covenant') or whether Lev. 19.13–18 may go back equally far into early Israelite history.

The Decalogue is in two slightly different versions, Ex. 20 and Deut. 5. It has some similarities with the ancient codes in other nations, especially with the Code of Hammurabi from Babylon.[1] The outstanding difference is that no other national code presented itself as a bond of obligation which had been revealed by God (or the gods). In Israel, the Decalogue was revealed to Moses on Mount Sinai in a decisive act of God; its authority lay in its origin in God's will. The codes of the other nations were more in the mould of civil law, that which the nation deemed best for the general ordering of its social life.

The Decalogue is regarded as being in two parts, known as the first and second 'tables'. The first, which consists of four commands, determines man's direct obligations to God in worship. The second, consisting of six commands, determines man's social obligations. As noted above, the second table is mainly negative. This, incidentally, may partly explain its appeal for us right up to the present day, since there is a streak in all of us which would like God's commands to us to be mainly negative, since these are much easier to keep than positive ones.

The Book of the Covenant, Ex. 20.22–23.33, appears at first sight to be an elaboration of the Decalogue, but most scholars regard it as a later code reflecting the needs of a people who practise agriculture in a settled community, and have encountered all the problems that arise with widespread slavery as well as with foreigners living amongst them. It is detailed; it has a noticeable element of harshness and includes the 'law of retribution' or *lex talionis* whereby one must repay life for life, eye for eye (Ex. 21.23–25); it insists on the land lying fallow in the seventh year; it includes a few references to the practice of the cult, but is not dominated by ritual concerns.

The fourth set of codes, the Deuteronomic, is very much more elaborate and includes many new features. The word Deuteronomy means, strictly, the 'second law'. It is usually held that this corpus of laws was prepared as a result of the teaching of the great eighth-century prophets, was then hidden in the Temple, and was discovered in 621 BC during the reign of Josiah, as described in II Kings 22. This led to the major reforms which

Josiah carried out, described in the following chapter. Von Rad comments, 'Never again did Israel express herself so comprehensively and in such detail as to the meaning of the commandments and the unique situation into which Yahweh's revelation of his will put her.'[2]

Deuteronomy claims that the 'whole law' is provided here (see 5.31). There is a constant appeal to Israel's gratitude for her calling under God, an appeal to the heart (see 6.4–9 or 30.6, 11–14). There is a shuddering sense of horror about worshipping other gods and great stress upon the one God of Israel (see 10.17 or 12.29–31). There is a new humanitarian flavour and a strong commitment to the poor (see 10.18, 19; 16.18–20; 23.15, 16; 24.10–13), although the *lex talionis* is still cited at 19.21. The code is set within a doctrine of history, in which it is claimed that when one obeys God one experiences 'blessing' and when one disobeys one encounters 'curse' (see 11.26–28, or chs. 28–30).

The fifth set, the Law of Holiness, is found in Lev. 17.26. It probably comes from the sixth century BC and aims to be another reforming code, but not as comprehensive as Deuteronomy. There is constant stress upon 'holiness', the basic phrase 'I am Yahweh', and the whole land as being polluted by sin. Much of it is taken up with cultic matters, but it also includes the highly significant command 'You shall love your neighbour as yourself' (19.18).

The final set, the 'Priestly Code', embraces the earlier section of Leviticus together with the law of holiness and some passages in Exodus and Numbers. It is reckoned to be the 'Book of the Law' which was the basis upon which the new community was to be established after the return from exile and the renewal under Ezra and Nehemiah, as described in Neh. 8.

2. The Prophets

From the early days of the settlement in the Promised Land the Israelite tribes were bound together by a loose confederacy in which the worship of Yahweh united them in a covenant brotherhood. Yahweh had established that covenant with them all, as described in the story of the founding father, Abraham, in passages like Gen. 12.1–9, 15, 17. Nobody was able to stand above the covenant obligations as if he were exempt from them, not even a king. Nobody was so low as to be unable to qualify for inclusion within the brotherhood, not even the most poor, or the *ger* (stranger). Responsibility was shared corporately, and there was less sense of individual than of common guilt; hence the sin of Achan affected his whole tribe (see Josh. 6 and 7); David's sin in calling for a census affected everyone (see II Sam. 24); the sin of King Manasseh brought the whole people into guilt (see II Kings 21.10–15).

The 'prophet' appeared as a man called by God to recall everyone to the obligations of the covenant bond with Yahweh. He rebuked the king if necessary, as with Nathan and David (in II Sam. 12), or Elijah and Ahab (I Kings 21). His irresistible sense of his calling was the driving force in his work, but all his awareness of God was vivid. This meant that new and powerful words began to be minted by the prophets, words to express the nature of Yahweh and his giving of himself to man. Four of these words dominated the prophetic messages – *qodesh* (holiness, meaning God's separateness from man together with his utter abhorrence of all sin), *tsedeq* (righteousness, meaning God's inherent straightness and rectitude), *mishpat* (justice, or the exercise of straightness between men), and *chesed* (covenant-love, steadfastness of mercy).[3] For the prophet, what is right is that which is derived from Yahweh's nature and is consistent with his covenant character.

This meant that often the prophet appeared to be opposed to the cult and denounced the callous religiosity that it seemed all too often to produce amongst the wealthy. Passages such as Isa. 1.1–17 or Amos 5.21–24 express the outrage felt at hypocritical religious observances. 'Let *mishpat* roll down like waters, and *tsedeq* like a mighty stream' (Amos 5.24). Israel was guilty not so much of ignorance as to what God wanted, but flagrant rebellion, so again and again she is bidden to *shub* (repent), and turn completely around. Again and again the practices of the people showed how far she was from knowing Yahweh, especially when the poor were seen to be down-trodden.

This inevitably meant that there was often a sharp tension between the teaching of the priests, in which right conduct is that which keeps the whole law (embracing social and ritual obligations enmeshed with each other), and that of the prophets in which the concept of law is often hidden beneath more powerful concepts relating to Yahweh's nature.[4] It meant, too, that the most constant questioning about the nature of morality was that which was promoted by the work and experience of the prophets. It was the prophets who asked questions about moral responsibility. Ought the individual to be solely responsible for individual sin, or ought the onus to be shared with the tribe or group or community? Ought morality to be demanded, or called forth from man out of a spirit of gratitude to Yahweh? Was the sense of covenant-people a snare and delusion, encouraging God's people to a smug self-satisfaction that they would be all right in the end whatever else happened in the world? Must we expect it to be profitable to obey God? In passages such as Ezek. 18; Hos. 11.1–4; Amos 5.18–20; Isa. 53, one senses an intense wrestling with those deep moral questions.

But such questions forced the prophets into even more thorough-going wrestling about morality. If God is sole God, Lord of the whole earth, is there then a moral answerability running right through all life and embracing all peoples, including those who do not know Yahweh? Isaiah 10 shows a response being hammered out. Is it ever possible for sinful man to become righteous and fulfil Yahweh's commands? Passages like Jer. 13.23 or Ezek. 20 show the question cropping up, and lead to the growing conviction that Yahweh must change man's heart if ever man is to be righteous (hence Jer. 31.31; Isa. 55; Ezek. 36.25–27). This would have to be a radically new act by Yahweh.

Undoubtedly the book of Deuteronomy showed how deeply the work of the prophets influenced the concept of law, yet the later prophets began to repudiate law as a way of determining right conduct. They hinted that morality was in essence much simpler, as in the famous summary: 'He has showed you, O man, what is good; and what does the Lord require of you but to do *mishpat*, and to love *chesed*, and to walk humbly with your God?' (Micah 6.8).

3. The Writings

The third strand in the Old Testament appears to have a quite different style, and to use a different vocabulary. 'Wisdom' is the supreme good and the key to the moral life. 'Happy is the man who finds wisdom' (Prov. 3.13) for, as that passage goes on to elaborate, this results in long life, 'pleasantness' and peace. What more could one want? With this writing there is little reference to the nature of God and what he wills from man, so that one gets the impression that the writers could almost have been moulded by some other tradition than that of Israel, provided that it were monotheistic. To be sure, 'the fear of the

Lord is the beginning of wisdom' (Prov. 1.7), but the wisdom being extolled is really a shrewdness about life in this sort of world, and a respect for the teaching of one's elders. There is much about everyday life and the contrast between the fool and the wise, little about holiness and obedience to God. Here folly is denounced, rather than sin. Yet this writing does represent a major intellectual achievement, for there is a highly developed sense of the order in life.

In the book of Ecclesiastes one senses even more how this wisdom tradition has moved far from belief in the covenant God who is rich in both judgment and mercy, law and promise. Here there is a pronounced streak of cynicism. 'Vanity of vanities! All is vanity' (Eccles. 1.2), and as for the God of history, why, 'there is nothing new under the sun' (1.9). The writer almost implies that worship is likely to be useless (5.1), and although he ends by declaring that one should 'Fear God and keep his commandments' (12.13), he does not clarify what these are.

Summary

The Old Testament contains, then, three fairly distinct strands of ethical teaching. The final one (the Writings) appears to be out on a limb as compared to the other two, and in the course of time has had little influence. The other two exist in tension with each other, the prophetic strand constantly exercising a sharp critique upon the advocates of the Law, so that it would be equally valid to cite a text such as Micah 6.8 as a summary of man's moral obligations as it would be to cite one of the great codes such as the Decalogue.

In the period between the return from exile and the re-founding of the people of Israel in Jerusalem under Ezra and Nehemiah, about 400 years passed before a major prophet appeared again – John the Baptizer – and then Jesus' ministry commenced. During that period the first strand appears to have dominated the moral scene, with the rise of the Pharisees and their intense devotion to every detail of the law. Whenever there is excessive concentration upon law there is strong possibility of various moral flaws appearing. Five of these are constantly cited.

(i) *Legalism*. This means trust that God is satisfied by our doing precisely what the law says. Inevitably this leads to self-righteousness, the conviction that one has become 'good' by the effort of keeping the law. Almost inevitably it also leads to the conviction that one can acquire 'merit' by such good works.

(ii) *Religiosity*. This means the conviction that by doing very religious acts very frequently, such as worship and private devotion, one meets God's moral demand.

(iii) *Formalism*. This is the conviction that the form of the command must be obeyed meticulously. It ignores the requirement that the motive for the act must also be pure and right.

(iv) *Eudaemonism*. This is the teaching that one should obey God's law, because then one will prosper or experience happiness for oneself. It makes obedience into a shrewd option for the most beneficial life. One obeys for the sake of enlightened happiness. There is a noticeable streak of this in the teaching of Deuteronomy.

(v) *Particularism*. This is the conviction that God has given his law, but it only applies to one's own group or nation, not to all mankind, and therefore makes one's own group vastly superior to the rest.

The Pharisees

The Pharisees receive harsh treatment in the New Testament. They are often presented as Jesus' most formidable opponents and as the most unpleasant of characters. The catalogue of their sins which fills Matt. 23 makes them appear almost as agents of the devil. They are there portrayed as being inveterate hypocrites teaching strict laws but not obeying them themselves, wholly lacking in compassion, ostentatious and proud, fastidious in their behaviour, nit-picking in their practice of tithing (so that they bothered themselves silly over presenting a tenth of even the mint in their back gardens), morally blind and unable to distinguish major moral concerns from petty ones, opposed to genuine prophecy. It is a formidable indictment. Were they all that bad?

The Pharisees seem to have originated about 200 BC as a disciplined body of laymen determined to preserve essential Judaism and stop it from being corrupted by foreign influences. This meant zealous attention to the Torah, the law, since this was at the heart of Jewish faith. They soon had an extraordinary list of achievements to their credit. They established synagogues wherever Jewish people lived in sufficient numbers, so that the faith could be preserved all over the 'diaspora' (the dispersion of Jews throughout the known world, but especially in the Middle East). The synagogues had their own special liturgy and acted as schools. The Pharisees worked to collect the scripture into a recognized 'canon'. They encouraged a strong sense of obligation to give regular tithes. Above all, they promoted the study of the Torah and, to prevent it becoming fossilized, developed the notion of the 'unwritten Torah', the subsequent reflection of later generations as to how the original was to be applied to changed circumstances.

They maintained that the Torah consisted of 613 command-ments, 248 being positive and 365 negative. They practised two types of teaching: *halakah* and *haggadah*. The former was prescriptive, the statement of what the Law commanded. The latter tended to be more imaginative and descriptive, since the Law's requirements were illustrated and expressed in stories or vivid pictures. They were inevitably theologians, always meditating both about the Law and the doctrine of God. Since they could not but believe that God is just, and since it is a matter of common observation that bad men often flourish, they became convinced that there must be an after-life in which God's justice would be vindicated.

Many Pharisees, utterly devoted to the living out of God's holy Law, found exquisite happiness and satisfaction in the religious life. To read Psalm 19 or the long Psalm 119 (an elaborate poem in praise of the Law) is to capture something of the profound joy the Pharisee found in God's Law. Many were extremely compassionate; for example, they sought all sorts of ways of avoiding the ruthlessness of the *lex talionis*, and by Jesus' time had devised an alternative system of payments. It is conceivable that when Jesus was presented with the woman taken in adultery (John 8.1–11), he too was being invited to find a way round the death penalty, a test which many a Pharisee could pass.

There were various schools amongst the Pharisees. In Jesus' time there were three main ones; the 'Haburoth' (extremists, isolating themselves as much as possible from normal every-day life and contacts); the school of Shammai (teaching a fairly strict attention to the exact letter of the law); and that of Hillel (who taught that the intention of the law mattered most, rather than its exact formulation).[5]

The teaching of Jesus

Before the development of biblical criticism it was assumed that when we read the Gospels and the teaching ascribed there to Jesus we find an accurate account of what Jesus actually said. It was fairly easy to decide what Jesus said about morality. One put together all the references to some moral issue (e.g. paying taxes) and harmonized them as best one could. But that was deceptive. It meant ignoring or explaining away a whole host of problems, particularly where the various Gospels reproduce the same item of teaching in a noticeably different manner. Which Gospel account is then the correct one? Biblical criticism is a highly developed skill which helps us resolve such problems. As an example of its value, let us first look at some of Jesus' teaching concerning marriage and divorce. There are four passages to be considered:

1. Matt. 5.31, 32. This reports the Jewish law on the matter of divorce, to which Jesus says that every man divorcing his wife 'except for adultery' commits adultery; a man marrying a divorced woman also does so.

2. Matt. 19.3–9. Some Pharisees ask if it is lawful to divorce a wife 'for any cause'. Jesus refers them to the statement about marriage in Gen. 1. They ask why in that case the Mosaic law permits divorce. Jesus replies that it is for their 'hardness of heart': whoever divorces his wife 'except for adultery' commits adultery against her. In the following verses the disciples express astonishment.

3. Mark 10.2–12. Some Pharisees ask if divorce is lawful. Jesus enquires about the Mosaic law and says it was for their 'hardness of heart'. From the beginning it was not so, and Jesus quotes Gen. 1. The disciples later query this and Jesus says that whoever divorces his wife commits adultery, and any divorced woman who remarries commits adultery also.

4. Luke 16.18. Every man divorcing his wife and remarrying commits adultery; every man marrying a divorced woman also does so.

There are various important differences in these statements. To begin with, only Matthew in 1. and 2. reports the exception clause – 'except for adultery'. The others make divorce wholly wrong, whatever the cause. Next, 2. and 3. are obviously reports of the same discussion, but have numerous variations including the form of the initial question. In 2. this includes the clause 'for any cause'. Only 3. mentions divorced women seeking remarriage; 4. knows nothing of the 'exception clause' utilized in 1. and 2. by Matthew.

It is helpful to realize that these teachings were also the subject of a lively debate amongst the Pharisees at the time. The law, in Deut. 24.1, says rather baldly that a man who 'finds something shameful' in his wife may divorce her by writing her a note. The Pharisees argued over the meaning of the 'something shameful'. Shammai interpreted this strictly to mean adultery; Hillel was more concerned with the inner meaning and held it to be some basic failure of the wife, which could include inadequacy in running the home. Others interpreted this in an even wider sense, meaning almost anything that offended the husband.

This means that in 2. Jesus was being asked if he agreed with the widest interpretation ('for any cause'), but in 3. he was being asked the general question. However, in 1. and 2. he sides in his reply with Shammai, whereas in 3. and 4. he repudiates divorce altogether and therefore corrects the Mosaic law. The 'exception clause' would agree with Shammai; the repudiation of all divorce would contradict Deuteronomy.

In such a case, how are we to proceed? What did Jesus teach? Almost all biblical critics, whose task is to help us through such quandaries, would claim that 3., the version in Mark, is almost certainly the original statement of Jesus. It denounces all divorce, whether or not it is sanctioned by Deuteronomy. But the early church found it desperately difficult to live by that absolute rule, especially in the midst of a Jewish people who permitted divorce and found it justified in the Torah. Therefore the saying became subtly altered by Matthew, who wrote later and had Mark's Gospel in front of him; he reported it so that it tallied with the strictest interpretation found amongst the Pharisees. Luke, in 4., reproduced that crucial conclusion to the whole matter as he too had picked it up from Mark or his other sources, but apparently he was not so concerned with the debate about the Old Testament traditions, possibly because he was writing mainly for Gentiles and not Jews.

This complicated problem has been a source of constant debate in the churches down through the centuries. Which version is to be regarded as authoritative? It makes a profound difference to many people, since marriage problems afflict all societies everywhere. It illustrates the dangers of going straight to the Gospels unarmed with the tools of biblical criticism. It is irresponsible to ignore the obvious fact that the Gospel records as we have them have been filtered through the life of the early church and then through the persons who compiled the Gospels. They had differing intentions in preparing their work, so there are marked differences in the styles and emphases found there.[6]

The ethical teaching of Jesus was not, of course, marked out by him as a separate and distinct item. For him, as for the whole Jewish tradition, ethics are an element in one's whole response to the revelation given by God of his will for human life. It is inextricably bound up with the doctrine of God, with the practice of worship, with all that is subsumed under the general theme of our 'obedience' and our responsibilities towards our neighbours. Nevertheless, the Gospel writers differ in their interest in ethical issues and Jesus' teaching about them.

Thus Mark's primary interest seems to be narrowly theological, to present Jesus as the Son of Man who portrays the mystery of the Kingdom, performs deeds of remarkable power and significance and, to begin with, bewilders the disciples until they grasp his Messiahship. His whole ministry seems to be conducted with a sense of the urgency of the time, for the End is near. There is no special interest in his teaching, and only a few of the parables and sayings are recorded. A great portion of the book is devoted to the events of the last week in Jerusalem. It is on the whole a brief account of the basic facts of Jesus' ministry.

But Luke has subtly different interests. He seems to be concerned to show that there is no inherent conflict between the Christian church and the Roman authority, and to show how Jesus' teaching and activity show an astonishing compassion for the outcast and despised, a compassion which surpasses the demands of the Law and throws it into question. It is obviously directed more to a Gentile than Jewish readership, and has much more concern for Jesus' teaching.

Matthew has a different character again. He is writing for Jews, has great interest in Jesus' teaching, especially as it affirms or goes further than the Jewish law. He portrays Jesus as a Messiah who is also like a new Moses, and his teaching is at times detailed almost to the point of it becoming a new set of legislation, (as was noted in the way he handles the sayings about divorce). The teaching is set more clearly within the framework of a coming Day of Judgment, and with constant echoes back to the Old Testament.

John is commonly accepted as being the last Gospel to be written, and to be cast more into the style of a series of profound theological meditations woven around seven great affirmations about Jesus and his significance ('the new wine', 'the bread of life', 'the light of the world', etc.). A constant theme is that faith means 'obeying my commands'; these are never spelled out in detail, but it is taken as axiomatic that they centre upon 'love for the brethren'.[7]

Our records of Jesus' sayings are, then, filtered through the writers, or collectors and editors, of the Gospels. They chose different material as being important, and presented it in slightly different ways, so that it would serve slightly different ends. But whilst they were doing this, the early church was experiencing its own growing pains, its conflicts with the Jewish and Roman worlds, its struggle to sort out its beliefs. These features of early church life also affect the materials found in the Gospels. Sayings such as parables, which may originally have been addressed by Jesus to his critics (e.g. the Scribes and Pharisees), may become turned into an appeal to the church to become a missionary one reaching out to the Gentiles; or they may become comments about the need for church discipline.[8] Sayings which anticipate an imminent End may be slightly transposed so that they become appeals to patience whilst awaiting the End, which by now may seem a long way off.[9] The audience to which Jesus spoke may be deftly changed to a different one; this can obviously happen if an original teaching was addressed, say, to Pharisees, but was seen later to be of such memorable importance that the early church wanted it preserved and, although in many a place there were no longer any Pharisees being a problem to its life, did so by regarding it as originally addressed to all disciples.[10] The detailed study of these issues is not our concern here, but a classic introduction is that in Jeremias, *The Parables of Jesus*.[11] But we should also heed the warning that 'the recovery of the precise use made of the parables of Jesus by Christian evangelists . . . is no easy task, and that the critical scalpel . . . cannot by itself ever decide for us when the authentic "lowest layer" has been reached'.[12]

However, the problems connected with discovering precisely what the original statement must have been, and to whom spoken, are not so great as to permit a basic cynicism about the

Gospel records. We can indeed hear what, in all likelihood, Jesus said. The main problem is always that of obeying it and moulding our lives by it. As Mark Twain is reported to have said once, 'It is not the parts of the Bible which I cannot understand which trouble me, but the parts I can.' Let us attempt a brief outline of the basic character of that teaching in so far as it throws light upon Christian ethics. This will be done through making three affirmations about it, and then citing three questions which constantly beset every disciple or interpreter.

First Affirmation. Jesus taught that nothing, absolutely nothing, mattered more in human life than to love God and live within his Kingdom. Every other claim upon us is secondary. The one all-embracing reality is the ever-present merciful love of God. To live in response to it must, of course, mean loving our neighbour as ourselves. This constitutes the 'great commandment'.[13] Much of his teaching was illustration after illustration of what it means in practice, the basic trust with which we can and should approach all life, the readiness to make traumatic decisions in abandonment to God, the forgivingness which we can now share freely with others.[14]

A previous generation of theologians used to say that Jesus' message could be summed up as 'the Fatherhood of God' and the 'infinite value of the human soul',[15] but this weakens the element of urgent demand within Jesus' teaching. Mark summarizes this teaching as the message: 'The time is fulfilled and the kingdom of heaven is at hand: repent, and believe in the gospel' (1.15). It is difficult to adjust this to the two generalized principles above; the key phrase 'kingdom of God' has virtually been abandoned there, the urgency has gone, the demand for repentance has been forgotten. As for 'the infinite value of the human soul', it is not possible to find this asserted as a central theme by Jesus. Instead, he teaches the astonishing extravagance of God's forgiving love whereby all men are undeservedly blessed, so his main assertion is that God gives remarkable value to human beings in the outgoing powerfulness of his love.[16] It is not put in the form of human beings having some inherent value in themselves, as the second generalized phrase implies.

More recently, great concern has been expressed by Rudolf Bultmann about the general framework of belief in which such teaching of Jesus was cast, that is, the 'eschatological'. In the text from Mark quoted above, Jesus refers to the Kingdom of heaven being 'at hand'; in many other texts he expresses his conviction that at any moment the End of the present order will occur and the whole universe as we know it will be transformed in an act of judgment and renewal. Bultmann says bluntly that modern man cannot be expected to believe that, or to view everything from that sort of standpoint. Therefore we must see this framework as a dynamic and powerful way of Jesus' stressing the crucial nature of our commitment to him, the crisis nature of the decisions we must make for him, the supreme importance of our obedience and its total and urgent demand. Thus the eschatological framework is a way of underlining the need for whole-hearted and constant obedience as the essential character of Christian living. Bultmann has a programme of 'demythologizing', but the effect of it is to make Christian discipleship one of total demand. The need for conversion and wholesale trust is by no means explained away; it is underlined.[17]

All readers of the New Testament have to come to terms in some way or other with this problem; Bultmann's solution may appear far too drastic and far too determined by a particular philosophical school (the existentialist). Others see 'the Kingdom' as inaugurated on earth in the person and work of Jesus, or in his cross and resurrection and giving of the Spirit, and to be fully consummated later, in the fullness of time. There are many subtle differences of interpretation here; what is common is the need to come to terms somehow with the urgent teaching of the imminence of the End.[18] But all agree that Jesus' primary demand was for radical and total obedience to the supreme will of God – nothing matters more in human life and for human destiny. God must be loved for his own sake, because he is the supreme good and source of all worth. The neighbour must be loved likewise, because God himself showers love upon the neighbour even if he is 'an enemy'.[19]

Second Affirmation. There is a complex relationship between the ethical teaching which springs from Jesus and that found within the Torah and taught so zealously by the Pharisees. In so far as the Torah guides and helps man into love for God and neighbour, it is to be strongly affirmed. Hence Matthew (the Gospel writer most concerned for Judaism) quotes Jesus as saying: 'Think not that I have come to abolish the law and the prophets; I have come not to abolish them but to fulfil them' (5.17), and there are other similar references implying deep respect for the Law.[20] But in so far as zealous adherence to the Law frustrated love for God and neighbour, it is clearly over-ridden by Jesus. The sharpest instance is in the matter of sabbath observance. 'The sabbath was made for man, not man for the sabbath', reports Mark (2.27). Matthew and Luke do not record that revolutionary saying. Matthew makes it clear that Jesus was standing in the great prophetic tradition, 'I desire mercy and not sacrifice' (Hos. 6.6), in his protest (see 12.1–8); Luke agrees with the two other synoptists that the conclusion of the whole incident is the declaration 'The Son of man is lord of the sabbath' (Matt. 12.8; Mark 2.28; Luke 6.5). Repeatedly, it seems, Jesus overrode the Jewish law concerning the sabbath.[21]

But Jesus over-rode the law on other matters also, including its liability to manipulation against the obvious needs of parents for support from their children (e.g. Mark 7.9–13 and parallels); its concentration upon the outer form of the deed rather than the inner motivation (e.g. Matt. 5.28); its obsession with formal cleanliness rather than inner purity (e.g. Mark 7.1–8 and parallels); its tendency to produce the over-fussy conscience and thereby people who lose sight of the major requirements of God (e.g. Matt. 23.23); its inevitable promotion of self-righteousness amongst its most zealous adherents (e.g. Luke 18.9–14); its exclusive character, being the way for the Jews only, the Gentiles being abandoned (e.g. Mark 11.17 and parallels, or Matt. 13.31f. and parallels, where the 'birds of the air' symbolize the Gentiles).

Thus Jesus asserts an authority to interpret the Law and to go far beyond it in critique, or in drawing out its inner essence, in a manner that appeared terrifying to the Pharisees. Nevertheless, in doing this he was often developing themes that were already appearing in their own teaching. He was not being totally novel, either in his concern with inner motivation or in his style of teaching, but he was drawing out the Pharisaic concern for the inner disposition, and the Pharisaic method of *haggadah*, in startlingly fresh ways.

Third Affirmation. In what, then, lay Jesus' originality? Many Christians seem quite desperately anxious to find in Jesus someone who is a totally novel teacher, the like of which the world has never known before nor since. As we have seen, he built upon the foundation of Jewish tradition, with a fundamental respect for the law and the prophets. His originality seems to have consisted of one minor feature and one major one. The minor one was his complete rejection of asceticism. Indeed he was not married, and apparently lived a very simple life, being content with elementary provision for his needs. He constantly warned against riches.[22] In those respects he shared the commonly accepted style of life for the 'prophets', as did John the Baptizer, and shared too something in common with the ardent community at Qumran. But, in sharp contrast, he seems to have revelled in good parties, to have enjoyed feasts, to be only mildly in favour of fasting, to have enjoyed the company of women and to have caused enough scandal as to be branded a 'friend of sinners'.[23] He was no ascetic.[24]

Jesus' originality lay primarily in the way he completely lived out his own demand for total obedience to God and total trust in him. In his ministry, the deeds and the words were wholly consistent with each other. He trusted God utterly, even to the abandonment in the garden of Gethsemane. But he gave himself wholly to human need. He was 'the man for others', in Bonhoeffer's memorable phrase. This integral consistency of word and deed led, by a remorseless sequence of inevitable tragedy, to the crucifixion. We return to a comment I made earlier: we cannot separate out Jesus' ethics from the total event of his ministry. He does not principally appear as a highly original and imaginative mentor whose aphorisms and stories excel in sublimity anything uttered by anyone else; he appears as the one who was totally devoted to God and man in an extraordinary power of loving; nothing whatever could deflect him from the course of that loving, and his most startling teaching is, ironically, to die on a cross.

Three nagging questions immediately beset every interpreter and every disciple. They are closely related to one another. The first concerns the imitation of Jesus. Is the Christian to see in Jesus the ideal example which is to be copied? Is the Christian ethic a matter of not having a string of rules to obey but, instead (and better) a person to emulate? Jesus himself never said so – at least, not directly. He did not say, 'You must learn to forgive just as I forgive'; instead, he told a parable about an unforgiving servant (Matt. 18.23–35) in which there is a sharp contrast between the merciful generosity of the king (who obviously represents God) and the niggardly attitude of the servant. The parable is then left to us to meditate about, and to be challenged by. The implication is that we are to model our attitudes upon those which we know to be true to God's own character, but no mention is formally made of Jesus himself embodying them. 'You therefore must be perfect, as your heavenly father is perfect' (Matt. 5.48). Elsewhere Jesus seems to want to divert attention away from himself and towards God (e.g. Matt. 19.17). Moreover, he had a special calling to fulfil; he was the Messiah, and nobody else is called to that office. There may well be hints of this in the way that the temptation story is presented in Matt. 4 and Luke 4. The series of three temptations follows Jesus' experience of God's call – 'This is my beloved Son, with whom I am well pleased' (Matt. 3.17; Luke 3.22) – when he goes into the desert to work out the implications of that calling. They are not temptations which we experience, but only those with which a Messiah would have to wrestle so there are no further references to them, and no teaching is based upon them and then related to the disciples. The temptations are peculiarly those for Jesus alone.

Yet we cannot be content with any reflection upon the New Testament which would result in our saying that Jesus is not, in some way or other, an example. Some later teaching affirms clearly that Christ's openness to suffering is to be emulated by us (e.g. I Peter 3.13–4.1), as is his willingness to be poor (e.g. II Cor. 8.9), whereas John's Gospel explicitly presents Jesus as commanding his disciples to love in the same manner as he has loved, 'For I have given you an example, that you also should do as I have done to you' (13.15). Jesus displays in his ministry as in his teaching what the royal way of love for God and man is like. The whole style and character of Christian ethics is unthinkable without that ministry. As T. W. Manson put it: 'In the last resort the Christian ethic inevitably comes back to Christ himself. It is from him that it derives its content, its form, and its authority.'[25] But Jesus is not to be slavishly, woodenly copied. It would be absurd, for example (and contrary to Jesus' teaching) if someone were to assume that because Jesus was not married, every disciple must remain single.

This leads us into the second, related, question. Is Jesus' teaching to be regarded as immediately binding and practicable? Should every would-be Christian read Matt. 5.38–42 and then practise total non-resistance whilst giving property away to every beggar and borrower? Should the passage that follows in Matt. 6.25–34 be taken to mean that the Christian need have no bank account or insurance policy or emergency supplies in the larder, but live trustingly from day to day, believing that somehow God will provide? Should we 'follow Jesus' by having 'nowhere to lay our head', and, presumably, not owning any property or hiring a house from someone else? Is discipleship a calling that removes us from the normal daily web of commitments and responsibilities to home, family, jobs, the state, etc.?

Nobody finds this question easy to resolve. At one extreme, some have held that indeed Jesus' teaching must be regarded as normative and practicable. At the other, very devout Christians have asserted that it is in no way normative and that it would matter little to our discipleship if Jesus had actually *said* nothing whatever. In between, there are a great range of subtleties of interpretation, with most Christians seeing the teaching as an absolute command which simply cannot be observed in the ordinary experience of living with normal obligations.[26] Many of these would say that Jesus taught 'first order principles', that is, absolute commands which seem sublimely removed from everyday practice and yet which should determine our attitudes and perspectives on life. Therefore we need to live by 'second order principles' which can be practised daily in this sort of muddled, fallen world, and which are derived clearly from the first order ones. They are not so sublime or timeless, but are possible in today's world; inevitably they tone down the astringency and absolute demands that are in the primal teaching, yet they still reflect it, even if in a diluted manner.[27]

The third matter concerns moral rules or laws. All of us long for moral questions to be simple and clear-cut; we yearn for uncomplicated ethical rules or directives, so that we can know with a certainty exactly what we ought to do. For this reason the Ten Commandments are so popular, whereas the summary of the prophetic witness (do justice, love mercy, walk humbly with God) remains virtually unquoted. This longing for simplicity and certainty means that Christians constantly go to Jesus' teaching in the hope of finding simple moral legislation there. Some claim to find it in the so-called 'Golden Rule' of Matt. 7.12, 'Whatever you wish that men should do to you, do so to them; for this is the law and the prophets,' but 'by itself (it) is neither the full statement of Old Testament teaching nor the adequate summary of what Jesus taught. Its actual wording any atheist might accept,'[28] and it is so generalized as to be quite inadequate for the formulation of rules.

Did Jesus ever legislate at all? When asked for a specific ruling by an aggrieved man Jesus repudiates a role such as 'judge or divider' (Luke 12.13–15). When asked to give a more detailed interpretation of the command 'Love your neighbour', he does not do so. Instead of defining the 'neighbour' so that everyone would know the extent to which the command should be obeyed and to whom, Jesus told one of the most famous of the parables, the Good Samaritan, asked his questioner 'Who behaved like a neighbour?', and then told him to go and do likewise. The request for legislation gained a reply which was a command to be loving; not at all what the questioner was hoping for (Luke 9.29–37). Almost all of the parables lead to a general but profound challenge: be alert, be trusting, be forgiving, be adventurous, be decisive. They never end in moral rules or orders. When a biblical scholar sought for a list of the 'commands of Jesus' he ended up with the following nine:

> Let your yes be yes
> Keep it secret (i.e. your piety)
> Love and lend
> Become last
> Sell and give
> Ask, seek, knock
> Be carefree
> Watch and pray
> Do this in remembrance of me (the last supper).[29]

These describe fundamental attitudes to God and to others, with the final one to be interpreted possibly as a worship command. There is no 'legislation' here.

Thus although Jesus was like a Rabbi in many respects, in this one he was not. He did not supply rules. He did not elaborate on known laws nor explain their applications. Like the prophets before him, he provided the sharpest of critiques against contemporary understandings of God's law. But he went further and deeper than the prophets had been able to go, making his whole ministry into a living embodiment of God's ultimate demand. There was no legislation, but the most vivid of all illustrations by word, act, dying and rising.

The teaching of Paul

A glance at the contents of some of Paul's letters shows that he had a tendency to divide them into two parts. The first described the nature of God, his work in Christ, the gift of the Spirit, the essence of the Christian life in the forgiveness, freedom, salvation thus enjoyed. Then there is often a benediction, followed by the second section dealing with the consequences of this glorious relationship with God through Jesus Christ. This contains a great deal of discussion about the forms which Christian life takes, with ethics. This pattern can easily be seen in Romans, Colossians and I Thessalonians, where the 'ethical' portions begin at Rom. 12.1; Col. 3.1; and I Thess. 4.1.[30] This gives the impression that for Paul theology was one subject, and ethics another. But that is most misleading, since the two are integrally related to each other, with ethical comments often cropping up in the first parts, and theological ones in the second.

It also might suggest that Paul had some sort of ethical system, some clear scaffolding of ethical theory which will appear in the second parts of letters. But that is quickly shown to be false. He had no standard way of approaching ethical issues, no stock syllabus of teaching, no ethical system at all. He did not apparently know much about Jesus' teaching, and only quoted two of Jesus' sayings – that the preacher/apostle is worthy of his pay (Luke 10.7 quoted in I Cor. 9.14), and the declaration about marriage in Mark 10.9 which seems to lie in the background of the whole discussion in I Cor. 7, but wittingly put on one side. Again and again, where his case would be greatly strengthened by reference to Jesus and to sayings which are well known to us, Paul did not cite them. Presumably he did not know them. What, then, did Paul do?

Paul taught that with the coming and ministry of Jesus a new age has commenced. It is in sharp contrast to the old. This contrast is illustrated by a considerable wealth of imagery and concepts. It is the contrast between 'law' and 'grace'; between 'sin' and 'righteousness'; between 'flesh' and 'spirit'; between 'death' and 'life'. Christians live in the new age, made plain by Jesus' death and resurrection. Christian ethics is that style of life which is fitting for the new age, appropriate to grace, righteousness, spirit, resurrection life. Paul's ethics are as simple as that – the working out in love of the faith whereby you are now living in the new age of Christ. The phrase 'faith working itself out in love' is often used as a simple summary of his position.[31]

Undoubtedly Paul at first thought that the End of the new age was imminent. His attitude towards marriage, in I Cor. 7, reflected this, since he was advising Christians not to marry in such an emergency situation unless they were so sexually excited that they simply must. His writing often reverberates with a spirit of earnest hope despite the trauma about to take place (as in I Thess. 4 and 5), although the consequence may be a rather simple injunction (as in II Thess. 3 where the thrust of the passage is that people should work hard and not be idle). By the time that Ephesians came to be written, when probably a disciple of Paul gathered together his major ideas and re-issued them to the churches, this imminence has receded into the background, and the teaching on marriage, for example, becomes much more positive and rich (see Eph. 5.24–33).

Paul's ethical direction to the new Christian, then, is 'live appropriately for the new age'. This may be expressed in various ways. 'Present your bodies as a living sacrifice, holy and acceptable to God . . . be transformed by the renewal of your mind' (Rom. 12.1f.). 'Do you not know that your body is a temple of the Holy Spirit within you, which you have from God? You are not your own; you were bought with a price. So glorify God in your body' (I Cor. 6.19f.). 'Make love your aim, and earnestly desire the spiritual gifts' (I Cor. 14.1). 'Working together with him then (i.e. Christ) we entreat you not to accept the grace of God in vain' (II Cor. 6.1). 'If we live by the Spirit, let us also walk by the Spirit' (Gal. 5.25). 'Have this mind among yourselves which is yours in Christ Jesus' (Phil. 2.5). 'If then you have been raised with Christ, seek the things that are above . . . put to death therefore what is earthly in you . . . Put on then, as God's chosen ones, holy and beloved, compassion . . . ' (Col. 3.1, 5, 12). 'Since we belong to the day, let us be sober, and put on the breastplate of faith and love . . . ' (I Thess. 5.8).

When outlining the character of this new life, Paul may freely utilize the various lists of vices and virtues which were a common feature of much of the best contemporary morality. Such lists of vices occur in passages like Rom. 1.29–31 or 13.13; I Cor. 5.10; II Cor. 12.20; Gal. 5.19–21. Lists of virtues occur in Gal. 5.22f.; Phil. 4.8; Col. 3.12–15. It would be a mistake to try and make the lists of vices all agree with each other in a standard form, or the virtues likewise, or to imagine that the virtues exactly contrast with the vices. There is nothing systematic happening here in Paul's writing, but he is freely and spontaneously illustrating the new Christian way in contrast to the old pre-Christian one. One great virtue constantly dominates the Christian life, however, and Paul can be at his most lyrical when describing it; that is love (*agape*), by which Paul means the deliberate, constant, sacrificial caring for others' total well-being which is seen in Jesus Christ. This love fulfils the law (Rom. 13.10; Gal. 5.14) and is the supreme gift of the Spirit (I Cor. 13) which Christians make their ultimate 'aim' (I Cor. 14.1). When it is put into practice in the life of the church it will mean the 'bearing of one another's burdens' (Gal. 6.1–5), concern for the weaker Christian (Rom. 14.15), constant efforts at reconciliation (II Cor. 5.19), the promotion of common harmony (Col. 3.14), sharing of goods with the needy (II Cor. 8.1–9), and it will overflow to all men (I Thess. 3.12).

There are some issues which cannot be easily resolved, however, by an earnest appeal to 'love'. When presented with these, Paul may simply cast about for any argument that seems to him to be helpful and convincing. Thus when asked about the conduct of women in church he affirms that their heads should always be covered, and produces different reasons. It is 'proper' or 'seemly' (13). It is according to 'nature' (14) and thereby protects her from angels (10). It is customary (16). When asked about Christians sharing in meals which involve food previously offered to idols he makes rather heavy weather out of the issue, saying both that it is perfectly all right for the Christian to do so because he is 'free' and the food has been dedicated to 'no gods' anyway, yet he is deeply concerned that the harmony within the brotherhood should not be broken by some too tender Christians being offended by such freedom (Rom. 14; I Cor. 8 and 10).

It is widely believed that the early church had developed a simple system of instructions for its converts. This included a series of ethical admonitions, material from it being incorporated into at least one Pauline epistle (Colossians), the later 'Pauline' epistle which is closely modelled upon Colossians (i.e. Ephesians), I Peter, and possibly James.[32] This series, or paraenesis, is usually known as the 'household code' because it included four simple directions for 'submission', the first three pertaining very much to household life:

> wives submit to husbands,
> children submit to parents,
> slaves submit to masters,
> citizens submit to the state.

In the one indisputably Pauline letter – Colossians – this list is reproduced with the exception of the final one (submission to the state), but it is clear from Rom. 13.1–7 that Paul argued this on grounds of God's appointment of all rulers, and that he would readily embrace the code. It is quite consistent with his general method (or lack of rigid method) that he should incorporate such simple instruction into his own writing.

It also appears that Paul had a concept of a 'natural law' – a moral sense of right and wrong which is held by everyone whether Jew or Gentile, whether aware of God's revelation or not. This idea had been widely taught by Stoics, who held that all men had some 'spark' of the divine within them. Paul makes use of this concept especially in Rom. 1.18–2.29 and possibly, as we have seen, in I Cor. 11.14, but he does not develop the notion very fully.

Finally, does Paul completely dispense with the Jewish law as a means of providing ethical guidance? He had, after all, been an intense Pharisee, thoroughly trained in the meaning and application of the Torah. Does he wholly repudiate his respect for the law? This is a very complicated matter because Paul uses 'law' in at least five subtly different senses, which means that he does indeed repudiate the notion that the keeping of the law is a way to salvation. Paul is adamant about that. If one tries to effect salvation in that way one becomes obsessed with self-righteousness and fundamentally misled. But does the law offer a legitimate picture of the truly obedient moral life? Here we are bound to say that to some extent it must do, otherwise we are postulating a strangely inconsistent God who reveals the law to Israel and then tells Christians to repudiate it. The 'law' as a guide to the pattern of living which God requires must have some positive elements in it, especially if love is its 'fulfilling'. It must also be legitimate to talk about the 'law of Christ', which Paul does in I Cor. 9.21, meaning that moral obligation under which Christians now live and which has a clear shape and form, determined by Christ.[33] Thus although it seems paradoxical, Christians live under a glorious 'freedom' because their allegiance is to Christ who, in his Spirit, stimulates all the spontaneous originality of agape-love,[34] yet this way of living is not completely shapeless and unpredictable; it has clear continuity with the Jewish moral code and can rightly be termed a 'law'. This is why Paul can earnestly oppose any criticism of Christian living or teaching as being amoral or morally anarchic (as he does in Rom. 6.1; I Cor. 5.9–11; 6.12; II Cor. 6.14–17; Gal. 5.13). Instead, in the glorious freedom of the Spirit, Christians live in glad and grateful obedience to the law of Christ.

The early church

As the church grew, new converts had to be instructed in Christian belief and given some clear guidelines for Christian behaviour. The household codes were almost certainly included in such instruction, and the Gospels were written to supply the essential story of Jesus for both the instructional and the liturgical needs of the churches. It is fairly easy to trace five tendencies in the development of ethics.

First, as a formal church organization arose, with its baptized membership and its rules and discipline, a great deal of attention was concentrated upon these, and the focus of ethical concern seemed to narrow. Love for the neighbour (which meant love for all in need) began to be narrowed down to love 'for the brethren' (meaning love for fellow Christians within the church). This is especially clear in the Gospel of John and the Johannine letters. The writers are absolutely adamant that to be a Christian is to embrace a new style of life in which love is the over-ruling feature, and that it is the love which we encounter through Jesus Christ. But the 'command' to love is normally applied to the circle of the brethren (as in John 13.14; 15.12–17; 17.26; I John 3.11–24; 4.7, 20). The early church did not confine its charity to its own members, since it shared with its parent Judaism a profound concern for the poor, so 'the practical application of charity was probably the most potent single cause of Christian success',[35] but its teaching concentrated more and more upon love for those within the church circle.

Issues arose which were of internal concern only as, for example, the problem of whether or not one was to receive back into the church community someone who had been baptized, had lapsed, and had committed grave sin. Echoes of this debate are clearly heard in passages like Heb. 6.1–6 or I John 5.16f., but teaching about the unforgiveable sin may have fuelled this debate (see Matt. 12.31f.; Mark 3.28–30; Luke 12.8–10). The debate may also have influenced the forms in which the saying appears in the Gospels, since in Matthew and Luke blasphemy against the Son of Man is forgiveable, but Mark implies that it is not.[36]

To read the Pastoral Epistles (probably written forty or fifty years after Paul's death) is to experience a different set of concerns from those which dominated Paul. In I Timothy, for example, the writer is concerned with the behaviour of bishops, elders, deacons, widows and women in general. The moral virtues required of the church leadership are those one would expect in any healthy community, so the bishop is to be 'above reproach, the husband of one wife, temperate, sensible, dignified, hospitable . . . etc.' (3.2), and such qualities could equally well be sought in a present-day political or industrial leader. One misses, then, the clear theological framework in which Paul cast his ethical teaching, and the result is a more domestic scene, with great stress upon those virtues which keep a community tolerably in harmony. But widows are regarded as a special problem, and woman's submission to man is firmly asserted (2.9–15). The unity of which Paul talked in Gal. 3.28 has now faded somewhat into the background.

This general domestication can be noticed in much of the writing that comes from the sub-apostolic age. People are to be generally 'well behaved', slaves are not to be refractory (Titus 2.9f.), arguments that may be divisive are to be avoided and we pray to lead a 'quiet and peaceable life' (I Tim. 2.2). In James the straightforward virtues are fervently advocated, often on very simple grounds – beware of the tongue, a 'restless evil, full of deadly poison' (3.8), needing control as do horses need bits in their mouths. Here especially one senses that the writer has almost lost sight of Jesus Christ, but writes in a plain rumbustious style that could almost as well come from someone with a deep respect for God but no explicit Christian commitment. Sometimes these writers make sweeping simplifications, such as 'the love of money is the root of all evils' (I Tim. 6.10).

Second, the church had to live in a complex world and quickly found that some ethical issues were far from simple. The most obvious instance was that of the relationship between Christians and the state. Paul, in a famous passage in Rom. 13.1–7, had argued that the state was a divine institution to be accepted positively by Christians. Jesus had taught that one should pay one's taxes (Mark 12.13–17 and parallels), and had submitted to Pilate and Herod even though he had been critical of the way 'the great ones of the earth' behave (Mark 10.42–44). The early instructional codes taught submission, as we have seen. There was, however, a noticeably different attitude in the Johannine writing, where the 'world' is believed to lie under the 'evil one' in darkness, ruled over by 'the prince of this world' (John 12.31; 14.30; 16.11). Whilst these references appear to be about Satan, the implication is clear that the world's rulers are caught up in a direct way in Satan's empire and doings. One must still submit, but not to a ruler who is ordained by God (as with Paul), but to one who is part of the devil's domain, which will pass away.[37]

The first rather haphazard persecution broke out under Nero in about AD 65; that under the Emperor Trajan in about AD 110, and so on sporadically until the very vicious one in the reign of Decius, AD 250. One of the disturbing features of the persecutions was their unpredictability, so that Christians never knew for long how they stood with the civil power. But the effect was to emphasize the deep misgivings about the nature of the state which appeared in the Johannine literature; these came to full fruit in the book of Revelation, where the Roman state is pictured as the Beast, the Great Whore. Christians are to endure its horrid reign with patience, for in due time God will destroy it.

Third, there was a slow and almost imperceptible slide back into many of the features of Judaism which Jesus and Paul had so firmly opposed. It was inevitable that Christians wanted clear rules, but the result was a reproduction of the Torah in Christian dress, most noticeable in writings which did not find a place in the canon of the New Testament, but which had great influence, such as the Didache. This was written in the second century as a manual of instruction which described the two ways of Life and Death, and purported to be the teaching of the apostles. Here some very Jewish features are most apparent. There is a complete confusion of deeds and dispositions; a self-righteous complacency appears, together with excessive scrupulosity over minor details; that the Christian life is lived under grace is almost ignored, the whole stress being on the keeping of the laws; obedience seems to replace faith as the key to the Christian life, so that God appears primarily as the Lawgiver; much stress is laid upon rewards and the accumulation of merit. One of the saddest features is the way in which there is a reaction against the Jewish institutions, but not the spirit of them. Thus whereas the Jews fasted on Monday and Thursday, the Christians were ordered to do so on Wednesday and Friday. In general, legalism has appeared again, with its attendant dangers.

Fourth, the early church was pitted against all sorts of rival religious systems in the big whirlpool of ideas within the Roman Empire. Many of these systems had a rough affinity, and could be loosely called 'Gnostic'. They taught that the human being is a divine spark trapped within an evil physical body, redemption being secured by special 'knowledge' or 'gnosis' whereby at death the saved soul could be ensured of flying back to God. Two different attitudes could be taken to morality. Either one could assume that, once initiated into the special wisdom, behaviour did not matter at all, or one could develop a profound distaste for the physical and material. The first attitude leads to moral indifference; the second to asceticism. The early church had to oppose both positions, and traces of that conflict are only too clear in I John, Colossians, and possibly Corinthians. Christians asserted that the physical was not essentially evil, for Jesus had come 'in the flesh'; that salvation was not for a select elite of initiates, but for all men; that morality was neither an indifferent matter nor one of denying the physical.

But there was one unfortunate result of this whole struggle. Some Christians began to teach that there are two Christian paths, one which involves a total acceptance of worldly, material life and its obligations (such as marriage), but the other involving withdrawal from the world to concentrate upon the spiritual. The latter began to be held up as superior, and thus the 'double standard' appeared in Christianity. Those who were first-class Christians took the way of withdrawal, with various degrees of asceticism; those who practised the normally involved life had to be content with some sort of second-class status. As Maurice Wiles remarks: 'The concept of the two standards cannot be allowed to stand unchallenged. Its root conviction is that God is to be found pre-eminently in withdrawal from the world. The early church . . . never really accepted that God can be as fully served within the affairs of the world as in seclusion from them.'[38] All this had, as we shall see, a profound effect upon the emerging Christian sexual ethics, but there were other important consequences too. This takes us beyond the period of the New Testament literature.

Questions for Discussion

(a) How would you summarize, in a few phrases, the ethical insights within the Bible?

(b) How important is for the Christian to try to follow out Jesus' teaching? Is it impossible to obey literally? If so, what should one do about it?

Chapter 3

How can we Utilize the Bible in Christian Ethics?

IN the imaginary family conversation outlined in Chapter 1 the daughter counselled her mother to find the answer to the morality of abortion in the Bible. The Bible will tell us. Later she said that we need a much better set of everyday rules 'based upon . . . the Bible'. The father was less sanguine at this point. He did not see the Bible providing help over many of today's problems. In the light of the last chapter, outlining the type of reflection and teaching upon ethics that occurs within the Bible, we return to those assertions and to the value which the Bible has, or should have, for Christian ethics.

It is clear that there are many Christians today who feel that all features of our lives are changing with bewildering rapidity; all the authorities that were previously regarded as stable – church, scripture, tradition – are now so challenged as to appear tentative and mutable; the familiar sets of *mores* which outlined the 'good life' for our forefathers now appear dated and defective; there is therefore an irresistible longing for some clear-cut, permanent directions for the Christian life. We can live with a good deal of uncertainty and change as long as some fundamental matters, beliefs and outlooks don't change very much at all. Since it is widely held that ethics shouldn't change very much (since what was right in one generation ought to be right for any other), there is a constant longing for immutable ethical laws or rules or orders to be dispensed from the Christian churches, and for these to be rooted and grounded in the Bible or, preferably, to be presented as if they were the quintessence of ethical wisdom in the Bible.

That longing cannot be dismissed out of hand as being childish or silly. If you were invited to a party and asked what you should wear and what would be happening, you would be disturbed if the reply were: wear absolutely anything and do what you fancy. You would press the question further. What will most others wear? What clothes would in practice be unsuitable? What activity or clothing would cause offence to the sort of people there? Can you not give me any sort of guidance? If, after a lot of questioning, the answer were to be more specific, even directive, you would feel relieved and more confident in going. We need to know what is expected of us before most of us can feel secure and assured. In a fast-changing culture in which many ethical landmarks are being removed, that need grows more insistent. But because Christians always relate matters of faith and morals in some way or other to the Bible as one of the major sources for authoritative guidance, the longing expresses itself as a desire to know 'what the Bible says' or 'what the Bible teaches'.

To a limited extent, the longing can be satisfied. There is indeed invaluable ethical guidance to be gleaned from the Bible. But it is not possible to glean a detailed code of behaviour which will be adequate for Christians in today's world and will provide extensive indications as to how to resolve the moral problems we encounter most frequently. There are four main reasons for this:

1. There is a considerable diversity within the various biblical traditions, with three somewhat different strands of teaching within the Old Testament, and several different approaches by the major writers within the New.[1] Further, there is sometimes a noticeable discontinuity between the Old and New Testaments, yet in other respects the attitudes within the Old seem to flow into the new very smoothly. Thus in the Old it is assumed that moral teaching applies to the whole nation, which can be exhorted to become a 'holy people'. In the New it is assumed that Christians are a minority people within situations in which other faiths may predominate. There is thus a very different style of social teaching within the New, and some Christians even go so far as to suggest that there is no teaching there about society as a whole. Yet in other matters we can easily sense the continuity. Take almsgiving as an example. It is upheld in the Old as a fundamental and constant duty; you must give to the poor and needy.[2] This teaching is carried slightly further forward in the New; you must do it without any sense of self-righteousness and in as secret a manner as possible.[3] But this is of course a fairly non-controversial matter of personal ethics, one which does not normally raise big or awkward problems.

2. The biblical writers were living within a very different culture and thought-world from that of today. The distance between them and us is immense. There is a great distance between us and the Victorian world, one which requires imaginative efforts from us before we can properly identify with Victorian problems; but the distance between us and, say, the church of the first century, or, further back, Israelite society of the tenth century BC is colossal. One simply cannot transpose teaching from two or three thousand years ago into today's world and imagine that the culture gap can be ignored.

This problem is sometimes countered by the claim that God's will remains constant, so that what God willed for the peasant community in Amos' time can be assumed to be congruent with what God wills for the industrial communities of today. That is half true. Of course there is congruence between the God of Israel and the Lord of twentieth-century civilization. His nature has not experienced some sort of transformation; as the biblical writers put it, God is 'faithful'. But man's whole thought-world has been massively changed: our whole way of thinking about and feeling after God, our way of talking about him, reflecting about him, our expectations of him, our awareness of him. This problem can undoubtedly be exaggerated,[4] but that does not invalidate the contention that we cannot neatly derive a body of moral teaching from the Bible and apply it to a culture that is many thought-worlds away.

An obvious instance arises from the sphere of economics and money. In the Old Testament the economy was primarily one of barter, with money playing a more secondary role in the affairs of the rich. There are a few hints as to how money was to be handled, but remarkably few. Especially, usury is forbidden.[5] It was wrong to lend money and then charge interest on the loan in addition to expecting repayment in due course. Every seven years there was to be a year of Jubilee in which all debts were to be cancelled. It is simply not possible to transfer that teaching into current economic life. Money has now become almost the sole means of exchange within social economic life; interest has to be charged on borrowed money because it is a legitimate reward for the use of that money; debts cannot be cancelled every seven years because our complex institutions have to have considerably more permanence than such short-term arrangements could permit; money today is a means of exchange not merely between one individual and another, but between large groupings of persons and other similar groupings. It is not possible, then, to extract some economic rules from the Bible and impose them on to contemporary society, however necessary it may be to construct some sort of morality for modern commerce and business.[6]

3. As an extension of the previous point, many modern ethical problems have no apparent precursors in biblical times, so that it is not possible to surmise from a reading of the Bible any general principles or more specific injunctions which could govern our approach to them. Take, for instance, the important ethical problem of abortion. There is no apparent precursor of this in the Bible, no discussion about the significance of the foetus or embryo. Or, again, the problems posed by the development of nuclear energy. Here the ethical issues centre upon the issue of risk. When is a risk legitimate, and when is it not? Is it morally acceptable to run a slight risk of the occasional accident, of workers' exposure to radiation, of terrorists capturing the installations, or of the long-term dangers from the waste products? There is hardly a clue in the Bible as to how to evaluate risks, what criteria one uses when doing so. Or, again, the moral problems posed by police work in the advanced urban societies. Should police be armed? Should they be answerable to citizens' control? Should they have access to confidential information? There are no helps to be derived from the biblical literature. These very significant problems are largely the product of the societies spawned by the industrial and technological revolutions. Despite their being unmentioned in the Bible they are, however, extremely important matters affecting the well-being of millions of people and the forms which human society should take.

4. A more debatable and highly-charged point must also be faced. It is normally dodged, or fudged, in books on Christian ethics. It is baldly this: must one assume that the teaching in the Bible was necessarily and in every respect right for the time in which it was written, let alone for our time? If, for instance, a law was adumbrated in the book of Deuteronomy and does not appear to be refuted or amended later, is it still to be regarded automatically as a valid one for that period as well, perhaps, as for ours? Might it not have been to some extent in error even for the community in which it was initially known? Or, coming to the New Testament, must one assume that all of Paul's reflections upon ethical issues were wholly adequate? Or those

of James, or Peter, or John, or the authors of the Pastoral Epistles? Or the writer of Jude? Or were there deficiencies about these reflections even for the communities of that time, to which they were addressed?

All Christians have such a fundamental respect for the Bible that they tend to react to such a threatening question with abhorrence, as if it is an implicit blasphemy. But is it? We have noticed that Jesus repudiated some Old Testament teaching and laws, amended some, but confirmed some. He did not apparently regard them as immutable merely because they were to be found within Scripture. Matthew 5 contains a whole sequence of references to such laws and, in contrast, Jesus' teaching. 'You have heard that it was said . . . but I say unto you . . . ' We have noticed, too, how a writer like James can write with little apparent reference to the ministry of Jesus, how the Pastorals appear to be somewhat pedestrian, how John can narrow down the arena within which Christians should be loving, how all sorts of limitations began to creep into the teaching of the early church. That teaching is not infallible, not inerrant, was not regarded as being so at the time, and did not automatically resolve the ethical dilemmas of the time.

There is no need for us to squirm at this unpleasant assertion. It does not mean that there is no permanent value in the biblical witness, or that we cannot postulate some sort of authority for the Bible, or that we must discount any sort of inspiration in the biblical writings. A book or poem or vision can be inspired without being infallible. A modern theologian of the Bible puts it like this: 'That (the Bible) contains statements erroneous in scientific and historical regards has already been implied . . . But there is every reason to agree that theologically also the Bible is imperfect. It is not a textbook of the most refined Christian doctrine . . . The status of the Bible is one of sufficiency rather than of perfection.'[7] We have to read the Bible, he says, with 'critical awareness'. A highly orthodox theologian of a previous generation, still revered as one of those who refused to duck the most significant problems, wrote of the reverence Christians ought to feel for the scriptures, the church, and the sacraments, and remarked: 'When they have done their proper work, when they have introduced us personally to God and left us together, it is not fatal if we find flaws in their logic, character, or faith . . . Defects . . . need not destroy the real religious witness they bear . . . Secure in the God to whom they have led us, we turn at our ease and leisure to examine their flaws with a quiet and kindly mind, knowing that they do not cost us our soul's life.'[8]

One of the most vivid examples for the modern world is the biblical teaching on the status of women. In the Old Testament woman is regarded as inferior to man in every respect. Judaism was a religion which exalted the male and kept the female in submission; a wife was in effect the property of her husband. In the New Testament there are no traces of Jesus teaching that woman was subordinate, but clearly that was a feature of the early household codes and was assumed by all the biblical writers. There is a tiny trace of a different attitude in Paul, when he wrote that, 'In Christ there is neither male nor female . . . ', but this insight does not appear to have been consistently applied and its full implications worked out. Instead, Paul can order women to be quiet in church and can produce a variety of not very satisfying arguments why their heads should be covered.[9] The writer of I Timothy justifies this attitude by reference to Adam and Eve; Adam was made first, and Eve was the one to first succumb to sin.[10] This strong assertion of male superiority, that runs almost unchallenged throughout the Bible, contributed substantially to the subservient role women have had in European culture up to the present day.[11]

A common method of some Christian apologetic is to argue that the biblical teaching does indeed assert the equality of status of man and woman, but that it was wholly inexpedient for the early church to assert it.[12] It would have meant such a challenge to existing society that the church would have been branded as a 'feminist revolution'; it would have meant that great numbers of people would have rejected the Christian faith for the wrong reasons (i.e. because it implied the exaltation of women, whereas the one true ground for rejection is that the faith implies the exaltation of Jesus as Christ); it would have been fundamentally bad tactics, making it impossible for the faith to spread so rapidly. But there is no scrap of evidence that the New Testament writers thought of the issue in these terms. It has never been asserted within the Bible that one should not do something held to be essentially right on the grounds that it may cause people to reject God for inadequate reason. There is no hint that what we moderns regard as 'tactics' was ever seriously considered by the early church. These unconvincing arguments are usually deployed to escape the disagreeable conclusion that perhaps the early church was to some degree in error, and does not offer to us the sort of teaching in this area which should be regarded as finally authoritative.

There are, then, four reasons why Christians cannot go in a simplistic way to the Bible and extract from it straightforward ethical direction or instruction for life today. The Bible is not, therefore, a 'problem solver'. It is not an equivalent of the books of maker's instructions which accompany machines or gadgets today. If the car goes wrong, you look up the appropriate advice in the manual; if the hair dryer falters, you refer to the accompanying leaflet. You cannot, however, look up some passage in the Bible if you are bothered by a dispute at work and are not sure what to do (as with the father in the family conversation). You cannot refer to the Bible in order to discover which way to vote in the next parliamentary or local elections. The Bible is more significant, more valuable, more profound, than are instructional manuals or political commentaries, or, indeed, books on Christian ethics. The Bible is the assembled witness of the Jewish and Christian communities to the central events of their faith, as authorized by the Christian church by about AD 376. It was never intended to be a short cut to the problems of Christian living, or an encyclopaedia of moral instruction, or a compendium of moral rules. In the end we merely devalue it if we try to make it into any such thing.

Is Jesus' teaching binding upon us?

Granted the difficulties cited above in regarding the Bible as an unambiguous moral authority for Christians today, can we not regard Jesus' teaching as binding upon us? After all, for Christians, it is regarded as a normal approach to the Bible to see Jesus Christ as the supreme authority *within* scripture. That which clearly points to Christ, that which clearly derives from Christ, that which clearly explains the significance of Christ, is to be regarded as the ultimate authority. Passages of scripture can be roughly assessed by those criteria. This makes some portions of the Old Testament of minimal value to the Christian – e.g. those which describe the details of the sacrificial rituals, now superseded by the ministry of Jesus. It also provides criteria for evaluating New Testament passages – e.g. the censoriousness of the Epistle of Jude is noticeably further away from the spirit of Christ than is the patient long-suffering advocated in I Peter, so the latter has more authority than the former. Using this yardstick, then, Christians can perhaps come to the Bible as a whole, not just to the New Testament, and find there the decisive authority for moral behaviour.

Again, this is not satisfactory. As before, we can group the difficulties into four main ones, some of them being the same as noted before in the previous section.

1. It is often impossible to establish with adequate certainty what exactly Jesus said or meant by what he is reported to have said. His teaching has come down to us through the memory and experience of the early church, and through the work and writing of particular people ('Matthew', 'Mark', 'Luke', etc.) who had specific interests they wished to promote, specific 'slants' upon the material. Thus we have the difficulties over Jesus' teaching on marriage and divorce, mentioned in the previous chapter. It is noticeable that Roman Catholics read the texts and see Jesus teaching the indissolubility of marriage; Protestants read the same texts and derive a different conclusion. The nub of the problem is, to begin with, in determining what exactly Jesus said. Again and again we are driven to the sombre conclusion that we do not know. We can surmise with a fair degree of assurance, but we cannot assert with certainty what Jesus taught us. Did he command Christians to fast regularly? To baptize infants? To give away all property? The textual evidence in the New Testament can be interpreted differently, and has given rise to endless controversy and different practices. It does not apparently offer clear-cut direction.

But the problems do not disappear when the original teaching seems to have been preserved in its original sharpness and clarity. When asked whether or not his disciples should pay tax to the Roman occupying power, a critically important issue for the day, we are fairly certain that Jesus replied, 'Render to Caesar the things that are Caesar's, and to God the things that are God's' (Matt. 22.21; Mark 12.17; Luke 20.25). The saying is very well attested and can readily be regarded as authentic. So far, so good. But what does its meaning embrace? Are 'the things that are Caesar's' to be understood as *all* money circulating within a regime? *All* taxes levied by the government? And what are 'the things that are God's' which remain quite undefined by the saying or the context? And might there not be some overlap between the two? Might a cruel government impose a tax which some poor people cannot pay unless they let their children starve? In that case, does the saying mean that the tax should be paid, or is the feeding of the children to be seen as 'the things of God' and the tax not paid? The text in itself offers no help to such problems. If we look at the commentaries it soon becomes obvious that Jesus' answer can be very variously understood. For example, in the Pelican New Testament Commentaries J. C. Fenton on Matthew makes no reference here to any presumed teaching on the roles of church and state;[13] D. E. Nineham on Mark says that, 'Essentially . . . Jesus is not enunciating any principle bearing on the problem of "Church and State"';[14] on the other hand, G. B. Caird on Luke says that, 'nothing in the gospels speaks more eloquently of the robust quality of his mind than his ability, in the momentary exchange of controversy, to enunciate a principle which has proved to be the basis of all future discussion of the problem of Church and State'.[15] To know what Jesus said does not then offer an immediate chance of incontrovertible guidance or moral direction but may only serve to raise fresh problems about which highly competent Christians will disagree.

2. If we were certain about Jesus' teaching, we would then almost inevitably have to ask ourselves, as was noted in the previous chapter, whether or not it is practicable in this fallen world. There we noticed how Christians have offered a wide range of interpretations of, say, the Sermon on the Mount, in serious attempts to resolve the gulf between Jesus' teaching and the normal considerations which Christians bear in mind in everyday conduct.[16] Again and again Christians of many differing dispositions have claimed that these commands can indeed be literally obeyed, but in the end have had to resort to some subtle interpretative device to bridge that gulf. Thus much Catholic theology has maintained that Jesus teaches both 'commandments', which every disciple can obey, and 'counsels', which only those with a special vocation can obey, but has often added the quick comment that this does not imply a morality on two different levels.[17] The 'gulf' has been narrowed down until the claim can actually be made that, 'in catholic moral theology the demands of Jesus are interpreted in such a way that they can be fulfilled by men with the help of the grace of God'.[18]

Or again, there have always been sectarian movements which have claimed that Jesus can be literally obeyed. They have been obliged to sit light to normal obligations to human institutions such as the state, and have run into the dangers of fanaticism sooner or later. They express LeRoy Long's 'intentional motif'.

3. As noted above, Jesus' teaching took place in a different sort of world and culture from that of today. What was significant or relevant then will not necessarily be significant or relevant now. His command to carry the pack of a soldier belonging to the occupying power not one mile, but two, is plainly a command which pertains to the world of his time. Nobody seriously argues that this can be done somehow in the modern world, for soldiers' supplies are now transported by lorry or helicopter.

4. Jesus did not refer to many of the pressing moral problems of our time. He lived long before the great revolutions in men's thinking which ushered in the complex modern societies able to utilize sophisticated technology, rapid transport, and vast resources of money and organized labour.

However, although we cannot go directly to Jesus' teaching, can we instead seek a slightly different, but related, goal? Can we try to determine what Jesus would *do* in our circumstances? That quest has a slightly romantic ring to it, yet it can be argued that Jesus' deeds were wholly consistent with his teaching and offer us both examples of moral rightness as well as clear indicators of the sort of principles and attitudes whereby Christians ought to live now. Jesus demonstrated a style of living in which he loved his enemies and forgave them; showed compassion to all sorts of people; sought to deliver everyone from fear, sin and oppression; lived with a care-free detachment from material goods; we should adopt the same, or similar, attitudes. We should do what we know Jesus would do.

But again there are fundamental difficulties. In a vast range of modern situations, if we refer to the gospel evidence and seek there some comparable situation, we do not know what Jesus would do. The trade union leader has no idea whatever as to what Jesus would do if in his shoes, because Jesus never was in a comparable situation, as far as we can tell. Jesus was never married, so he does not offer any obvious clues, from his behaviour during his earthly ministry, to the appropriate life-styles for married people. Jesus was never, as far as we can tell, a businessman, or a banker, or a politician, or a journalist. For many years he was probably a carpenter, and there is virtually nothing known about that period of his life. The writers of the New Testament regarded it as of insufficient importance to warrant even a few stories or anecdotes – a clear sign that they did not reckon to learn anything of vital importance from it, and did not expect it to be of any value to subsequent generations of Christians. After that Jesus was a wandering preacher; few Christians today are called to that sort of life, or needed in that sort of role. We cannot presume to resolve our ethical problems by discovering what Jesus would do in comparable situations.

The error which has been haunting the whole of the discussion so far in this chapter is that of assuming that the Bible on its own is a sufficient authority or source for Christian ethics. It never has been, and never will be. Always Christians have utilized in some way some other authorities and sources. Their reading of the Bible has been partly determined by their respect for these other authorities and sources. Thus those Christians who have believed that support for their own nation is an essential element in their discipleship have read the Bible in the light of that conviction, and have found a passage such as Rom. 13 to be particularly cogent and strong as the Word of God. Those who have been convinced that war is the ultimate blasphemy have read the Bible in the light of that conviction and have found Matt. 5 to be particularly cogent and strong as the Word of God to them. The first group has been willing to take part in most of the nation's wars; the second group has not. Both have appealed to the Bible, but both have in practice been needing other authorities as well as that of the Bible. There is nothing wrong in doing so, but both parties need to be aware of what is being done.

The original question with which this chapter began – how can we utilize the Bible in Christian ethics? – has to be preceded by an initial question before it can be properly answered. We first have to ask: what are the resources for Christian ethics? We turn, then, to that question, before returning to the original one.

What are the main resources for Christian ethics?

In practice there are four main 'resources', or 'centres of authority', often differently described in the different Christian traditions.

1. *The Bible*. On page 50 it was defined as 'the assembled witness of the Jewish and Christian communities to the central events of their faith, as authorized by the Christian church by about AD 376'. Acting on that definition, the Bible is both Old

and New Testaments; is witness to the 'central events' of the faith and not, therefore, to every element within the faith and to every problem with which the believer may be concerned; is that which was so authorized by the Christian church; was assembled and tested over a long period – over 300 years – and did not drop down from heaven as one finished and perfect product. It does not include some literature which Judaism regarded as authoritative, such as the Mishnah. This was the collection of oral tradition made by the Pharisees during the period 200 BC – AD 200, which related the laws of the Torah to every-day living. They held it to be as important as the Torah, a view which has great consequences for ethics. The Christian church did not so judge it, nor did it so judge many very inspiring and helpful books circulating in the church in the first three centuries. As a result, they did not become authorized as part of the canon of scripture.

2. *The tradition of the church*. This is the wisdom accumulated within its life and expressed in various significant ways such as the formulation of the creeds or the fixing of the canon of scripture. Since the church decided what was scripture and what was not, it is obvious that one cannot divorce the authority of the Bible from that of the church. The Bible was, in many ways, the product of the church's life, reflection, preaching and memory. If there had been no church able to attempt to formulate some sort of common mind, there could hardly have been a Bible consisting of the New as well as the Old Testament. On the other hand, the church owed its existence to those events about which the Bible testified, and its way of understanding them was expressed supremely in the Bible, so that the Bible is in some way a reference point for what is to be properly understood as 'church' and what is not. A church that does not see its life as determined by the Bible, tested and validated by the Bible, can hardly claim to be a 'Christian' church at all.

3. *Reason*. Reason is notoriously difficult to define; it is easier to sense what is unreasonable. It is unreasonable when an argument cannot logically be held to follow from the premises upon which it was formulated. It is unreasonable when a presumed conclusion is not demonstrated by the available facts or not validated by the criteria held to be relevant. It is in these senses that 'reason' is a resource, in that coherence with presuppositions and available evidence must be practised. Within this somewhat loose understanding of reason one must,

of course, include the experimental evidence provided by the modern 'sciences', without holding the view that 'science' is an ultimate authority in moral matters. It is based upon assumptions that constantly need scrutiny, and often has to adopt methods which are inspired guesswork, and to formulate 'results' which are general observations about the way in which matter normally appears to function. However, Christian ethics is rooted in respect for knowing 'how things actually are', on the facts of the case, which involves respect for scientific data.

4. *The current experience of Christians.* This is not to be subsumed under 'tradition', the second source, because that has an essentially and inescapably backward look. Tradition harks back to the foundation experiences of the church, and the build-up of insights, theology, regularized practices, liturgy, etc., which followed. Current experience is necessarily orientated to the present scene and is, of course, a continuation of tradition and will, to subsequent generations, be regarded as part of tradition. For the time being it has a freshness, a rawness, that tradition does not possess. It may include some new elements altogether, produced by modern living. Thus in ethics we can hardly regard the Christian reflection upon the problems of the atomic era as being part of tradition. They are current experience, and are requiring us to find new ways of discussing moral issues in order to cope with them. This is not merely a question of finding new words and terms, but new ways of understanding the character of the ethical issues before us.

However, if there are these four general areas of 'resource' or of 'authority' in Christian ethics, how much weight should be given to each? Which is the most important, the most authoritative? Are they equally important? That question has to be side-stepped, because it implies that they are of a like character and can be somehow balanced against each other, just as one can balance the claims made, say, upon one's weekly wages. Housekeeping requires some, the running of the car requires some, savings must be given a share, money must be given away to charitable purposes, etc. Each of these claims can be expressed in terms of quantities (of money): £60 housekeeping, £30 car, £10 savings, £10 charity, and so on. But the 'resources' cited above are not readily comparable, and cannot conceivably be quantified at all. The Bible is a collection of written witness to certain events and a key person (Jesus Christ). Tradition is an ongoing body of teaching, etc., which is nowhere written down in some authorized corpus of books. Reason is a facility within the human make-up. Experience is our perception of how certain truths or factors have impinged upon our existence. We cannot compare these and say that one is twice as valuable as one of the others and half as valuable as the final two. But in practice most of us tend to put the most stress upon one of these areas of 'resource', and to use the others to suplement this. Here, Christians differ markedly, and the different Christian traditions differ.

Protestants tend to put the greatest weight on to scripture, and often begin their ethical enquiries by trying to find out what the Bible says; they make constant reference back to scriptural teaching. Earlier in the chapter we noted the problems inherent in this practice. But we should also note the severe difficulty in identifying a practice as 'Christian' if it could not be shown as congruent with the general tenor of scripture and the character of Jesus' ministry and teaching. This difficulty has arisen in the contemporary scene over the practice of apartheid, for example. It is hardly possible to say that there is explicit teaching in the Bible on the subject of the relationships between the different races and the way in which they should live together within any one nation. Yet it is possible to show convincingly that the practice of apartheid is basically contrary to the whole style of life and understanding of human relationships which is assumed by the biblical writers and in the teaching of Jesus.[19] Apartheid can in this sense be shown to be 'unscriptural'; it can then be labelled 'un-Christian'. This is not to deny that some Christians have vigorously argued against such a conclusion, but they have been a very small minority, and have been those who have had such obvious self-interest at stake that other Christians are entitled to be sceptical about their case.

Catholics tend to have placed the greatest weight upon tradition, most especially as this is preserved and elaborated within the magisterium, or teaching office, of the church. That office is not, however, infallible. This means that the faithful owe to this teaching an internal assent of intellect and will, whereas to the infallible teaching an absolute assent of faith is required. The normal way in which this teaching office is expressed, as far as morals is concerned, is through the encyclical letters issued by the Pope and, less significantly, through the occasional pastoral letters issued by the hierarchy in any particular country. The assumption behind all such teaching is that it is a development of what has gone before, stretching back to the early Church Fathers and to the New Testament. This means that the Bible and early Fathers will be extensively quoted, and somewhat elaborate attempts made to show that current teaching is consistent both with them and other encyclicals on the subject. The event which threw this whole edifice into the greatest question in recent times was undoubtedly the Papal encyclical *Humanae Vitae* of 1968, dealing with marriage and contraception. The extensive questioning of the arguments, the discovery that large numbers of Catholics did not obey it, and the conviction that it represented the teaching of only a conservative section of the church, threw both its internal teaching and the assumptions about the magisterium and the general notions of a steady 'development' of moral teaching, into ferment.[20] We can sense Long's 'prescriptive' motif here.

Other traditions place a certain amount of weight upon the judgments of the church, but do not claim such a highly-developed authority for their pronouncements. There is a greater feeling of individual liberty to dissent from the church's judgments, and an explicit denial that she could be infallible in any respect. There is little attempt to claim any strong thread of inevitable continuity with previous judgments, and little attempt to try and build each judgment upon previous ones, thus implying some steady development.

It is with reference to these two general areas of authority that Christian ethics inevitably shows its differences with other styles of ethics. This is not the place for arguing that Christian ethics tend to be necessarily more satisfying, better argued, more appropriate to the business of everyday living, than the ethics of secularists, or humanists, or communists, or anyone else. It is merely to point out that in their ethical systems there is of course no need whatever to cite scripture or the church (except perhaps for polemical purposes, to show the dangers of referring to these two areas of authority). But in the next two areas of general authority one notices at once the high degree of overlap with the ethics of others.

The Catholic tradition has always stressed the significance of reason, especially since the major framework of Catholic thinking was set out most cogently by St Thomas Aquinas, who drew extensively on the teaching of Aristotle. Reason is that faculty which demonstrates the distinction between humans and the brutes. Moreover, by reason man may acquire a basic knowledge of morality by reflection upon the structure of life as he can perceive it directly, without any teaching from Bible or church. Aristotle had taught that there is a natural justice, and that most men can recognize it. Thomas taught that all men participate in the eternal law and use reason to direct themselves to it; they know that they must pursue certain good 'ends' in life; they must preserve the self; they must not voluntarily do harm to any other person. Thomas was not prepared to go very far in delineating the content of this natural law, but his teaching has had an enormous effect upon all Catholic teaching.

This stress upon reason is not, however, a solely Roman Catholic trait. It occurs strongly in a great deal of Anglican social and moral teaching, and has often been separated from a rigid belief in natural law, which has not necessarily been held to be convincing by Anglicans. It inevitably makes Christian ethics more willing to appreciate the results of enquiries within other relevant, more scientifically-orientated, disciplines (e.g. psychology, sociology, anthropology). But some Protestant traditions have been unable to lay such weight upon the human faculty of reason, holding that in the Fall the totality of man's condition was corrupted, including his thinking and rational powers. This has been particularly stressed in Lutheran circles, and those modern theologians most anxious to stress the inadequacy of man and the primacy of God's saving gracious acts in Christ. Karl Barth, determined to see ethics as our listening to God's gracious command and responding obediently in faith, states firmly, 'Reason cannot be the guide I meet in acknowledgment'[21] (i.e. in acknowledging God's commands).

But the Anglican traditional position does perhaps remind us of the perils of becoming unreasonable at any point, as the following quotation shows: 'One must seek economy and consistency within the conceptual scheme of a religion, coherence of the scheme with conclusions in other areas of human investigations, and adequacy to interpret and illuminate the data of practical experience. If these are not sought, one's religious beliefs will remain at a primitive and superstitious level; if they are not found, a religious scheme will, to that extent, become irrational.'[22] Here one senses Long's 'deliberative' motif.

The fourth general area is the one to which the most attention has been directed in current theology and ethics – that of 'experience'. This is true especially, but not solely, in Protestant circles which have been the most receptive to existentialism and the whole stress upon the importance of the decisions made deliberately by the self. These are what make us into significant human beings; 'authentic' life is that in which we make them in somewhat rugged independence from the other traditional authorities. This may, however, sound extreme to those who still want to assert that no authority is valid until it has knowingly and responsibly been accepted as such by the self. I must for myself accept the weight of scripture, or Church, or 'reason', and must for myself test out their contribution to my ethical quests.

It is here that one encounters again the inner sense of moral obligation which we all possess and which seems as if it has come to us 'from outside'. It seems to be true of almost all human beings (hence the belief that natural law is a universal human awareness of obligation). It is most noticeable when, looking back upon an act, one feels an accusing finger somewhere within one, telling one that one did wrong. We call it 'a bad conscience', in which case we are meaning by 'conscience' the faculty for moral evaluation. It feels as if it comes from God, or from some source much greater than ourselves, hence our sense of awe about it. Christian teaching has been adamant that we must not immediately identify the reflection of conscience with the voice of God, despite this feeling of awe that often goes with it when we believe that we have sinned. But it is a Christian duty to train our conscience, to nurture our ability both to perceive and do the right acts, and to cultivate the right motivations.[23] However, there is a tendency in charismatic Christianity to claim immediate awareness of God's will, either in terms of guidance for tasks to be done, or in evaluation of past acts, and thus a tendency to put almost all the weight upon this area of 'experience', despite the warnings from much of Christian tradition. In charismatic Christianity one meets an extreme example of Long's 'relational' motif.

Whilst these four areas of authority have often been identified fairly closely with one of the Christian traditions in the past, it is now apparent that almost all Christians are increasingly being aware of their need for all these authorities. The old distinctions are becoming more and more blurred. Roman Catholics, for example, are becoming far more consciously indebted to scripture; Protestants more consciously indebted to tradition. Indeed, each of these traditions seem to be steadily moving much closer to the other in general method.[24]

To return to the original question at the beginning of the chapter, how we can utilize the Bible in Christian ethics, our conclusion would be that in practice nobody actually uses the Bible alone as the sole authority, even if they claim that they are relying upon scripture alone. In practice ethical judgments depend upon several areas of authority, with the scriptures being claimed to hold a central place in almost all Christian schemes even when the basic sources are probably elsewhere.[25] But is there some standard, or ideal, method of holding these four areas of authority together? Alas, no. At this point there are inevitably many different methods and many different theories. It is beyond the wit of man to formulate a wholly satisfactory theoretical model as to how this should be done. Moreover, in practice, these four areas must be of differing usefulness depending upon the matter being considered. As we have already noted, there are scant resources made available in the Bible for assessing the problems posed by nuclear energy; when considering that matter a great reliance must necessarily be placed upon scientific data, with little help derivable from the Christian tradition and teaching of the church. But when considering the question of truth-telling there is a great deal of reflection available in the Christian tradition, some resources in the Bible, and very little from what one may term 'scientific data'. Thus the Bible is of varying use, along with the other resources. When we encounter teaching that cannot be reconciled with its central witness we can perhaps class it as 'un-Christian'; normally we need all four sources in varying measure.

Questions for Discussion

(a) To what extent can the Bible be a 'final authority' in ethical matters?

(b) Are there any ethical problems in which the teaching of the Bible must give way to other sources of authority (e.g. subordination of women)? If so, how can one justify dependence upon those other sources?

Chapter 4

The Development of Christian Social Teaching

JESUS did not outline any social theory to his disciples, nor any critique of existing social structures. The early theologians, such as Paul, were not primarily concerned with doctrines of society, and showed little interest in tackling what we would understand today as 'social ills'. There was a noticeable attitude of acceptance towards the existing social structures; ethical teaching concentrated powerfully upon the nature of the new person who confessed Jesus as Lord and sought to live 'in the Kingdom'. The new person was commanded to love God utterly, and to love the neighbour as himself. The result was a new community of those who made that confession and tried to practise that love, but a community with no pretensions to being able to put the rest of the world right. It was a small minority community in a largely hostile world, living under a vivid expectation of the imminent end of that world upon the return of Christ.

It soon had to sort out every-day ethical problems as best it could – what do we teach about marriage, about eating food offered to idols, about making vows, about paying taxes, about people who won't work, etc.? Inevitably, teaching which had all sorts of social implications had to be provided, but on an immediate basis of responding to questions as they arose, and without the benefit of some major doctrine of society. Soon all this became caught up in the struggle to sort out the boundaries of the faith. What should Christians believe, and what is outside acceptable belief? What is to be shunned as heresy, and which teachers or teaching is to be distrusted?

Some themes dominated the ethical teaching all along. The Christian must give primary loyalty to God and, if this meant refusing to confess the Emperor as divine, must honour that primal loyalty at the cost of his life. The Christian must practise love to all. The Christian must share all that was possible with the poor and needy. The Christian must abhor violence and killing. But soon, within the first two centuries, other notes were sounded also. The current notions of a universal moral law, mainly Stoic in origin, became steadily assimilated into Christian belief and led to a constant stress upon the equality of all men and thus to constant efforts to ameliorate the lot of slaves. The stress within Greek ethics of cultivating virtues made its way into Christian teaching, so that the cardinal virtues of prudence, justice, courage and temperance were especially upheld. As Maurice Wiles points out, 'it is hardly the most natural classification for discussing the moral teaching of the Bible or of Christ'.[1]

In AD 312, an extraordinary event occurred which transformed almost overnight the whole setting in which the growing church was living. The Emperor Constantine conquered Rome, the key to his asserting his rule over the Empire, and confessed Christianity. The church suddenly found itself the official religion throughout the sprawling and somewhat chaotic world of southern Europe, and saddled with enormous social responsibilities. It had no 'social theory' to work with, but a very considerable experience of the work of charity, plus a lot of shrewd commonsense. As Troeltsch puts it: 'The Church, which acquired great wealth in capital, slaves and land, whose bishops finally played a great part as large landowners, whose assistance was enlisted by the State – which was no longer equal to its responsibilities – for police work, the care of the poor, and the control of the population, possessed on the practical side an extraordinary intelligence in practical matters.'[2]

This meant the rapid creation of a new class of people – the bishops, owners of land and property on an enormous scale, expected to act as judges, guides, teachers, rulers, organizers – in effect, a new aristocracy. The doctrine of natural law was steadily developed so that the state was reckoned to be grounded in this fundamental law of nature, which was then identified with the Law of Moses (and especially the Decalogue), in turn identified with the Law of Christ. No doubt this looks deceptively simple to us today, but it provided theological justification for accepting the role which had so unexpectedly been thrust upon the young unprepared church, as handmaid and partner to the state. It provided no means of offering criticism to the state, of course, so that (as Troeltsch rather acidly puts it) 'All that this "Christianization" amounted to in the end was that everything was left outwardly exactly as it had been before.'[3]

Whilst most things were outwardly as before, much thorough heart-searching went on concerning the use of money. By the end of the fourth century, a pattern of teaching had developed which can be summarized thus:

1. A realistic acceptance of God as Creator, recognizing that all things come from him and are not, in any strict sense, owned by anyone else.
2. We are therefore stewards, or tenants in God's world – to care for and dispense to others on God's behalf.
3. All things are created and provided by God to support all people.
4. Hence ownership has a communal reference prior to any private one.
5. Private ownership makes relative sense, (*a*) so that things be well administered for the social whole, and (*b*) so that a man can support the basic needs of his family and dependents.
6. What is 'earned' comes from one's abilities, intelligence, social setting; these are God's gifts also.
7. Wealth is for using, not hoarding, because it exists precisely to bear fruit.
8. To hold back what could be given to those in need is not merely a lack of kindness, but is an act of injustice, may be theft, and possibly murder.[4]

This teaching stressed stewardship under God, the communal reference, the sin of holding back one's hand from giving to the needy. It is set within a whole attitude towards material possessions which we hardly ever encounter in twentieth-century church life, and about which the churches offer little consistent teaching.

The other major development in the Christian social tradition during this period was the growth of monasticism. Beginning with the flight into the Egyptian deserts of those who despaired of leading the holy life within the normal constraints of social living, and deeply influenced by the prevailing gnostic notions of the evil of the body and its desires, the movement produced its fanatics as well as its saints. It produced the solitary hermit seeking the holy life in isolation, obsessed by the fantasies which his rigours brought forth within his troubled mind. His withdrawal from the world and his fellows implied a denial of the doctrine of creation, that God has made the world in goodness; it implied a denial that one discovers the service of God through service of one's fellows, that one must love the neighbour. But the growing church was generally unmoved by such extremism. It would have agreed with a modern ecumenical statement such as this: 'Complete pessimism regarding the world, which releases the called community from responsibility to withdrawal, is not possible. God has not withdrawn himself . . . '[5], and whilst we moderns would cite our belief in the God whose purpose runs throughout history to promote salvation, the church of the time would have probably laid more stress upon the incarnation as the decisive sign that God is not 'withdrawn' from the world.[6]

The Western and Eastern churches encouraged the monastery as the ideal setting for the holy life. Inevitably this implied the creation of a double standard of morality: the monk was the first-class Christian and the layman caught up in the duties of earning a living and supporting a family became second-class. Maybe that was a price worth paying? It led to the creation of communities in which there was the threefold pattern of work, study and worship laid down in the classic rule of St Benedict in about AD 540, in which the holy life was not pursued in isolation from one's fellows nor in indifference to the world. It led to the creation of centres for learning, piety, education, culture, poor relief, medicine, evangelism, spreading across the whole of Europe in a remarkable network.

In AD 410 another traumatic event shook the ancient world and the young church. Rome again fell, before the armies of Alaric the Goth (an Arian Christian). It was as if the symbol of the world's order and stability had been shattered. To many Christians it caused the most appalling heart-searching and despair. Had God abandoned his world to chaos? Augustine, Bishop of Hippo in North Africa (now known by the French name of Bone), set out to write a major work which would help fellow Christians keep their bearings in such a tumultuous world, and would also rebut those pagans who attributed the fall of Rome to the Christian religion. It ended up a colossus of a book entitled *The City of God*, nearly 1100 pages long in the Pelican translation, and taking sixteen years to write, itself composed of twenty-two 'books'.[7] It was not designed, of course, as a compendium of Christian ethics, but inevitably it includes most of Augustine's mature teaching on ethics together with his understanding of how God works in human history. Thus it includes the sort of material which could be labelled as 'social teaching'.

To Augustine, the supreme 'end' of man is to love God totally as the final satisfaction of all needs; all other 'goods' (e.g. love of neighbour, love of the human race) are to be 'used' as they contribute to the supreme end. But sin has corrupted man so that he loves himself in his pride and is enslaved. When his will is wholly given over to love for God, the 'chief end' can be realized. In popular thought Augustine is often credited with the apparently glib maxim that the Christian ethic is 'Love God and do what you like'. His teaching is better expressed as 'Love God with a wholly devoted will, and then do as that will directs you'.

His social teaching is in essence a profound reflection upon the biblical image of man as a pilgrim seeking a city. We live in two cities at the same time, says Augustine, the one being 'Babylon' in which man's pretentious love for self predominates, the other being 'Jerusalem' in which love for God prevails. All history is an unfolding drama of these two co-existing cities. 'We see then that these two cities were created by two kinds of love: the earthly city was created by self-love reaching the point of contempt for God, the heavenly city by the love of God carried as far as contempt of self. In fact, the earthly city glories in itself, the Heavenly City glories in the Lord . . . in the former, the lust for domination lords it over its princes as over the nations it subjugates; in the other both those put in authority and those subject to them serve one another in love.'[8] The latter city must steadily transform the former, and harmony and good order is especially to be prized. But the earthly city is not equated with the state, nor the heavenly with the church,[9] so that a social theory is not, strictly speaking, being propounded. Long can readily find the 'institutional' motif here.

In mediaeval times the acceptance of the structure of society continued. No significant Christian voices were raised to indicate some other way of organizing human communities. 'It is important to realize that the civilization which developed in the later part of the Middle Ages was perhaps the supreme expression in history of a welfare state in which men exchanged liberty for a measure of social security. The majority of the population were serfs. They were bound to the soil and bound to give labour, but equally they had rights . . . they might starve as the result of plague or crop failure . . . they were not likely to starve as the result of the collapse of the social system.'[10] The one alternative type of community or fraternity was that offered by the monastery or the religious order, but it was never pretended that this was for all men.

But mediaeval thinking came to its finest flower in the thought of Thomas Aquinas (1225–1274). He taught that the supreme end of man was to share in the beatific vision of God. To this end man must practise not only the cardinal virtues of justice, wisdom, prudence, courage and fortitude, but also the theological virtues of faith, hope and charity, which can only be infused into us through God's grace. This happens supremely through the church's sacraments. The natural-law teaching is developed very fully; the law of nature reflects the eternal law of God, which corresponds closely to what we normally mean today by the 'will of God'; that law is expressed in the Law of Moses and the teaching of Christ, and as known in the Decalogue is assented to by reason.

Thomas outlined a hierarchical view of society in which every person has his duties and obligations and rights. In each case those lower in the order have duties towards those higher, but the higher must faithfully exercise their responsibilities to the lower. There is thus a functional view of society, in which everyone has a place and task and is needed by the others. Above all, owing his position to God's authority, is the monarch. But Thomas docs not merely sacralize the existing social order. The monarch has a duty to maintain a law which corresponds to the Eternal Law; if he does not, or if he is incapable of ruling, those under him have a right to rebel. Moreover, Thomas was prepared to go to considerable lengths to clarify the Christian duty within the whole complex web of everyday responsibilities. He postulated a 'just price' for traders, which permitted them to obtain a small profit, sufficiently to meet their needs and those of their family, and sufficient for them to be able to exercise charity towards the needy.

The Reformation and after

The whole edifice of mediaeval ethics was fundamentally challenged in the Reformation. Luther's ethics were wholly different in structure and intent. To him, the fundamental and all determining reality of the Christian life was God's justifying act in Jesus Christ, to be received solely by faith. Therefore no good works could ever merit God's approval; but all works done 'in faith' (or in accord with the first commandment of love to God) would be approved by God, such works being able to be done in the 'freedom' of the Christian man and out of spontaneous love for the neighbour. Alongside his works the Christian will experience suffering, which is more important as the means of growing in faith. Reason will help guide the Christian in his actions, but it is darkened through the Fall and is constantly being reawakened through the preaching of the law and gospel (and even through the acts of governments).

When we turn to social ethics, however, Luther's contribution (1483–1546) has been monumental. He formulated the doctrine of the two kingdoms (or two 'realms' or two 'regiments') whereby God rules the world, these two being clear, Luther held, when one reads the New Testament. There one encounters two types of injunction – in Matt. 5.39 we must turn the other cheek, and in Rom. 13.1 we must obey secular authority. The one injunction pertains to life in Christ's kingdom, where he rules in love through his Word, a rule which only Christians can obey. The other injunction applies to life in the secular kingdom, the state, where God rules in wrath and justice by means of the 'sword' (i.e. the coercive power of the state to restrain and punish evil), using the secular power (or 'prince') to control all men. The former rule (through Christ) is the 'right-hand' rule of God; the latter is the 'left-hand' rule. The former is destined to be eternal; the latter is temporary. The church is an agent within the right-hand rule; the prince and magistrate and soldier are agents on the left.

Luther thus gave a divine mandate to princes, whether they were Christian or not (and reckoned a Christian prince to be unusual). The prince's duty was to practise stern justice in checking evil, to allow the church her liberty in preaching the gospel, to defend the state from all rivals and to honour God. He abolished all notions of there being one Christian pattern for the 'religious' (i.e. that of the monastery) and another inferior pattern for the laity, and taught that all Christians are called to live faithfully within both the secular kingdom and that of Christ. Duty within the former was to be expressed within the 'orders of creation' such as the state, marriage, and the world of work and commerce. A Christian was to recognize that with a secular calling he might have secular duties which required wholly different behaviour from that which he would exercise in a personal capacity as a private citizen (thus as a magistrate a Christian may have to be very strict towards thieves, but in a personal capacity should be generous towards the needy).

Luther's highly complex position has been massively criticized on three main counts. First, it is suspected that he has allowed the state a rule which is not subject to Christ, and has thus appeared to drive a distinction between God's reign operating 'without Christ' and his reign operating through Christ. How can God rule other than through his trinitarian being? Modern Lutherans have striven hard to show that Luther's position can be reinterpreted here and that the left-hand rule through the 'orders' or 'mandates' can be understood as a rule in Christ.[11] Second, the autonomy he has granted to the secular spheres has really been thoroughly conservative, enabling them to exist without a sharp prophetic critique from the Word of God. During the German church struggle against Hitler which developed in the 1930s, many observers held that Lutheran theology was preventing the church from making an appropriate witness, a criticism which Karl Barth was making as early as in 1939 when he noted that, 'Those who want to make a too clean-cut division of the Two Kingdoms or Offices are as ready, today as ever, to appeal to Luther. And unfortunately a good bit of this is justified.'[12] This is usually countered by pointing out that Luther 'stands midway between the long, intricate mediaeval disputation between the Spiritual and Temporal powers in Christendom and the modern dilemma of Church and State. He will not easily fit into either set of problems.'[13] That is, Luther worked at a time when the interminable struggle in Europe between the emperor (wanting a church which was subservient and whose influence was restricted to the spiritual realm) and the church (headed by a pope who wanted to direct emperors and princes) had well-nigh exhausted Europe and produced devastating wars. Luther, in effect, produced a solution which gave the princes considerable scope, but was not advancing the sort of social theory required by the political conditions of our own day.

Next, as an extension of the previous point, Luther does not sense how all political systems, all states, stand under the eschatological and final judgment of God and therefore must be improved. There is no inspiration nor vision for reforming society,[14] and therefore little specific guidance for the amelioration of social ills. As Niebuhr puts it: 'The weakness of the

Lutheran position in the field of social ethics is accentuated . . . by its inability to define constant criteria for the achievement of relative justice . . . Since it rightly has less confidence than Catholicism in the character of reason, it relegates the "natural law", that is, the rational analysis of social obligation, to the background as an inadequate guide. But it has only odds and ends of systems of order to put in the place of "natural laws".[15]

The mediaeval world had seen perpetual struggle between emperor and pope, but a common understanding that the state originates in man's essentially social nature. Luther's view was fundamentally different – the state originates in man's essentially evil and anti-social nature, which must be restrained by law backed by force. There were other Christian voices, those of the various sectarian movements, which saw man's essential nature as evil, and therefore the state as evil, and sought to withdraw from social life into holy communities, or promoted a revolutionary temper. With these Luther had no truck whatever. But a different type of social teaching emerged within the work of John Calvin (1509–1564), both for basic theological reasons and because the city of Geneva, in which Calvin spent the greater part of his ministry, was able to experiment with Calvinist politics. The times were favourable, both economically and politically. The influence of Calvinism has been much more extensive upon the British Isles, Holland, Switzerland, America and South Africa, so much so that Troeltsch even credits it with producing what he calls 'Americanism'.[16]

To Calvin, the good life is one of complete submission to God and his will, so that there is a powerful streak of self-sacrifice and self-control in all his teaching. God in his inscrutable wisdom has ordained some men to salvation, others to perdition. How do we know that we are of the elect? Because we believe in the saving, justifying work of Christ, and because we then find that we produce the good works which the elect will achieve. Good works, especially the works of love, are not a means to salvation, but a sure sign of it. Moreover, the Law of God is an immediate guide to us in these works; here he developed the famous 'third use' of the Law, which drives us to repentance (because we do not fulfil it), requires the coercive power of the state to ensure it (in a world of sinners), but also directs us in the way we should go. Calvin's teaching produced, then, an energetic people who gladly accepted the circumstances of social and economic life as a means of glorifying and serving God. As he put it: 'We must, therefore, administer them (i.e. earthly blessings) as if we constantly heard the words sounding in our ears, "Give an account of your stewardship." At the same time, let us remember by whom the account is to be taken – viz.: by him who, while he so highly commends abstinence, sobriety, frugality, and moderation, abominates luxury, pride, ostentation, and vanity; who approves of no administration but that which is combined with charity, who with his own lips has already condemned all those pleasures which withdraw the heart from chastity and purity, or darken the intellect.'[17]

But Calvin held that God had created mankind unequal; to him, that was obvious. Some had been born to rule and authority, others to serve, but all had equal place within his mercy and purpose. He was adamant that whilst riches may be a sign of God's favour, poverty was definitely not a sign of his disfavour. To help the poor was an essential duty. In economic life Calvin reluctantly agreed to the charging of interest on loans, but only up to 5%, and explicitly condemned any interest on loans to the poor. His ethic has been accused of promoting, and even producing, the spirit of capitalism, about which an interminable argument has ensued.[18] It is probably more accurate to suggest that capitalists have arisen in many settings, and there were several about before Calvin's time, but Calvinism provided a very favourable soil in which the capitalist spirit could grow. Tawney comments that, 'It is perhaps the first systematic body of religious teaching which can be said to recognize and applaud the economic virtues.'[19]

Calvin, unlike Luther, would not permit the state to go its own way with a limited amount of admonition from the church. He saw a much more intimate inter-relationship between the two and, as in so much current Catholicism (but for slightly different reasons), saw the two as virtually co-extensive. The church was the gathering of the elect, which must both feed them with the Word through preaching and sacraments and fellowship and exercise a 'godly discipline' amongst them. Further, the state must facilitate the church's life, must protect the realm against opponents, must maintain law and order, but must also inculcate a 'godly discipline' amongst its citizens, for which it needs the church as indispensable guide and mentor. Calvin could even anticipate a state of affairs in which the ruler should be deposed by the magistrates (in effect, a form of oligarchy); moreover, in the last resort, Calvin seemed to see the ultimate authority residing not in the ruler and his appointment 'under God', but in the will of the people (to which the church could appeal especially through preaching). This latter notion was to have immense consequences, especially when allied to the generally expansionist temper of Calvinism. Those adventurers who were to extend the known world and develop an industrial revolution which would assist them in dominating it would obviously find here the most congenial religious teaching, and where opposed by king or emperor would find the firmest ground from which to justify their wresting of power from ancient authorities.

The Reformation produced nearly two centuries of convulsion in church life in England and Scotland. Lutheranism was never a serious contender, but Calvinism came over the channel as Puritanism, and a long struggle ensued for the soul of the English church. In the end it did not triumph, but the Anglican *via media* did, expressed in its most persuasive form in Richard Hooker's *Of the Laws of Ecclesiastical Polity*, which began to appear in 1594. By the end of the seventeenth century the Puritan party had been forced into a conforming minority within the established Church of England or else forced out into groupings of Presbyterian or Congregationalist order and denied many civic rights, even though in Scotland Presbyterians had acquired an unassailable hold upon the established church. The battles had ended with a fairly clear delineation of the roles of church and state, and a new respect for the Bible. In Scotland a lad of eighteen was hanged in 1697 for denying the authority of the scriptures.[20]

These tumults had hardly contributed to a clearer Christian social ethic, even though Cromwell had been able to appeal in the end to the 'will of the people' (an echo of Calvin) in order to persuade Parliament to cut off Charles I's head, and the power of the monarch had been reduced and trimmed. That ferment of ideas which we know loosely by 'democracy' was only slowly taking hold, although again Puritanism was a fertile soil for it. It was to find its most conducive setting in the New World, and its most persuasive advocate in John Locke (1631–1704), to whom the American constitution was so profoundly indebted. But at home Tawney gloomily commented that 'the social teaching of the Church had ceased to count, because the Church itself had ceased to think'.[21] Nor was the following century all that much better; its saving grace was that the churches were largely instrumental in founding schools and hospitals. 'This age was by no means one of the ages of faith; but few epochs have given more convincing proof of their faith by works . . . in providing the rudiments of elementary education for social classes which otherwise would have been left wholly illiterate, and in establishing hospitals for the sick, and particularly for women in childbirth, it was mindful of the blessing bestowed upon the Good Samaritan.'[22]

The Christian social conscience received a powerful jolt in the evangelical revival which swept the greater part of England under the leadership of John Wesley (1703–1791), but it was not a jolt demanding a reconsideration of the social structure. Wesley's passionate concern was holiness, and the saving of as many souls as possible, whether inside the existing church or outside it. His passion for souls was matched by his competence in organization, so that the Methodist societies were bound together with a tightly-organized connexional system under his autocratic leadership. Methodism was a missioning holiness movement with an acute social conscience in which poor relief featured prominently and converts were expected to lead disciplined lives of sobriety and mutual care. Wesley was a High Church Tory, a staunch supporter of King George and adamantly opposed to all revolutionary tempers. Locke's notion that power belonged to the people by inalienable right appalled him. 'The supposition, then, that the people are the origin of power is in every way indefensible. It is absolute, overturned by the very principle on which it is supposed to stand; namely, that a right of choosing his Governors belongs to every partaker of human nature,' and Wesley proceeded to scorn the notion that it belonged to women, or people aged eighteen, and ended by saying trenchantly, 'There is no power but of God'.[23]

Wesley's detailed advice to his people included 'Rules for the People called Methodists' and a deceptively simple injunction concerning the use of money – earn all you can, save all you can, give all you can – which he qualified in many significant ways. Wesley was passionately generous, passionately devoted to social welfare and the care of the poor, and a fervent supporter of the anti-slavery crusade. The last letter he wrote, ten days before his death, was to implore Wilberforce to keep struggling against that 'execrable villainy'. But there are no signs of any fundamental doubt concerning the social structure; sharp warnings to rich men, but none about the economic order itself. 'Wesley's economic ideas may be designated pre-industrial;

indeed in some respects they may have been more mediaeval than modern. Even so, they were founded on sympathy for human need . . . '[24]

The same evangelical vigour for the poor and their relief was evident in the Clapham Sect, laymen who gathered around John Venn, Vicar of Clapham from 1792–1813, which also launched numerous missionary causes. Its most famous member was Wilberforce, and its most famous success the declaration by Parliament that the Slave Trade was illegal (in 1807) and, later, its total abolition in the Empire (in 1833). But the turbulent revolutionary events on the Continent worried the English deeply; almost to a man English Christians espoused law and order and were aghast at the chaos in France. 'Throughout the period 1791 and 1848 the various Methodist connexions usually supported law, social order, the monarchy and non-violent politics,'[25] in which they reflected the prevailing religious attitudes. But one of the Methodist secessions became an exception to this – Primitive Methodism. Originating in 1812, it spread like wildfire in many areas in which Wesleyanism was weak. It was a movement of the poor which shunned a leadership class of ordained ministers; its ministers were at first more like full-time paid workers and preachers. It was powerfully involved in all the emerging struggles of Chartism and what we term 'the labour movement', so that it played a big share in the judgment that, 'It is one of the fortunate peculiarities of the English religious tradition that the political parties of the left, first the Liberal and then the Labour Party, have been to a very considerable degree influenced directly by Christian individuals and principles.'[26]

As the nineteenth century drew to its close the general Methodist concern for sobriety and a diluted form of the Puritan virtues was linked to a growing agitation against the restrictions under which historic Dissent had always laboured, an agitation with a pronounced anti-Anglican tone. The result was what was loosely called 'the non-conformist conscience', which found allies in the Liberal camp. It wanted to promote social equality for non-Anglicans, campaigned against drink and gambling and the havoc they were wreaking in the urban slums, and tried to make political life more 'moral'. A famous maxim of one of its leaders – Hugh Price Hughes – was that 'what is morally wrong can never be politically right', a principle he used to help bring down the Irish leader Parnell, who was held to be a party to adultery. Hughes exhorted his hearers, 'Do not be afraid of the rising and advancing tide of democracy',[27] but politically he did not get much further than arguing that we must look at the masses through the eyes of Jesus Christ. Henry Rack says of the whole movement, 'The real trouble was that the temporary political influence held by the Nonconformists in those years was exercised so dubiously; over the Parnell divorce case; and eventually to sabotage educational progress by campaigning against Church Schools. The Conscience was hopelessly divided over the morality of the Boer War.'[28]

But within the Anglican church there were profound rumblings. Thomas Arnold had written in 1831: 'I cannot understand what is the good of a national Church if it be not to Christianize the nation and introduce the principles of Christianity into men's social and civil relations; and expose the wickedness of that spirit which seems to think that there is no such sin as covetousness; and that if a man is not dishonest, he has nothing to do but make all the profit of his capital that he can.'[29] Anglicans began to see that ambulance work amongst the poor and needy was indeed admirable and an utter necessity in the sprawling new cities and their wretched slums; but it was also necessary to enquire into the fundamental causes of poverty. It was a theologian who gave that enquiry a most significant boost – F. D. Maurice (1805–1872) – and around whom the term 'Christian Socialism' came first to be used. Maurice himself hardly ever used it, nor did he write or speak much about socialism. His over-riding conviction was that God in his order had established Jesus Christ as the head of all men, thereby creating a universal brotherhood, whether men recognized it or not.[30] Baptism was a sign of it; so was the national church. Within this order the basic rule was one of co-operation, not competition, and on this score Maurice was appalled by the social order in which he lived. He initiated co-operative guilds and enterprises, most of which failed, and educational efforts which had much more lasting success. He disliked 'democracy', or mob rule by the greatest number, and sounded almost patriarchal in his advocacy of king and government. A prophet before his time, his teaching germinated and later brought forth much good fruit in the formation of socialistic societies which captured some of the best minds and leaders of the church. Hence the formation of the guild of St Matthew in 1877, by a remarkable curate named Stewart Headlam, and then the founding in 1899 of the Christian Social Union. Similar ideas were affecting Roman Catholics also, hence the Catholic Social Union (1893) and Catholic Social Guild (1909).

As a result the ancient sense of incomprehension and alienation which had existed between the Anglican church's leadership and the working classes with their rising aspirations began to be removed; here and there were bishops, and even academics, who espoused some sort of socialism both intellectually and with their hearts. It provided a few rays of light on an otherwise sombre scene of church failure. 'From 1877 onwards the Guild of St Matthew . . . was in the forefront of any movement for pressing the claims of the oppressed. Riots, marches of unemployed, even expeditions for breaking the windows of West End clubs were often led by the curate of Bethnal Green. But the Church as a whole took a quieter course. Many were, of course, antagonistic to radicalism in all its forms; but the remarkable thing is the sympathy which so many showed with Socialist idealism and the identification of so many of the clergy with the Labour movement.'[31] Bishops became involved in the solution of strikes and grievances, whereas a century before that would have been unthinkable because it would have been assumed from the start that they would be hopelessly prejudiced in favour of the powerful. When Westcott, Bishop of Durham, addressed the Church Congress in 1890, he said: 'Individualism and Socialism correspond with opposite views of humanity . . . individualism regards humanity as made up of disconnected and warring atoms: Socialism regards it as an organic whole . . . the method of Socialism is co-operation: the method of individualism is competition . . . The aim of Socialism is fulfilment of service: the aim of Individualism is the attainment of some personal advantage, riches or place or favour.'[32] That was Maurice all over again, but spoken by one of the most respected scholars and leaders of the time.

Into the twentieth century

It was inevitable that the American churches should be stirred by a similar movement, since there, too, the huge new industrial centres were productive of appalling slums and privation. But there was a distinctly different flavour to this movement, which from the first was animated by much more basic confidence in human nature than was Christian socialism. The movement became known as 'the social gospel', and was to have some influence in England also, mainly within the Free Churches. It arose chiefly around the remarkable person of Walter Rauschenbusch (1861–1918), a Baptist pastor whose first charge was a largely middle-class church in New York which was very close to a large slum area (from which few worshippers came). Rauschenbusch set himself the task of trying to understand that situation, only to discover that none of the current Christian interpreters could offer any sort of satisfying view of the massive social inequality, its causes and its cure. But in 'socialism', as presented mainly by agnostics, there was such an interpretation to be found, so he set out to try to produce a synthesis between Christian theology and (mainly secularist) socialism. This was no intellectual game, but a vital task for the sake of the Christian mission.

The key idea was that of 'the Kingdom of God', which Rauschenbusch believed was the centre of Jesus' message, by which he meant the immediate practice of love and goodwill here and now, involving the repudiation of force, free voluntary co-operation (which he called 'the democratic spirit') and human solidarity. The Kingdom was already substantially realized in some spheres of American social life – the family, the church, education, political life (citing the virtues of the American constitution). But in one sphere – the economic – this was manifestly not so. It was 'the unregenerate section of our social order', competitive, autocratic and commercialistic, in practice sheer materialism. It needed to be replaced by a new order based on 'equal rights, the democratic distribution of economic power, the supremacy of the common good, the law of mutual dependence, the uninterrupted flow of good will'. This could come gradually, especially if the church raised a band of men who accepted for good and all the Christian law.

It was very utopian. The Kingdom of God had become one of moral growth, with Jesus as the exemplar of moral ideas. It crassly over-simplified Jesus' message and took it out of its eschatological setting. It assumed that men can be made good by exhortation; it underestimated the tragic power of sin, and the way in which social institutions buttress self-interest. It was often criticized for neglecting the life of prayer and worship, but this is almost wholly wrong; Rauschenbusch was a deeply devout person. Yet on the other hand it roused the American churches from their individualistic pietism and created a wholly new climate of social concern. It had a marked effect on subsequent legislation. 'Whatever its limitations, the social gospel made a permanent contribution to Christian life and thought in America by effectively calling attention to the social dimension in all religious thought and by emphasizing . . . the importance of the quest for social justice.'[33] Long's 'institutional' motif is clearly seen.

The 'social gospel' teaching was to be savaged by the American ethicist who came to dominate Christian social thinking during the middle part of the twentieth century – Reinhold Niebuhr (1892–1972). Christian social ethics owes him an immense debt, for he both contributed an extraordinary string of powerful and seminal books over the course of nearly fifty years, and through the journal *Christianity and Crisis* kept up a constant stream of Christian commentary upon contemporary politics, so that all his ethics was translated into critique of current policy and never remained purely theoretical. He did not claim to be a theologian, but his dominant concerns were the nature of man and the means whereby the norm of love which must direct all human activity and all efforts to create human community could be translated into practicable justice. His doctrine of man was probably the clearest element in his exposition. Man is both spirit (and therefore able to transcend the self, experience freedom and the unconditioned) and nature (therefore bound by necessity, the finite, the limited). All Christian witness must begin by exposing every other view of man as illusory. On this count Marxism, atheism and much which goes with the cult of 'science' is tragic illusion – it has not grasped that man is spirit. But so too are all utopian and liberal dreams, all perfectionisms, mysticism and the holiness movements – they have not grasped that man is nature. Sin is the anxiety which this dual structure produces in man; sin is also the wilful refusal to see it.

Social structures all derive their power from human self-interest. They have a collective 'sin' which means that they are not to be regarded as individuals writ large. The individual must aim to practise *agape* love, the love seen supremely in Jesus' cross; but social structures must embody justice, which is the appropriate approximation of love. To Niebuhr, man is thus a complexity; social life is even more of a complexity. His teaching became strewn with pithy but infuriating aphorisms to express this: 'Sin is overcome in principle but not in fact,' 'Christ is the revelation of the very impossible possibility which the Sermon on the Mount elaborates,' 'Man's capacity for justice makes democracy possible, but man's inclination to injustice makes democracy necessary.' But there is no blueprint for human society. 'We need a pragmatic attitude towards every institution of property and government, recognizing that none of them are as sacrosanct as some supposedly Christian or secular system of law has made them, that all are subject to corruption.'[34]

Niebuhr's position could possibly be classed as 'Christian realism', and a good example of Long's 'operational' motif, but this hardly does justice to its scope and range. It is true that he had little interest in several areas of Christian theology – in the doctrines of the church, or the Holy Spirit, or salvation. Yet he had a peculiar grasp upon the stuff of political thinking and a vast shrewdness about the ways of power amongst men. He was not fundamentally a pessimist, even if human pretension features largely in his expositions, for he constantly pointed to the God who is Lord of history. To him more than any other contemporary we owe the incisive way in which the necessity for justice is upheld, and social structures which balance one power against another so that some sort of tolerable justice may result. Yet many theologians keep asking for a clearer connection between the justice he wanted established between groups, and the love which must be the supreme norm.[35]

To return to England. The Christian Socialist tradition, deeply rooted in Anglicanism and there given a deep theological base, but also deeply understood in many sections of the Free Churches, found a superb expositor and champion in the leading churchman of his day – William Temple (1881–1944). His massive theological competence and grasp, his immense qualities of leadership and his passionate concern for social justice, made a profound contribution to Christian life and thought, to the national life, but also to the developing ecumenical movement which he assisted with all his powers. 'It would be difficult to name any more impressive Christian of the twentieth century,' wrote David Edwards.[36]

In many ways Temple stood in the line stretching from Maurice.[37] His theology centred upon the incarnation, but to him the theme of atonement was inseparable from it. He, too, held a strong view of the 'solidarism' of all men with Christ, and believed that the atonement should become realized, and must meanwhile be expressed as well as possible, in social organizations. Like Niebuhr he was sharply aware of sin and self-interest, and held that: 'The art of government in fact is the art of so ordering life that self-interest prompts what justice demands.'[38] He believed that the church has an inescapable duty to keep pointing towards a social order which reflects man's true nature under God, and one of his most effective short books, *Christianity and Social Order* (1941) was designed very largely to justify and expound that view. He believed that it was possible to set out the basic convictions of Christian belief, and then to indicate 'middle axioms' (half-way positions between doctrine and practical guidance for specific occasions, themselves arrived at as a result of experience in that field as well as doctrinal theology).[39] From them one proceeded to detailed ethical judgments. In the short book just quoted he did this with some precision, setting out the basic theology and middle axioms (about which there should be little disagreement amongst Christians), and then in an appendix setting out how he saw the outworkings (about which he freely accepted that Christians would differ). The appendix includes such propositions as: urban land needed for housing should be compulsorily bought but the owner should not obtain profit from it; there should be family allowances (after the second child) and free milk and meals at schools; some spheres of work should be retained by the state to ease unemployment; workers should have a far greater say in industry; maximum rates of dividend should be fixed, and so on.

It is time now to stand back a little and try to gain some perspective on the whole of the story being unfolded. It is evident that Christians have, in the course of Christian history, taken up a wide variety of stances towards the social-political orders in which they have lived. Is there any way of assessing the relative merits and demerits of all such stances? The well-nigh classic work which has most succeeded in doing this is Richard Niebuhr's *Christ and Culture* (Richard being brother to Reinhold, mentioned earlier).[40] This is a study of the relation between 'the Jesus Christ of the New Testament' and 'culture', meaning 'that total process of human activity and that total result of such activity to which both "culture" and "civilization" are applied in common speech'. He finds that there have been five main ways of expressing this relation:

1. *Christ against culture*. Christians deny that culture has any authority over them and seek to live only in direct obedience to Jesus, often by withdrawing into sectarian communities to practise the holy life, or else by living as if free from normal secular obligation. Political activity is always abhorrent (Long's 'intentional' motif dominates).

2. *The Christ of culture*. This is the complete opposite of the former, since here obligation to Christ is identified with obligations to culture. The tension between the two is virtually absent; Christian belief is identified with the prevailing philosophy; political activity is encouraged in a somewhat uncritical manner.

But those two positions are extremes. In between stands the basic conviction that Christ is above culture, that obedience to him is always transcending obedience to the secular and social realm. But here Christians may take up three distinctly different stances, hence:

3. *Christ and culture in synthesis*. The common ground between the two is much stressed, usually by means of natural law. A noticeable tendency is to maintain the status quo, so it is essentially conservative and often supports a hierarchical view of society (Long's 'institutional' motif again).

4. *Christ and culture in paradox*. The two realms are sharply differentiated, yet God requires obedience in both and different styles of obedience will be needed.

5. *Christ transforming culture*. Culture is not essentially evil, but has been twisted so as to need conversion and reorientation to its true character. Christ seeks to redirect, reinvigorate, regenerate culture from within (Long's 'operational' motif).

For each of these positions Niebuhr provides ample illustrations from the history of Christian social thought. In each case he offers a trenchant critique of the underlying theologies, so that no position can be held to be wholly satisfactory. Within Christian history he holds that all five constantly occur within the life of the church, almost as if she needs them all in order fully to express herself. The result can be easily put into a diagram, indicating the thinkers mentioned in this chapter, thus:

Christ against culture	Christ above Culture			Christ of culture
	Christ and culture Synthesized	Christ and culture in paradox	Christ transforms culture	
Sects, some forms of monasticism	Thomas Aquinas	Luther Reinhold Niebuhr	Augustine Calvin Maurice Temple*	Social Gospel Locke

(*Temple is not cited by Niebuhr, but this is undoubtedly where he would locate him.)

This outline has only taken us up to 1945 or thereabouts. Before then the impact of the ecumenical movement was beginning to be felt strongly; since then it has had great effect upon both the materials and the methods of Christian social ethics. But that must remain for a later chapter.

Questions for Discussion

(a) What do we learn from the early Christian thinkers which is of value to us today in social life?

(b) Into which of Niebuhr's five categories would you place yourself? Your church? What are the weaknesses of such a position?

Chapter 5

War and Violence

THE early church abhorred violence, and drew deeply upon Jesus' teaching and example. Jesus of Galilee died unresisting and unprotesting on a cross, whilst praying to God for forgiveness for his opponents. In his teaching he had repeatedly stressed the duty to forgive; God forgives our sins, but to receive that forgiveness must involve us in having forgiving natures too.[1] He had shunned violence and the spirit of revenge. His approach to others seems to have been marked by acceptance, graciousness, gentleness, deep concern and compassion, forgiveness, and a constant will for their good, for their whole restoration into God's image. He taught and showed that that was what the Kingdom is like.

Did Jesus then teach pacifism, the complete repudiation of force? Did he urge this upon his followers? Here the evidence becomes more problematical. He did not stop them having swords, yet on one famous occasion rebuked Peter firmly for using one.[2] He did not apparently urge his followers to avoid the soldier's calling. He expected them to pay taxes and thus acknowledge the jurisdiction of the Roman Empire and also the local Jewish temple tax system.[3] He submitted to crucifixion.

Frequent attempts have been made throughout subsequent Christian history to claim that because of this teaching and example Christians must be 'pacifist' and repudiate all use of violence against other persons. But the modern issue of 'pacifism' was not quite the issue with which the early church had to wrestle. The first Christians were a small minority in a situation in which the dominant Roman power preserved law and order, sometimes cruelly but generally with fairness and efficiency. When persecution broke out it was fitful, haphazard and patchy; Christians were not, however, politically conscious.

It was some time before a Christian king had to decide what to do about the defence of his realm; the first to have this problem may well have been Agbar of Edessa, converted in AD 202. It was even longer before Roman soldiers had to resolve whether or not they could continue as Christians; it seemed most clearly right on the frontiers where the army was keeping barbarians at bay, more questionable nearer home or when the soldier had to pronounce total allegiance to the Emperor. The most famous early martyr who found he could no longer bear arms was Martin of Tours (AD 336). The early monks were, of course, almost totally unarmed and opposed to any violence against other persons.[4]

To attempt to draw a direct line between that early situation and the modern world is mistaken. It would represent a misuse of the Bible, such as has been rejected in earlier chapters. Nevertheless many attempts are made to appeal directly to the New Testament; where these do not merely produce a string of proof texts but handle the main thrust of the New Testament teaching they cannot be dismissed as irrelevant to Christian decision-making, for these are highly authoritative teachings that have left an indelible mark upon the Christian scene.[5] As a result, this issue has throughout the ages been one of the most difficult ones with which Christian ethics has to deal. In Christian history there have been three main types of response, each of which must now be considered: the 'crusade', the 'just war', the rejection of all war (sometimes loosely termed 'pacifism') – of which the last has produced a great variety of positions.

The crusade

Some wars have been seen by Christians as 'holy wars', those in which God's cause has been opposed by thoroughly evil causes so that it has been a Christian's clear duty to God to fight upon the good side. The cause has been identified with 'the right' or 'the Kingdom of God' or 'God's righteousness' or 'Christian principles' or 'Christian civilization', or some such phrase implying that the cause is most certainly God's. Inevitably this has been done by grossly over-simplifying the issues at stake, by blinding the Christian participants to the causes, and by vilifying the enemy so that he can be presented as an agent of the devil. In practice all wars come about as a result of a whole complex of reasons, a tangle of factors that may include historic grievance, economic factors, shortage of land or resources, the claims of ethnic minorities, frontier squabbles, accidental insults by either party, efforts by unpopular governments to divert internal unrest to external enemies, territorial ambition, and a host of other forces. But when a crusade is launched all these are covered over with a veneer of total righteousness; the cause is God's cause. The enemy is wholly evil; there is no moral ambiguity in either position. All moral subtleties are deliberately obscured. The issue is made into an elemental one of right versus wrong, of good versus evil, of God versus the devil. Modern states are particularly liable to this, since they have at their disposal all the resources of propaganda through the mass media which, when at the service of an efficient totalitarian police state, can be massively effective in brain-washing a people.

In these cases extensive use is made of imagery culled from the Old Testament and the Book of Revelation. There, many battles are fought which are represented as those of God's people versus the evil ones. It is usually forgotten that the battles in the Book of Revelation which depict God's forces deployed against evil ones are almost always battles in which God's angelic forces (not human forces) are involved. There is great stress upon God's wrath, God's justice, God's righteousness; little reference is made to his compassion, forgiveness and mercy. Great stress is laid upon the basic divisions amongst men, the gulf between the saved and unsaved, the righteous and the unrighteous, the elect and the damned; little stress appears upon the ultimate purpose of God to save all men, upon the solidarity of us all in sin and grace, upon the call to reconciliation. Thus Calvinism has a tendency to lend itself to this thesis much more so than does its theological opposite, Arminianism.

But the character of the Christian is portrayed in these instances as being essentially military, with great stress upon the military virtues – resolution, courage, physical strength and recourse, obedience, military skill. Virtues such as gentleness, forgivingness, long-suffering, self-control or peaceableness are pushed into the background. Those New Testament passages which draw upon military imagery are greatly prized, such as Eph. 6.10–17, and it is hardly noticed that such passages refer to spiritual, not earthly warfare. References to Jesus upon the cross are few; references to the 'victory of the cross' are many.

Of course the term 'crusade' is taken from that long series of cruel, bloody, and finally disastrous campaigns which were launched against the Turks in the eleventh and twelfth centuries to liberate the holy places of Palestine from the infidel Moslem.[6] The church had identified the crusaders' cause with the will of God and identified the Moslem with Satan, which was not difficult to do in a European world that knew very little about anybody living beyond its borders. But crusades have recurred with monotonous regularity ever since. The expansion of the European powers into Africa, Asia and Latin America was often portrayed in these terms, with the native peoples being classed as 'heathen'.

The twentieth century has had more than its share. The distressing feature has been the readiness of Christian churches to baptize wars and make them into crusades. It is an especial tendency with established churches in which church and state co-exist as two aspects of one nation, but it has also been effected by the non-established churches. The most appalling instance was the first Great War (1914–1919). The English churchmen, almost without exception, interpreted the conflict with Germany as a crusade for the Kingdom of God against the devil (the German Kaiser). Very few voices were raised against the jingoistic appeals to the whole populace to 'fight for God and nation', or the massive recruiting campaigns that swept almost all the young men into the forces, or the outpouring of crude propaganda against the Germans. The constant appeals to the moral purity of the Allied cause were all heartily endorsed by most of the spokesmen of the churches.[7] If examined closely, the war memorials in every parish in the land, listing a great string of casualties, are all too frequently mute witnesses to the uncritical alliance of the Christian churches with the national cause.

Commenting upon this evil tendency to portray the other power as implacably wicked so as to strengthen resolution to fight a protracted and costly war, Herbert Butterfield remarks that, 'In view of the crimes, sinister movements and aggressions of Tsarist Russia in the years before 1914, the pillorying of Germany as the sole wicked power in Europe – or even as so darkly wicked as Russia herself – deserves to stand on record for a long time as the slickest ethical conjuring trick in the whole of modern history.'[8] Thus is the evil of war baptized and made not only acceptable to the Christian conscience but so righteous that it becomes an essential element of Christian obedience to go to fight in it.

The same tendency has prevailed since. The Vietnam War in its early phases was seen all too often by American Christians as a war of the 'free' (and righteous) West against the communist (and unrighteous) East. The war which Ian Smith fought in Rhodesia was presented as one to 'defend Christian civilization'; the long struggle in South Africa is often presented by its government in those terms.

The grievous thing about the crusade mentality is its presumption. It presumes to know exactly what God requires in a complex situation in which two sets of interest are mutually opposed, presumes that God can be wholly identified with one of them, that which the crusaders also support. The simple warning of Jesus needs to be heard very loudly: 'If anyone says to you: "Lo, here is the Christ!" or "There he is", do not believe it' (Matt. 24.23). But presumption, which stifles self-criticism, almost inevitably leads into fanaticism and intolerable cruelty. Crusades are amongst the most hideously vicious of all wars, inspired as they are by corrupted religion.

The 'just war'

In practice the vast majority of Christians have held that some wars are a regrettable necessity in a fallen world, that they are the lesser of the possible evils in some situations, and that therefore they can be described as 'just'. That does not apply to all wars, but only to those which meet certain criteria. During the course of Christian history these have been steadily refined and elaborated. The process began principally with Augustine, who reluctantly had to decide whether or not violent action against Donatists was legitimate. They were a Christian group, living inland, who had no basic quarrel with Catholic Christianity on grounds of doctrine (they were not heretics) but insisted on controlling their own church life and, to a large extent, their political life, thus bringing them into conflict with both church and state. Their major complaint against their fellow Christians was on the question of the re-admission into the church of those who, in times of persecution, had abandoned the faith and been apostate. Catholics were generally willing to re-admit them after some disciplinary probation; Donatists were not. In the end Augustine sanctioned violent action against them, a terrible thing for a Christian bishop to do against fellow Christians. But it was Thomas Aquinas who put Augustine's original thinking into much more refined shape, and produced three criteria. It is important to note that these were mainly for rulers, whereby they could practise some moral adjudication; they were not originally devised to guide the consciences of individual soldiers. It was of course the hope that if these criteria were available then fewer wars would happen, especially on the part of Christian rulers, and such wars as did occur could be less cruel and more ordered.

1. The war must be fought on the authority of the ruler. It was illegitimate for small-scale captains to unleash war. Here the context was decidedly mediaeval and Thomas was wanting to restrain the petty princelings and their ambitions.

2. The cause must be just. It must be a war to resist aggression or to support the rights of some outraged group.

3. It must have a right intention, the advancement of good and avoidance of evil. It must not be motivated by a passion for revenge or killing, must have clear aims and thus always be ripe for negotiation since its objectives are plain (and in themselves just).

A fourth condition was added early in the sixteenth century by Francisco de Vittoria, a Spanish moralist troubled by many of the wars being fought by the conquistadores in their conquests in the Americas. He taught that the war must be fought by proper means. There were two elements in this; the war must not directly involve non-combatants, the civilian populations, and there must be proportion in the means used. Thus one should not destroy a whole village because enemy forces are hiding in one house; that is a violation of civilian immunity, but also is disproportionate.

For many centuries these conditions seemed to meet most cases, but with the advent of the nineteenth century and the creation of large and highly organized armies utilizing weapons of a greater destructive power, and with the formation of larger and more sophisticated nation states, requiring new political awareness and techniques, other criteria had to be formulated. Three more were constructed, making seven in all.

The war must be a last resort, all peaceful attempts at a solution having failed. Next, the war must offer the possibility that the good achieved by it would outweigh the inevitable evils involved. Next, it must be fought only when there was reasonable hope that justice would be triumphant – i.e. when there is reasonable hope of success. The gravest weakness perhaps in these later criteria is the assumption that a war is a predictable contest. In practice all sorts of unforeseen things happen once a war has started. Other nations get drawn in. Morale is affected by a variety of contingencies. A bad harvest can cripple one opponent; the weather may help one side and hinder the other. Wars have a momentum of their own which very easily develops into a headlong rush to a state of affairs which had never been planned or desired by either participant.

It is debatable whether or not the final form of the doctrine of the just war has been of genuine benefit to the Christian conscience. At least it meant that Christians were not automatically sanctioning all wars, and were officially teaching that war must be restrained and tightly controlled.[9] That nations and their leaders probably took little notice of the doctrine, especially in recent times, is not in itself a weakness in it. There have been occasions when it has enabled Christians to make significant contributions to ethical debates, as for instance in the Second World War when on 9 February 1944 the House of Lords debated the morality of the practice being developed by the RAF of obliteration bombing of German cities. Bishop George Bell opposed it because it violated clause 4 above of the just war doctrine, and incurred much public odium as a result. He also opposed the call to unconditional surrender which, in just war theory, can never be a 'just cause'.[10] Alan Booth, commenting on the doctrine of the just war, points out that it is rooted in a concept of human solidarity in which mutual obligations persist even when hostilities have begun: 'However profound our hostility to another nation . . . we remain tied in a human solidarity with our enemy. Thus we may never contemplate total war or his liquidation, nor even the destruction of his society.'[11] So the doctrine enables Christians to keep a parlous hold upon some ground of morality even in the midst of the terrors and distortions and ambiguities of what they feel to be legitimate war.

'Pacifism'

This term has been put in inverted commas because there is no one single pacifist position; the term covers all those who for various reasons believe that Christian faith inevitably leads to refusal to participate in war by killing opponents, or enabling them to be killed. They have been classified by an American theologian John Yoder into no less than at least sixteen, or possibly twenty-two, varieties, but much of this is hair-splitting.[12] For our purposes there are seven main groupings of pacifist positions, as follows:

1. There have always been some Christians who have held that despite all the problems involved, Jesus' teaching must be literally obeyed in the world, that this is an essential element in genuine Christian faith, and that therefore his command to love enemies and turn the other cheek when attacked must be implicitly followed. They usually repudiate the use of coercive force by the police and military personnel. Their position is most accurately called 'utopian purism' (Yoder's term), since they stress living with the pure intention of love and as if the kingdom is to be regarded as here in its fullness, hence the utopian streak in all their teaching. In England the most outstanding example of this position has probably been George Fox (1624–1691), a mystic with a vivid sense of the Word of God who believed that God has given to each of us an 'inner light' to discern the truth and enable us to obey him implicitly. Fox held that Jesus' teachings are to be obeyed literally and is generally regarded as the founder of the Society of Friends (Quakers), a body which has consistently maintained a 'pacifist' witness. In more recent times the most persuasive and powerful advocate of this position has probably been the Russian novelist Count Tolstoy; in Catholic circles the most illustrious exponent was probably Saint Francis of Assisi (1182–1226).

2. In most generations there have been Christians who have held that the life of non-violence was essential to Christian obedience and, if it cannot be practised in normal community living, then it must be lived out in simple communities in some way separated from the normal pressures of social life. These communities would be sanctified ones, developing a style of life which is distinctive in its mutual respect for all members, its refusal to employ any form of coercion or violence, its stress upon forgiving and accepting love, its sharing of common resources. The great problem with such communities has always been the degree to which they can in practice make some sort of agreement with surrounding society and claim exemption from society's requirements (e.g. military conscription, payment of taxes which will support armies and police forces, etc.). Monasteries are an obvious instance of such sanctified communities, usually able to come to amicable terms with the state

because of the exemptions given to clergy and monks, who have rarely been obliged to bear arms (at least, in Europe).

But other communities have flourished which were in no way monastic, being composed of men and women in family groupings of various sorts, but bound together in community by a strong common faith and discipline. Most forms of Christianity have experienced such communities in their midst: the Doukhobors originating in Russian Orthodoxy, the Hutterites and Mennonites and Moravians within European Protestantism, the more recent Bruderhof founded in this century. In our own time there has been an explosion in the formation of small communes, or community-style groupings, many of which have been profoundly 'pacifist' in their whole intent and ethos. Many have quietly accepted the basic provision which the state makes for all its citizens, have paid taxes and rates, and have not found too great a problem in membership of wider society until, say, military conscription has been introduced. This happened in the United States in the late 1960s as a result of the Vietnam War and raised acute problems of conscience for young male members, who were obliged to register as conscientious objectors. Some countries (e.g. Germany) did not make provision for such tender consciences until very recently, but in any case all such communities came to some sort of amicable compromise with the state, since they shared in its protection and services. They could do no other.

A variation on the principle of the sanctified community is the notion that Christians bind themselves together into a company of people who create, within the normal setting of social life, a 'pool of peace', or a whole atmosphere of loving and trusting, of eschewing violence, without necessarily living together in some shared community structure. It is most easy to opt for this possibility where such bondings of Christians can exist alongside each other in a sub-culture such as a university campus, hence John Pairman Brown's concept of the 'liberated zone',[13] an area of thought and culture within which pacifist ideals have wholly permeated. This comes close to the concept of the 'pacifist church', an area of thought and worship which is dominated by the belief that pacifism can be practised daily. The great problem with the notion of the pacifist church is that it is, by definition, uncatholic, excluding the vast majority of Christians who do not believe that their Christian obedience must issue in pacifism of any form (and who probably support the doctrine of the just war).

3. There are Christians who simply have an utter hatred of war and all its monstrous works. War brings them a terrible revulsion. It denies everything they believe about God and man; they are bound to repudiate it with all their being, whether this seems sensible or not, whether it will produce a better world or not, whether it brings them into contempt or not. This is essentially a negative position, but its proponents do not see that as invalidating it at all. The most powerful example of this position was the Anglican chaplain who had served through the Great War in some of the most horrific battles – Dick Shepherd – and who became Vicar of St Martin-in-the-Fields afterwards. He called on everyone who wished to 'renounce war' to send him a postcard, and founded the Peace Pledge Union with the simple basis 'I renounce war'. The PPU was not specifically Christian, since persons of any faith or none could share such horror at war that they would refuse to participate in it. The main and lasting result of the PPU was its founding of a newspaper – *Peace News* – which has survived up to the present, even though the PPU is virtually defunct.

4. A more positive development concerning war can be seen in what is best termed 'prophetic protest'. Whereas Dick Shepherd recoiled against the huge evil of war, and can be accused of making an emotional reaction to the endemic problems of war in human society, prophetic protest attempts to penetrate much more deeply into the attitudes running through our whole social structure which seem inevitably to produce war and the war mentality; it seeks to expose these to the light of the gospel and to conquer them by the power of that truth. It is finely demonstrated in our own times by the Berrigan brothers, Jesuit priests in the USA who led the initial student revolts against the Vietnam War and acted as goads to the developing sense of guilt which slowly percolated through great areas of American society, beginning with student campuses. The Berrigans saw American political life as a morass of lies and illusions, fostered on to a hysterical public by a cynical and deluded government egged on by the vast power of the military and industrial machine. They were sent to jail for encouraging the burning of draft cards, but said: 'We are in jail, we insist, because we would neither remain silent nor passive before the pathology of naked power, which rules our country and dominates half the world, which shamelessly wastes resources as well as people, which leaves in its wake racism, poverty, foreign exploitation, and war.

In face of this we felt, free men cannot remain free and silent, free men cannot confess their powerlessness by doing nothing.'[14]

In this position war was not seen in isolation as one abhorrent feature of modern society; it was seen as an integral part of a much bigger social sickness. The task of the prophet was primarily to help people see it all clearly, with the stark vividness of those gripped by the word of God. This imparts a passion into the writing, equally evident in the work of the Catholic monk, Thomas Merton.[15]

5. A very few Christians have gone one stage further. They have denied that the state can have any significant authority at all for Christians and, in the extreme, have identified it with evil. They have advocated pacifism because they have opposed the right of the state to order anyone to kill another and, in some cases, have opposed almost totally the right of the state to order anything. It is an extreme position, rarely found amongst those in the major stream of Christian orthodoxy, but constantly appearing on the fringe of church life.[16] It is noticeable today in the semi-Christian sectarian movement known as Jehovah's Witnesses. The Witnesses suffer constant persecution mainly because they refuse military service, on the grounds that the state does not have authority over a believer to oblige him to kill another human being.

6. This position, which is much more overtly theological, is seen with especial clarity in the Fellowship of Reconciliation.[17] It could be classed as 'redemptive personalism', for it holds that by suffering in love, as Jesus did, one lets loose a potency for promoting good and reconciling enemies that is essentially unpredictable in its outcome. Christians should embrace the vocation to such suffering love as an essential element in their discipleship. No doctrine of society is put forward; instead it is believed that such personal activity will act as a creative and reconciling force in all human affairs. The FOR was anticipated in 1914 when two Christians – a German Lutheran and a British Quaker – parted knowing that war would soon divide them, but saying, 'We are one in Christ and can never be at war'. By the end of 1914 about 130 Christians in England formed a continuing society to maintain that witness. For many years the Basis of the Fellowship began:

1. That Love, as revealed and interpreted in the life and

death of Jesus Christ, involves more than we have yet seen, that it is the only power by which evil can be overcome and the only sufficient basis for human society.

2. That, in order to establish a world-order based on Love, it is incumbent upon those who believe in this principle to accept it fully . . .

3. That, therefore, as Christians, we are forbidden to wage war, and that our loyalty to our country, to humanity, to the Church Universal, and to Jesus Christ our Lord and Master, calls us instead to a life-service for the enthronement of Love in personal, commercial and national life . . .

However, in 1975 the Basis did not seem to give a sufficiently positive or specific ring; it encouraged others to think of 'pacifism' as a negative protest against excessive violence, and not as a positive pattern of living. The Basis was extended by a 'Manifesto' issued in the name of the International FOR. This had a different theological starting point, viz.:

God is our Father and we are brothers and sisters to all mankind. But especially we are one in Christ with all who believe in him. We are called to commit ourselves to Christ's way of love, no matter how unpopular it may be – not expecting to know all the answers but as a venture of faith. In the Cross we see that suffering love is the way God uses . . . therefore we are called to repudiate violence and war . . .

and there follow twelve consequences including support for the poor, rejection of the arms race, opposition to racism, etc.

Included in this list is a commitment to study 'non-violent techniques for resolving conflicts'. This leads us into a seventh category of 'pacifist', those who hold that non-violence is the most effective strategy for achieving human rights, the resolution of conflicts, etc. This position owes an incalculable debt to Mahatma Gandhi, who pioneered the practice of non-violence by mass movements during the British occupation of India. His tactics were brilliantly successful and hastened the British desire to grant independence in 1948.[18] His most famous disciple was Martin Luther King, who used Gandhi's techniques to secure civil rights for American negroes, and was assassinated in 1968. This has led to a profound searching for ways of organizing non-violence in groups involved in conflicts, and to a large literature, much of which cites examples from European history, from

Gandhi and King to support its theses. Inevitably the focus of interest can then move on from questions like 'How can I best live out Jesus' love?' to 'What is the most likely and satisfactory strategy for gaining the group's rights?' The concern can then become one of securing the most efficient tactics against oppressors; it is fairly obvious now, in the light of history, that Gandhi's tactics against a Britain utterly exhausted by the Second World War, and willing to transform the old imperial empire into a more fraternal commonwealth of nations, were quite superb. Thus non-violence can be advocated both from theological presuppositions (one must practise the love seen in Jesus) and from more practical ones (the group will succeed more quickly by non-violence). Again and again one finds the advocates moving between these two main poles of conviction.

The suggested seven-fold typology for pacifism is not wholly satisfactory. Often a particular pacifist, or a group, could have their position in one or two of the categories outlined above. One may sense this particularly with a towering figure such as King. He believed profoundly in non- violence and taught it to great masses of Negroes despite the constant cries of the radicals calling for violent revolution. He believed it to be the right strategy. But he believed this not as a strategist who had studied political movements and their effectiveness, but as a believer in the almighty power of redemptive love. He believed that agape could transform opponents. 'Love is the only force capable of transforming an enemy into a friend', but such considerations 'are not the ultimate reasons why we should love our enemies. An even more basic reason . . . is expressed explicitly in Jesus' words: Love your enemies . . . that ye may be children of your Father which is in heaven.'[19]

Kenneth Slack, assessing King's work in the light of criticisms from both black and white, comments that, 'King was committed to belief not in the value of abstinence from violence, but in the creative power of the Christian agape', and that therefore 'King's movement was probably the last chance which white America had to accept a revolution within its society on peaceful lines'.[20]

When pacifist ideals have often been espoused so movingly by superb Christian leaders and thinkers it is at first sight strange that the vast majority of Christians have always been non-pacifists. There have been some smaller, usually Protestant and sectarian churches that have been 'peace churches' (e.g. the Moravians, the Mennonites, the Society of Friends), but none of the churches claiming a majority of Christians in a country has been officially pacifist. There must be formidable reasons for this. One factor has been the tendency of Christians to lump all pacifists into one general category of starry-eyed idealism and to ignore the important distinctions between the varieties mentioned above.[21] Yet Count Tolstoy and Saint Francis are not the archetypal pacifists for all time. The most thorough theological assault upon the pacifist traditions was that expressed in 1936 by Reinhold Niebuhr when giving, ironically, the Rauschenbusch lectures.[22] Walter Rauschenbusch, the major exponent of the Social Gospel, had been very close to some pacifist positions, and had had great influence upon the young Niebuhr, who became for a short time the Chairman of the American FOR. But Niebuhr became totally opposed to that whole tradition and resigned from the FOR; in these lectures one sees why. He makes seven main criticisms (which apply in varying degrees to the different pacifist stances).

1. The ethical teaching of Jesus does not deal with immediate human problems. It is solely directed to our relationship with God. It is therefore absolutist, perfectionist and impossible to practise now. It makes no allowance for consequences, so it has an essential element of the impracticable within it. Not to see this is an elementary theological and ethical blunder.

2. When you turn Jesus' teaching into an immediate programme you always blunt and modify it (inevitably), but also you make Jesus into a legalist. Instead his moral teaching is intended as a perpetual judge transcending all our ethical systems and programmes, subjecting them all, in their partiality and finitude, to the light of God's everlasting truth.

3. Jesus gives no advice whatever on how to restrain sin, how to keep violent men or groups in check.

4. Pacifism is tragically naive about human nature, assuming it to be readily reformable. But man's selfishness is built into all human structures and societies, where it is inherent in the total system.

5. Pacifism concentrates attention over and over again on individual morality, and when talking about groups or nations it uses the same terminology and understanding as if inter-personal relations were being discussed. But this is a cardinal error; groups do not behave like individuals; there are hardly any hints in the New Testament about inter-group behaviour.[23]

6. It is afraid of power, including coercive power. But in an imperfect world God has given us levers of power; Christians must unhesitatingly use them so as to promote justice and restrain evil. We cannot opt out and leave the exercise of power to others, or we abandon our responsibilities under God for our neighbours.

7. It is naive also about salvation. It assumes that men can be made good and loving by pious exhortation, by appeals to their 'better nature'. But that sort of optimism is fatuous and inept.

Most of these criticisms are reproduced today in slightly different form, using different theological terms. Thus the first criticism is now expressed thus: pacifism assumes that the Kingdom of God is here in its fullness and we can live 'as in the Kingdom'. The fourth criticism recurs constantly, particularly against those who see non-violence as an effective strategy; the critics point out that this is only so when you arc protesting against a society which has a fairly compassionate streak in its whole ethos, and which has sufficient guilt to know that it ought to be giving in (e.g. the British in India, the whites in the USA). But 'ruthless modern despots do not play good-natured games with their critics. It is hard to imagine Hitler or Stalin blenching at the prospect of Gandhi fasting to death. They would have helped him on his way, exterminating him secretly so that there was no mark of his passing except for a blood stain on some cellar wall.'[24]

One further criticism is often made, again of some (but not all) of the pacifist stances. This relates to the example of the cross. Pacifists may affirm that in the cross we see God's way of handling evil; that way must be our way; we must therefore be pacifist. To this it is objected that the whole doctrine of salvation is here being over-simplified. Jesus' going to the cross was a unique, once-for-all event, in which God subsumed within himself the guilt and tragedy of humanity's sins; it was completed in the resurrection where Jesus' act of self-sacrificial oblation was vindicated and God's new era inaugurated. But the individual Christian is not thereby called to crucifixion (and resurrection) except in an internal and mystical sense. The individual Christian is not a little copy of the Messiah, the Saviour of the World, not a little redeemer of mankind. Only Jesus the Christ could be that unique one. 'Christians are not themselves individual redeemers,' as Davies puts it.[25]

Nevertheless, despite these severe strictures, the pacifist case has a haunting hold upon the Christian conscience. Some Christians, pacifist and non-pacifist, would say that the whole

Christian church needs the pacifist element within it but that not every Christian is thereby called to pacifism. Instead, within the general economy of God, a few Christians are called to make this witness, but not arrogantly as if they alone have the sole insight into God's truth at this point. This is 'vocational pacifism', the belief that some Christians have a specific calling to make this witness in and for the church as a whole, even though the church as a whole cannot (and maybe should not) make this witness. It is parallel to the belief that some Christians have a specific vocation to celibacy but the church as a whole does not, or that some are called to be teetotallers but not all. Those with the vocation are a constant goad to the church's conscience, preventing her from too easily slipping away from her fundamental rootage in the New Testament and from regarding one of the most significant moral problems in terms that are uncomfortably like those adopted by those with no allegiance to Christ.

But is that position satisfactory? Virtuous minorities who feel a special calling to take up a different stance from most other Christians have a notorious tendency to self-righteousness. All too often they become arrogant spiritual prigs. They are saying, in effect, that the majority may make unethical compromises but the really sincere good minority will not do so and will thereby indicate that there is a 'better way', a 'higher morality'. Yoder adds, 'In the experience of the peace churches, the "vocational" label is a cover for failing to decide how clear one is on one's own convictions and their relevance to one's brethren, while still taking credit for a righteous stance.'[26] But maybe Yoder is being unduly astringent here?

Since the close of the Second World War the standard arguments about the just war, Christian pacifism in all its varieties, and the nature of Christian witness in the world political community have been dominated by two concerns, one of which is inevitably a modern one whereas the other has been always with us but in muted form, though it is now a very crucial concern indeed. These are nuclear war and violent revolution; we need now to outline the character of the debates on these two topics that have ensued amongst Christians.

The new issue of nuclear war

The first atomic bomb to be used in warfare was dropped on Hiroshima on 6 August 1945; 80,000 people were immediately killed. The scale of weaponry was suddenly given a quantitative jerk upward; more quantitative jerks have followed as bigger bombs have been developed, together with highly accurate delivery systems. These 'jerks' have produced a whole new tangle of moral problems for which all traditional moralities were unprepared, and all standard moral discussion had inadequate terms and procedures. Christians, along with all others, found themselves facing unprecedented ethical perplexities. How have they responded?

To begin with, it was soon recognized that the doctrine of the just war was not adequate to handle the new situation – that is, it could not afford the necessary ethical guidance. Clearly no nuclear war could be a just war, since clauses 2. (just cause), 3. (right intention), 4. (proper means), 6. (good achieved to outweigh evils incurred) and 7. (reasonable hope of triumph of justice) were all to be violated. As early as 1947 the Vatican stated that the doctrine was now inapplicable. Only one major attempt has been made to justify the use of the doctrine as a guide to nuclear powers in the conduct of nuclear wars. This was by Paul Ramsey, in *War and the Christian Conscience* written in 1961,[27] in which he maintained that the doctrine is still of some use, that nuclear weapons are in some limited senses still morally permissible. It was a convoluted argument; the subsequent escalation of the arms race and capabilities of the latest weapon systems make the case ever more difficult to maintain.

However, the moral and ethical issues cannot be blandly settled by arguing that nuclear warfare cannot possibly be 'just'. That would make Christian witness relate to only one of the problems being encountered. The major justification for the possession and development and threat to use nuclear weapons originates in the concept of 'deterrence'. The West must possess a strong and varied armoury of nuclear weapons and must be willing to use them against the East because otherwise the East will not be adequately deterred from its avowed intention of ruling the whole world in a communist style. If, however, a nuclear exchange takes place, then the deterrence has of course failed; meanwhile, in order to keep the peace, nuclear weapons must be available and there must be willingness to use them (since it is pointless in having them at all unless this willingness also exists). The deterrence argument, utilized in the context of threats to rule the world or threats to destroy the world, is new, since no nation has previously been in a position to destroy the world.

Christian response has been understandably varied.[28] 1. Some Christians have advocated the immediate abandonment of nuclear weapons by the nuclear powers. Whilst this has been argued on various grounds, the basic conviction has been that nuclear weapons are so monstrously evil that their use can never be justified, the threat to use them cannot be justified, and therefore to possess them is never justified. Obviously the many sorts of 'pacifist' would argue thus, and would have to argue either that the West must then develop very strong conventional forces (sufficient to be a counter to the East) or that a new sort of encounter must be permitted to take place between East and West in which there would inevitably be a strong probability that the East would attempt to enforce communism world-wide. This scenario is so difficult to envisage that few Christian attempts have been made to present it.

2. Some Christians have endorsed the present policies of the West to build up a nuclear arsenal always one stage ahead of the East so that deterrence is always credible. This policy results inevitably in an arms race, but this must be accepted. Few official church statements have ever been made of this type, however, even though some have at times come fairly close to it. It is usually most apparent when Christians have spoken in endorsement of official government policy, as happened when the so-called 'moral majority' supported President Reagan during the 1980 campaign for the Presidency, or when similar support has been expressed in Britain for government policy. This support can be preferred for a variety of reasons – because it is believed that the government alone knows the full dimension of the case and can alone make a responsible moral decision, because 'political' matters belong in their essence to the sphere of politics and must be left to the political experts, or because the political-ethical case is patently right and the grounds on which it is argued are acceptable to Christians.

There are many fundamental problems about this stance. It ascribes astonishing wisdom to governments, abdicates from genuine involvement in the making of public policy, but, more grievously, equates Christian opinion with government opinion and denies any element of Christian critique. It is not often noticed in the current debate that this stance most glaringly commits Christians to making the defence of the state into an absolute good. For politicians that must be so; national politics is the business of preserving the national self-interest and the existence of the state. But the state is not an absolute good to Christians; only the will of God for all humanity can be that. There comes a crucial point at which Christian ethics cannot concur with national political self-interest; clearly that point is passed when there is the intention of acting in a manner that is a blasphemy against mankind as a whole (as in a major nuclear exchange). 'The Christian conscience does require us to be ready to surrender the political purposes of our nation if the only alternative is intolerable devastation for mankind.'[29]

At times another variant on this stance has appeared, in that Christians have asserted that God may well be pursuing his own inscrutable purposes through the current dangers and, more especially, may be using a nuclear holocaust as a means to effect his will. The doctrine of providence asserts that God is able to make even the wrath of man to praise him; who knows but that his eschatological purpose might not be effected through nuclear war? This argument was once deployed by no less a person that the Archbishop of Canterbury, Dr Fisher, in an essay in 1958, and caused an understandable furore.[30] The trouble with it is not that Christians should disbelieve in providence, but that they should not use the argument to imply passivity, or a retreat from a searching criticism of the ways in which purely political considerations distort the ethical issues at stake.

3. Another position (somewhat vaguely termed 'multilateral disarmament') asserts that the arms race should be checked at its present level and 'frozen' by multilateral accord. Then, in progressive stages, the levels should be steadily lowered. This has always elicited strong support from the churches. The majority of the official or semi-official reports during the period from 1950–1980 come roughly into this category. Some of them were greatly preoccupied with descriptions of the general scene and of the options open to government, expressed horror at nuclear war but guarded support for the doctrine of deterrence, and held that the West has to negotiate the reduction of arms from a prior position of strength. The Report to the British Council of Churches entitled *The Search for Security* is of this type.[31] Its title is indicative of the general priority given to the concept of security; the value of the report is that it clearly starts from ground which is shared by the politician. But is there anything that is distinctively Christian in such an approach? Is this another instance of the absolutizing of the state and 'national security'?

Within this position there is bound to be a toleration of the doctrine of deterrence. It is, after all, the lynch-pin of current Western policy; indeed, that policy goes further and asserts NATO willingness to initiate nuclear warfare in some cases. It is generally easier for British Christians to be critical of the doctrine, since the major Western power acting as the great pillar of nuclear military might is the US. There has been some Christian critique, however, in the US, notably by the eminent social ethicist John Bennett.[32] Bennett has had great doubts about the policy, not least because it over-simplifies the relationship between East and West and assumes that the world must be regarded as inevitably divided into two opposing camps. Christians, he says, cannot so view the world and cannot therefore see the global policy of the West in the restricted way which deterrence doctrine seems to require.

In Britain one interesting thesis concerning deterrence has recently emerged, that Christians should formulate a notion of 'just deterrence' so that limits are set upon its acceptability similar to the limits set by the doctrine of the just war. Richard Harries suggests three limits:

1. Not to arouse unnecessary fears in potential adversaries,
2. 'Men are not as reasonable as they think they are', so the cause must not be identified with Christ (as happens in the crusade), and
3. Only those weapons which are necessary to make deterrence credible should be deployed.[33]

4. This position, somewhat vaguely described as 'unilateralist', asserts that for Britain at least there is the immediate possibility of scaling down her nuclear deterrent posture by unilateral action, and that she should do so even if the East shows no willingness at first to make comparable gestures. This position is sometimes linked with political arguments about Britain's economic ability to stay in the nuclear arms race, or the future role of Europe as a 'nuclear free zone', or Britain's remaining in NATO, or British action setting in motion a new climate, having effect upon present non-nuclear powers even if it does not have immediate effect upon Eastern policy, or arguments that it would in the end make Britain safer from nuclear attack. There is a wide range of argument that can be utilized to support this case. The great attention devoted to the Report to the Church of England's General Synod entitled *The Church*

and the Bomb (published in 1982 and debated in 1983)[34] derives from the fact that for the first time a 'unilateralist' case was being formally argued within that church. This represents a shift in general Christian opinion around the year 1980, when most Christians began to feel that the West did not intend to pursue disarmament negotiations seriously and that the escalation of the arms race was actually being promoted by the West. Some unilateral initiatives are essential to stop the inevitable spiralling of that 'race'; the dangers inherent in that policy were reckoned to be greater than those involved in unilateral action.

It is from within this stance that deterrence doctrine is most likely to be heavily criticized. Thus Kenneth Greet[35] raises six basic objections: deterrence cannot be proved to have been effective, it increases the danger of accidents, it involves the risk of widespread proliferation, it encourages unrealistic talk about limited wars, it assumes that Russia is the greatest and permanent threat to the future world order, it blurs some essential moral theology. It is also from within this stance that the most serious consideration will be given to what unilateral action should be like and can achieve. Thus a Report to the Methodist Conference of 1983 on *Nuclear Disarmament – Some Theological Considerations* made careful use of the work of Charles Osgood,[36] who wrote that for unilateral action to be most effective:

1. The opponent must perceive that the unilateral step proposed will actually reduce the external threat to him.
2. Each unilateral step should be accompanied by an explicit invitation to reciprocate.
3. Unilateral acts must be fulfilled whether or not the adversary agrees in advance to reciprocate.
4. The steps should be planned as a whole in advance, and persisted in whether or not the opponent responds as you intend.
5. The step should be announced before it is taken, to full publicity.
6. Initiatives should concentrate on areas of mutual concern and should offer opportunities for co-operation.
7. Steps should be graduated, so as to avoid undue danger during the early period.
8. Unilateral initiatives should be accompanied by firmness towards the adversary.[37]

Christians adopting these four general positions tend to base their cases upon different areas of Christian doctrine. The first group, regarding nuclear war as wholly abhorrent, tends to utilize the doctrine of creation and to point out that nuclear war is undoing the whole creative activity of God, dismantling the 'building blocks' of the created order. It will also lay stress upon God's purpose to reconcile all men, to create of humanity one genuine human 'family'. Those in the second group tend to lay great stress upon God's will to restrain evil in the world, and (as already noticed) the doctrine of providence. Those in the third group tend to favour 'realism' and hence lay most stress upon what is deemed practicable in a wicked world; again, the restraint of sin features largely. Those in the fourth group tend to lay stress upon God's 'unilateral' work, his taking of unprecedented initiatives in the incarnation and the whole work of redemption; they may even use the concept of 'resurrection' (as does the Methodist statement cited above).

Revolutionary violence

The arguments about the just war and about nuclear war look very academic to many Christians today. They maintain that neither of those situations is remotely like the one in which they live. Their nation possesses no nuclear weapons so far, thank God; their nation is not particularly prone to get embroiled in major wars with neighbouring states; but their social order is so manifestly unjust that every sensitive Christian conscience must be exercised with the pressing problem of how to effect a new social order. Revolution is what is required by God, not revolution in the sense of a major development of technology (the 'industrial revolution' or the 'cybernetic revolution'); not merely revolution in the sense of a fundamental change of heart by all persons (conversion, in classic Christian terminology); not the so-called 'palace revolution' in which one ruler is merely replaced by another with no change in the social structure; but a fundamental re-structuring of the social order so that each person within it has certain basic human rights acknowledged, can participate in social decision-making, and in which power and resources are divided justly between all. This has become the pressing ethical issue for vast numbers of Christians. How can this revolution come about? What means are legitimate to effect it? Especially, is it ever morally acceptable for a Christian to participate violently in a revolutionary process?

The issue is not totally new. Down through the centuries Christians have had to wrestle with the problems of how to depose tyrants or mad kings. But in recent times it has acquired huge momentum because of the rise to self-consciousness of so many social groupings which in the past accepted their humble and under-privileged lot in a quiescent and uncomplaining manner. Now the masses are arising from that ancient slumber, partly as a result of the preaching of the gospel all over the world,[38] partly because of the mass media making everyone aware of the good things which a privileged few enjoy, partly because a world-wide awareness is developing which suggests that the old order does not have to remain for ever and a new order can be created. The whole theme of 'revolution' (in the broadest sense of that term) has attracted much attention in modern theology.[39] Here, however, we must concentrate on the ..arrower issue outlined above – is it legitimate for Christians to attempt to change the existing unjust social-political order by violent means?

Inevitably there is no standard Christian response, but a range of responses. There have always been Christians who have held that such action is intolerable. Many pacifists would hold that revolutionary-style activity aimed at improving the social order is of course required of us, but in no circumstances could a Christian perpetrate violence against another human being on such a scale that injury or death might result. Peaceful revolution, yes; violent revolution, no. Those Christians who have always tended to deify the existing social order would argue that revolutionary violence is intolerable. Thus much Catholic social teaching has been of this type; the horrors of the French Revolution meant that 'revolution' became a dirty word in that teaching afterwards. But Lutheran teaching has the same emphasis. Even with the German church struggle against Hitler becoming acute, Bonhoeffer could write, 'According to Holy Scripture, there is no right to revolution; but there is a responsibility of every individual for preserving the purity of his office and mission in the *polis*.'[40] This teaching has been grounded in the belief that the social order is instituted by God primarily so as to restrain sin and promote order in society; until very recently it was not held that the social order exists to promote *justice*.

There have always been Christians who have argued that in the last resort revolutionary violence is acceptable, but that normally it must be regarded as abhorrent. The difficulties then arise in defining what is a last resort and what is not. Calvin had asserted that magistrates, and not the general public, had the right to depose an ungodly tyrant; John Knox had argued that 'God has not only of a subject made a king, but also has armed subjects against their natural kings, and commanded them to take vengeance upon them according to his law,'[41] which implied that the 'armed people' were to be understood as the agents of God, rather than the ungodly ruler; Cromwell regarded his army as a lawful power raised up by God to oppose the king. But these arguments have a mediaeval ring about them; they are concerned with replacing or improving the highest layer in the pyramid of power; they are not, strictly speaking, the modern concern of liberating the lowest level of the social order by some revolutionary activity and programme.

Roman Catholic social theology has always eschewed revolutionary violence, even though Thomas gave a guarded place to a people's right to depose a tyrant. But it is impossible nowadays to contribute adequate guidance on matters affecting the social order without dealing, sooner or later, with the issues posed by violent revolution. In 1967 the Papal encyclical letter *Populorum Progressio* was addressed to the cause of man's complete development. The small sub-section dealing with 'Temptation to Violence' has subsequently become the most important, and most quoted, section of the whole letter. It reads thus:

> 30. There are certainly situations whose injustice cries to heaven. When whole populations destitute of necessities live in a state of dependence barring them from all initiative and responsibility, and all opportunity to advance culturally and share in social and political life, resource to violence, as a means to right these wrongs to human dignity, is a grave temptation.
>
> 31. We know, however, that a revolutionary uprising – save where there is manifest, long-standing tyranny which would do great damage to fundamental personal rights and dangerous harm to the common good of the country – produces new injustices, throws more elements out of balance and brings on

new disasters. A real evil should not be fought against at the cost of greater misery.

The exception clause in the middle of paragraph 31 gives sanction to a violent revolution in the last resort. It has been so interpreted by Roman Catholics all over the world, but most especially in Latin America, where the issue is so pressing. It has enabled them to claim that the Pope himself has sanctioned, in the last resort, and in a situation only vaguely defined, a revolutionary uprising.

Thus it had been virtually unthinkable for Christians to contemplate radical action until this century; now it has become essential to have some sort of criteria whereby civil revolution can be ethically assessed, so the 'last resort' position inevitably moves into one modelled upon the just war doctrine – the 'just revolution'. In 1970 a report was presented to the British Council of Churches which was a 'Christian assessment' of the emerging violent situation in Southern Africa. It gave a description of the pressures for liberation and national freedom that were engulfing that part of the continent. It then addressed itself to the awkward question whether or not Christians (who in this case would mainly be black Africans) could ever participate in the various revolutionary movements. It did not go very thoroughly into the theological issues involved in that ethical question, but said, 'There can be a just rebellion as well as a just war and we cannot sincerely withhold support from those who have decided to face the certain suffering involved in such rebellion.'[42]

It made no attempt at delineating the just revolution, but shortly afterwards such an attempt was made by a Church of England report presented by the Board of Social Responsibility to the General Synod.[43] This had been prepared because of the widespread concern within the English churches at the grants made by the Special Fund of the Programme to combat Racism of the World Council of Churches. This concern arose largely because English Christians were appalled lest Christian money should be going directly to movements fomenting revolution and practising violence. The report noted that 'within limits international law recognizes a right of revolution', and cited the recent 'Statement concerning Moral Questions' issued by the Roman Catholic Bishops on 31 December 1970 which said, 'It is not possible . . . to issue a blanket condemnation of all who under any circumstances resort to violence. Where protests against injustice have been stilled by promises of redress which remain unfulfilled, it is governments which bear the heavier responsibility for violence which may thus break out' (a statement which seems to owe a good deal to the section in *Populorum Progressio* quoted earlier). Finally the majority affirmed that there can be a just revolution and that it would need to fulfil these criteria:

The regime concerned must be palpably unjust and tyrannical.

The oppression it employs must be out of all proportion to the needs of government, including external threats to security.

Every effort must have been made to seek a solution by negotiation and reconciliation.

The good to be attained must be greater than the evils, material and spiritual, which would also ensue.

The rules of the just war must, as far as possible, be observed.

There must be a reasonable chance of success.

The difficulties inherent in this set of criteria are similar to those inherent in the whole notion of the just war. What is meant by 'every' effort at negotiation? Is it reasonable to expect rebels to 'negotiate' with a tyrannical government when that is precisely what they cannot do for fear of arrest? How are we to judge chances of success? Revolutions, like wars, are highly volatile; all sorts of unforeseen factors can enter later into the situation (e.g. intervention by foreign powers). Moreover, revolutions have to be steadily built up over the passage of time, beginning with small acts of defiance when there would be no immediate hope of success in all-out revolt, but designed to rattle the government and rouse the consciousness of the people. After many years of such mounting activity the final revolt can be staged. Are those preliminary acts 'just'? Yet some such effort at establishing such criteria must be made in order to guide the Christian conscience. The compilers of the report comment that 'we are impressed with the extent to which those who say they are irrelevant do, in fact, invoke them'.[44]

This leads us to a more explicit Christian commitment to violent revolution, which has featured in a great deal of theological and ethical work in the 1970s and beyond. It is rooted in the conviction that the social order must primarily be *just*; that the deep-seated conservatism of all human institutions, and most especially of the rich and powerful who benefit most from the present order, ensures that no radical changes can be effected; that therefore God's will can only come about by fundamental reform of the social order, which almost inevitably involves revolutionary violence. Christians should not be blind to this; they should wittingly work for justice and therefore for revolution and accept that along the way there may have to be some blood shed, especially if the rich and powerful obstruct necessary changes.

One of the great catalysts for this whole understanding of the Christian obligation (or 'apostolate', as he would call it) was the Columbian priest Camilo Torres. Son of a wealthy family, university lecturer and chaplain, he had studied sociology as well as theology, and was appalled by the poverty and helplessness of the masses. He was not a Marxist, but would collaborate with them to a considerable extent, and accepted some of the Marxist analysis of the social order. His whole revolutionary convictions originated in his Christian obligation to show charity to his neighbour, a charity that produced more food, better living conditions, a more just society. He saw that this required a revolution, so formed the United Front of the Columbian People in 1965 and also became laicized ('I will never again offer mass until after the revolution'). Believing that he was in great danger of assassination he finally decided to join the guerrilla fighters; three months later, on 15 February 1966, he was killed by government troops in an ambush.

Camilo said: 'It is necessary . . . to take the power from the privileged minority and give it to the poor majority. This, if done quickly, is the essential element of a revolution. The Revolution can be peaceful if the minorities put up no violent resistance. The Revolution is the means of obtaining a government that will feed the hungry . . . love their neighbours not only in a transitory and occasional way, not just a few but the majority of their neighbours. For this reason the Revolution is not only permissible but obligatory for Christians who see in it the one effective and complete way to create love for all . . . When there is an authority opposed to the people, this authority is illegitimate and tyrannical. We Christians can and must fight against tyranny.'[45] Camilo has had profound effects upon Latin America, and upon Roman Catholicism there. He has inevitably become a folk hero, as potent dead as alive. His commitment to revolution as an essential aspect of love for the neighbour was rooted in his understanding of what Christian living is all about.

A second important catalyst was the Conference held in Geneva in 1966 under the auspices of the World Council of Churches on the theme of 'Church and Society', or 'Christians in the technical and social revolutions of our time'. It was the first time that the ecumenical movement faced up to the great surge of desire sweeping the under-developed nations for a better life and a more just world economic and political order. The word 'revolution' appeared boldly in ecumenical literature from that time onward. The final report said: 'The Christian is therefore called to speak a radical "No" – and to act accordingly – to structures of power which perpetuate and strengthen the status quo at the cost of justice to those who are its victims. The task of bringing about effective social change, and in discerning in the protest of the poor and oppressed the relative historical justice at work is especially his.'[46]

This Conference also introduced on to the ecumenical theological scene what has subsequently been called 'political theology' by Europeans, whereas the Latin Americans have preferred to call their parallel work 'liberation theology'. It showed that theologians were wanting to work with a much more dynamic conception of the relationship between the triune God and the world's social structures. In the past the dominant framework of understanding had been that of a stable social order, graded in a hierarchy so that each person had a specific place and role, and generally presided over by God. It could almost be pictured as a strong secure pyramid with God as the supreme authority at the top, the governing class next, and so on down to the peasants or workers at the bottom. But now theologians were trying to work with a concept of God as the energy for transformation within the social order, as the one promoting health, human rights, human well-being, justice, free participation. These themes were being summed up as 'humanization', or by the biblical term of 'shalom'.

This appeared in the preliminary work for the Conference, notably in that by the American theologian Richard Shaull. He wrote: 'The Christian is called to be fully involved in the revolution as it develops. It is only at its centre that we can perceive what God is doing, understand how the struggle for humanization is being defined, and serve as agents of reconciliation. From within the struggle we discover that we do not bear witness in revolution by preserving our purity in line with certain moral principles, but rather by freedom to be for man at every moment.'[47] He saw it as a Christian imperative to be a wholehearted social revolutionary and, far from paying the traditional Christian respect to social order, went so far as to say: 'In those situations which are most rigid, our initial task will be that of introducing incoherence and violence.'[48]

The debate about Christian involvement in violent revolution continues unabated, an inevitable element within the larger debate on how to produce a more just and 'humanized' world. In its initial stages one other discussion flitted into it, and then out again. Was Jesus a revolutionary in the sense that he too espoused, as a last resort, revolutionary violence? Biblical scholars had for long noted the connections between Jesus and the Zealots, the revolutionary guerrillas of his day, but S. G. F. Brandon asserted that Jesus was a Zealot, with active Zealots amongst the Twelve.[49] Brandon argued his case on many suppositions, not least that Jesus was crucified as a Zealot (based on a somewhat strained interpretation of the account in Mark's Gospel). If Brandon's conclusions were accepted it would have had enormous consequences for the discussion about revolution. For example, in 1969 a Rhodesian guerrilla fighter, a Christian, asked a respected minister whether or not his action was consistent with Christian discipleship; the minister wrote a book giving him an enthusiastic yes; when referring to Jesus he quoted Brandon as 'the standard text for any Christian trying to make theological sense of the revolution of our time' and went on to say: 'You have the judgment of an eminent Christian scholar that Jesus anticipated you as a freedom fighter by two thousand years, and suffered a fate that you might well be called upon to share.'[50]

However, the Brandon thesis was savaged by a host of scholars, most especially by the acknowledged expert on the Zealots, the German New Testament scholar Martin Hengel. In a trilogy of pithy books he presented a wholly different view, supporting the traditional Christian understanding that Jesus resolutely did not participate in, or encourage, revolutionary violence.[51] The debate, much of which was extremely technical, was summed up clearly for the WCC by Hans-Rudi Weber in 1972 who found the Brandon case quite unproven;[52] since this there have been few attempts to enlist Jesus directly into the bands of the armed freedom fighters. More recently Hugh Montefiore has argued that Jesus was under intense pressure throughout his ministry to align himself with the Zealots, that he opposed this totally, and that the incident of the feeding of the 5000 was an occasion when the crowd tried to turn him into a military captain, hence his rapid dismissal of the disciples and then his escape to be on his own.[53] This debate in New Testament scholarship is a warning to ethicists not to grasp at the latest convenient scholarly straw, for straws can support little moral weight.

Questions for Discussion

(a) To what extent was the just war tradition accurate in its criteria? How would you improve them?

(b) Should every Christian be a pacifist? If so, of which sort? If not, are some pacifist positions more acceptable? Which?

Chapter 6

Sexuality and Marriage

EARLY Christianity was immediately indebted to Judaism, where sexuality was a sign of man's place within the creative purpose of God. The male carried within him the mysteriously potent seed from which human life was made. It enabled the Jew to live on (in his children) and for God's ongoing purposes in history to be continued. Sexuality was good, an element within the divinely-appointed vitality of man's nature. It must be regulated carefully. The seed must be honoured. Marriage is assumed to be normative for all. Yet sexuality must not be worshipped (as in Baalism).

It was, of course, a male-dominated society. Woman's role was to provide the necessary shelter within which the seed could be nourished and a baby produced; then she was to care for the child. Polygamy was accepted as part of a culture in which the large tribe-family was the basic social unit. There were still traces of polygamy in Jesus' day, and it is sobering to realize that the only strictures against it in the New Testament are the demands that bishops and elders should be monogamous.[1] Males were not subject to strict sexual *mores*, so concubinage and prostitution were accepted. But females were the sexual property of their husbands, their behaviour was rigidly controlled, they could readily be divorced.

Yet there were traces of two other features within Judaism. There was sometimes a warm delight in the companionship of man and woman, the occasional acknowledgment that love-making ennobled and glorified both partners. It was seen most obviously in the Song of Songs and the stories of the patriarchs, the former being a constant embarrassment to the early church. Alongside this there were the growing speculations of the rabbis on the nature and essence of sin, whether or not it was perhaps related to man's sexuality and this mysterious power which seems to be able to dominate his existence and drive all other thoughts out of his head, and all other desires from his will.[2]

Early Christianity inherited this along with the teaching and example of Jesus. He appears to have had a more exalted view of woman, to have held that 'in the beginning' God created marriage to effect 'one flesh', and to have taught a strict view denouncing divorce. Yet when Paul handled the problem in I Cor. 7, he was both aware of this and also willing to sanction separation in a marriage where a pagan partner did not want to stay married to a Christian (the 'Pauline privilege').[3] The early church in the circle from which Matthew's Gospel originated held that Jesus permitted divorce on the grounds of *porneia* (the 'Matthean exception').[4] But both Jesus and Paul were apparently celibate, as were some others in the apostolic circle.[5]

Early Christianity lived, however, in the whole whirlpool of ideas which made up Mediterranean civilization, within which many religious groups held that the physical body was evil, its desires sinful. Redemption was some form of escape for the spirit from this prison-house in which it had unfortunately been shut up. 'Gnosis' of one sort or another could enable that deliverance to be effected. Obviously that could produce two totally opposed views of sexual morality – either, that to the 'saved' person there was no longer any meaning whatever in physical acts and therefore indulgence could now be unfettered (leading to crass hedonism), or that heroic asceticism was the only way to live in the 'saved' situation.

The strong rootage of Christianity within Judaism prevented the first hedonistic response from occurring. God willed strict sexual responsibility as an essential response to his creative purposes. But despite hints in the New Testament that coitus is honourable and deeply significant to man as a creature of God,[6] despite hints that marriage is as profound a relationship as perhaps that between Christ and his church (as in Eph. 5), the second response gained more and more ground. Virginity became widely praised by the early Fathers. 'Spiritual' marriages in which the partners prayed together but never had coitus became exalted in many circles, causing endless scandal until finally forbidden in AD 420. The pressures became almost irresistible to exalt celibacy over and above the married state.

The early Fathers were not primarily interested in constructing what we would call a 'theology of sexuality'. Their interests were mainly practical. They wanted to produce some sort of authoritative moral guidance for their people. They struggled to establish an order of 'deacons' so that the celibate could all serve the church within a framework of discipline. They sought to avoid enthusiasm and extravagance, with the exception of fanatics like Tertullian and rigid authoritarians like Jerome. They were quite apathetic towards the family and regarded marital obligations as a nuisance (constantly quoting Paul in I Cor. 7). They steadily developed the whole notion that the married state was inferior to the celibate, and commenced the long struggle to impose celibacy upon the clergy. By the fourth century it was the rule throughout the Western church. They grudgingly acknowledged that marriage was good, and fervently asserted that celibacy was better. They denigrated coitus, and more often denigrated woman, typified after all in the figure of Eve. Clement of Alexandria even saw the orgasm as an experience as dangerous as epilepsy!

It was Augustine *par excellence* who constructed a strong theological framework within which to hold these views. His own bitter struggle with sexual passions, his previous conviction as a Manichee, his rapturous delight in God's grace, his towering intellectual power, all contributed. He noted that people practise coitus in private, and that sexual passion and its release in the orgasm so dominate the person that the reflective reason is utterly swamped. Surely, then, sexuality as we know it is the result of the Fall. If venereal desire was once good, it has now been corrupted utterly. It is evil. It leads to man's enjoyment of the flesh in oblivion to the one true good – the love of God. It is because man is the willing victim of 'concupiscence' (the overwhelming lust for self-gratification) that our practice of sexuality is evil, and through it we transmit the awful contagion of original sin.[7]

The consequence is that for Augustine celibacy is indeed the higher state, for within it venereal passion can be totally mastered by God's grace. But there is a clear duty to perpetuate the species, so there is a lesser place for the married state. Within it, coitus must occur to further conception, but venereal pleasures are inherently sinful and to be avoided. Practise coitus as rarely as is required for procreation, but never enjoy it! The 'good' in marriage can most clearly be seen in that it is a likeness of Christ's relation to the church, a symbol of this, a 'sacrament', for it involves duties and obligations, pledges and willing agreement, and it carries within it a blessing that should make the Christian thankful. It is wrong to try to dismember this union, for it is indeed God who has 'joined together', and only a separation that will enable both partners to pursue the holy life as celibates can be permitted. Thus Augustine established the massive framework for an understanding of sexuality which has dominated Western Christianity almost to the present day.

The following centuries saw several developments occurring slowly and fitfully throughout the sprawling church of Christendom, but always building upon Augustine's foundations. It was more and more clearly accepted that the married state was for second-class Christians and should be forbidden to the clergy. The true 'end' of marriage was seen to be procreative, but since uncontrollable lust is a constant social danger, marriage was also seen as a means of constraining it within a safe framework. Thus there is a lesser 'end' also to the married state, the remedy for sin.

The most tortuous and convoluted debates took place concerning the institution of marriage.[8] What makes a marriage? The many tribes being slowly converted into Christianity held different views. For some, marriage was constituted by the free consent of the two parties, made by their mutual will to be married. For others it was constituted by the giving of the *mundum*, or bride price, from the one family to the other and the transfer of the woman from her own parental family setting to that of the husband. For others, it was the first act of intercourse between the couple – the *consummatum* – that effected the marriage. Slowly the Western church asserted that 'consent makes marriage', but the way to a unified view was slow. Gratian's Decrees (c. 1140) asserted one major view, that consent is the efficient cause of marriage but establishes *conjugium initiatum* (the initiation of marriage); upon consummation it becomes a *conjugium ratum* (ratified marriage). To the latter applies the character of indissolubility even if impeded by imprisonment, absence, entry into monastic life, slavery or supervenient impotence. On the other hand, Hugh of St Victor and Peter Lombard (c. 1150) developed the notion of the double character of the marriage sacrament – the consent is likened to the union of Christ to his church in charity, whereas the consummation is likened to the incarnational union. The matter was finally expressed authoritatively at the fourth Lateran Council (1215), where Gratian's version triumphed.

Both these views shared in the developed concept of the indissolubility of the marriage bond. Augustine's view of *sacramentum* as a symbol had now become one of a sacrament mediating a supernatural saving grace which seals the marriage together permanently, only divisible by the death of one partner. Thus whereas the early Fathers held that marriage *should* not be severed, now it *could* not. Previously divorce was not permissible, now it was not possible, for an invisible sacramental seal binds the partners together despite any appearances to the contrary. Just as it is impossible to alter who one's parents were, so it had now become impossible to alter one's marriage partner. The consequence of this was that the theology of marriage had moved from the area denoted by the doctrine of creation (where Judaism placed it)[9] to the area of the doctrine of redemption.

Whilst the doctrine of marriage was slowly developing, so too was the church's control over marriage and marriage rites. No church rites were known before the ninth century, but steadily the church was acquiring control. By the twelfth century ecclesiastical courts were ruling marriage throughout Europe. But this raised the debate about the character of marriage all over again, for how was pagan or natural marriage to be understood? Gratian claimed that it was not indissoluble and that the Pauline privilege was operative, understanding this as Paul's permission to divorce, not merely to separate. But others were not satisfied because this introduced the concept of two sorts of marriage into a Europe which was part Christianized but coming more and more under the authority of the church. Nevertheless the distinction between natural and Christian marriage was generally maintained.

The requirement for a priest and two other witnesses to be present was not established until the decree *Tametsi* of the Council of Trent (1563). This was not aimed at asserting the church's rights over against those of the State, but was primarily designed to avoid the muddle of clandestine marriages throughout Europe. Interestingly, the priest did not have to be present at and active in the marriage ceremony until the decree *Ne Temere* of 1907. This reminds us that the traditional doctrine of marriage is that it is instigated and initiated *by the couple themselves*, by the expression of their consensus, and not by any act of the church or priest. At the exchange of vows, the couple are being 'priests' to each other; in the subsequent consummation they are establishing the sacramental character of their union.

It is useful at this point to comment upon the developments within Eastern Christianity, where Augustine's theology never found such widespread acceptance, and sexuality was never so closely related to sin and the transmission of original sin. In the East, marriage theology stayed in the area of the doctrine of creation; even though marriage later became a sacrament in the East, too, it was never established that the married state was inferior to the monastic in any decisive way. Thus the Council of Trullo in AD 691 forbad the marriage of bishops and the second marriage of clergy, but would go no further. This has remained the rule in the Orthodox Churches to this day. But marriage theology in the East has always understood marriage to be such a close and total union that not even death can dissolve it – it will extend into the after-life. Nevertheless, it can disintegrate from within and it is the responsibility of the church to deal graciously with its erring children when this happens, to mediate forgiveness and the chance for a new start. Thus a second marriage can be solemnized within the church, the form being almost identical for those who have been divorced as for those who are remarrying as widows or widowers, with a penitential element introduced. A third marriage is almost impossible, and a fourth cannot be entertained at all.[10]

Common to West and East was a profound contempt for the homosexual, who was regarded as twisted, corrupted, and peculiarly distorted by a vicious form of sin. The horror roused by homosexual practice was enormous; along with it went most extreme denunciations of masturbation. When the doctrine of natural law found much more precise form under Thomas Aquinas in the thirteenth century it became possible to define the sin of homosexuality as one 'against nature'; on these grounds it became more heinous than fornication and was held to be the cause of all sorts of outrageous maladies.[11]

The Reformers were totally opposed to clerical celibacy and the taking of monastic vows, and so to the whole concept of the married state as being in some manner inferior to that of the celibate. Luther held that every Christian had a calling to marriage – the man to be father of a family whom he would bring up in the fear and admonition of the Lord and to whom he would in some ways represent God; the woman to bear children, care for them and her husband and thus contribute to the family's well-being as the basic social unit of Christian living. Yet Luther did not direct himself to working out a fresh theology of sexuality; he appears to have held that there was a shame attached to the act of coitus and to have withdrawn slightly from the rigour of the Augustinian position (as, incidentally, had Thomas Aquinas earlier), but he still maintained that marriage was to be seen as a remedy for lust. Calvin was more positive than this, stressing the social significance of marriage and the virtues to be encouraged within the marriage bond. Luther permitted divorce for the innocent party in cases of adultery and desertion and cruelty, basing his case upon the Matthean exception; Calvin was stricter but still allowed divorce in the first instance cited.[12] Both were in effect laying the grounds for a more elevated view of the woman and of the value of home and family life.

Within the English church a different view of the sacramental character of marriage was emerging, whereby its indissolubility was no longer stressed, but instead the sacramental character of the total union and the family's whole life was being hinted at. From 1547 priests were permitted to marry. Whilst the three ends of marriage were seen to be procreation, the remedy for sin, and mutual care (as distinct from Catholicism which still held rigidly to the first two of these), three 'goods' were also cited: 'faith', 'offspring' and 'sacrament'. There was no uniformity about all this, so that Jeremy Taylor, for example, could cite the ends of marriage as those of mutual society, procreation and the remedy for sin (an order which has a decidedly modern ring about it). Nevertheless Cranmer's Book of Common Prayer maintained the order of procreation, remedy, mutuality, and this virtually settled any discussion on the matter for almost 300 years. Divorce was not permitted, but after 1604 separation was tolerated on the grounds that this was allowed in the Pauline privilege. Then in 1670 Parliament established the right of private persons with sufficient wealth to promote bills granting divorce, and the church was faced for the first time with the task of making some response, only to find itself clearly divided. Some (like Andrewes) were indissolubilists; others held that the essence of marriage was 'bed and board' and that if those proved impossible to maintain then divorce was tolerable. This basic division was to run through Anglicanism for hundreds of years afterwards.[13]

It was the Victorian era which caused the underlying differences to surface again. In 1836 the state set up its own registration procedures whereby it could authorize marriages;

the 1857 Matrimonial Causes Act then set up matrimonial courts which could grant divorce on the grounds of adultery, thereby taking over jurisdiction from the ecclesiastical courts. Bishop Tait and F. D. Maurice, for example, were in favour; Bishop Wilberforce and John Keble were against. The 'Matthean exception' became the most obvious justification for the first group, while the latter employed varieties of indissolubilist arguments. However, as the century went on there was a distinct hardening of opinion, and steadily the latter position gained strength. There were two main causes – the increasing alarm over the growing number of divorces and the discovery of widespread immorality and breakdown of family life throughout the nation, especially amongst the urban poor; and the development of biblical scholarship, which suggested that the 'Matthean exception' might well be a later gloss upon Jesus' original teaching to be found in Mark 10. By 1900 almost all the bishops were in the stricter school. The claim was widely made that a stable civilization required stable marriage, and therefore no divorce. Yet, although divorce was such a debating point, little theological attention was being devoted to the nature of sexual love. This did not happen either amongst Free Churchmen, who were usually more flexible than Anglicans, and normally took their stand with Luther in being willing to remarry 'innocent' parties.

Current concerns

The present century has caused enormous questions to be raised against the traditional Christian understanding of sexuality (which was primarily an interpretation of the nature of *marriage*, after all). The whirlpool of new discernments, radical questioning, colossal shifts of opinion, is extremely difficult to chart in any systematic way. There are six major areas, outlined below (but not in any sense of priority), with hints as to where there has been significant response from Christian ethics.

1. There has been virtually an explosion in our knowledge of the role of sexuality within the person, the contribution it makes to the inner dynamics of personal development. Prior to Freud it was generally believed that sexual interests only began to be aroused after puberty, that they were mainly directed towards the functions of procreation, and that male sexuality provided the norm. Freud blew those first two positions open, but

accepted the third in a remarkably uncritical way (hence his vilification nowadays by Women's Liberation circles). For Freud the sexual 'drive' is one of the most significant and certainly the most powerful within the person; it directs itself towards a sexual 'object' and is liable to repression by many processes, ultimately causing great damage; but it may be sublimated, and here Freud was less confident, and perhaps less interested. Thus sexuality was no longer a pressure within the person aimed at fulfilling procreative purposes; it was much more determinative of the person as a whole and aimed at many levels of personal satisfaction, especially the release of sexual tension and the satisfaction of the sex drive when roused by encounter with the sexual object. The nature of the orgasm became particularly important, since this release of tension could only adequately occur upon its success.[14]

One result has been a great growth in psychological and biological study of sexuality. The work of researchers like Kinsey,[15] or Masters and Johnson,[16] has provided a mass of information about sexual behaviour and characteristics, often validating some of Freud's hunches, but in some cases correcting them (e.g. he held that for women the 'vaginal orgasm' was the ideal, whereas Masters and Johnson show that no such thing happens). Christians can do no other than accept the new knowledge thus made available. But much of this research has proceeded upon assumptions that require constant critique. For example did Kinsey, formerly a world authority upon gall wasps, regard human beings as slightly more complex forms of animal life, and are our moral frameworks to be regarded as he indicated, as somewhat arbitrary 'taboos' inflicted upon us by society? Implicit within much of the work has been an assumption that there is a 'form' or 'essence' to sexuality which must be able to be expressed by the personality or serious disorder is bound to occur. This is itself a highly dubious assumption, as a careful study of the relevant literature soon shows.[17]

Christians inevitably have other serious reservations about much of the theorizing that has accompanied this research. In particular, there has been a long experience within the Christian tradition of the calling to celibacy, and a profound discovery by both men and women that this can be fulfilling, happy, healthy and productive of the whole range of virtues. Moreover, celibates have had experience of a depth of loving which has not of course been expressed in genital sexuality but has been flavoured with agape, the supreme gift of the Spirit.[18] Jesus, after all, was not married, and yet was man fulfilled to the utmost.

But other results of the recently-acquired sexual knowledge have been of great benefit. It has made us aware as never before of the whole spectrum of sexuality, of elements of homosexuality and heterosexuality within each person. It has helped us to see that many people are best to be understood as bisexual, able to experience erotic sexual attraction to either sex.[19] It has helped us to see the great range in sexual desire, practice and need across the vast range and variety of human beings. It has helped to promote much more tenderness, sympathy, understanding of those whose sexual drives might otherwise appear to be not merely bizarre but wicked. It has thus had great importance for Christian pastoral care, and has done much to destroy the old rigidities in Christian attitudes.[20]

2. The development of fairly efficient and widespread contraceptive techniques has meant that sexual intercourse can now be considered in its own right without reference to the 'end' of procreation. This is a matter of vast significance. For the first time in the whole history of the human race it is possible for a couple to experience sexual intercourse and be reasonably free from the fear of pregnancy, if they so wish. If the supreme 'end' or purpose of intercourse be procreative, then, of course, this is an unmitigated evil. Roman Catholic theology has always insisted somewhat woodenly that this be so, and as a result has had to oppose contraception with all its might, and to support its opposition with a whole battery of arguments. It is contrary to the natural law; it will result in a cheapening of the woman, who will become merely an object of sexual desire; it will undermine marriage and promote promiscuity and sexual licence. The traditional attitude was re-expressed powerfully by the papal encyclical *Casti Connubii* in 1930, but by the 1960s it was clear that this was not proving convincing to many Catholics. Moreover a new factor had appeared – the population explosion. For the first time ever there loomed over the world the threat of having far too many people.

Pope John XXIII responded by setting up a theological commission to investigate the whole doctrine of marriage and, implicitly, of sexuality. Then the Roman Church experienced Vatican II, the massive council that lasted six years and meant radical reappraisal of Catholic teaching and practice. The

Council did not address itself directly to marriage because of the ongoing work of the commission, but gave clear indication that it wanted new notes to be sounded. Thus the highly important 'Pastoral Constitution of the Church in the Modern World' stated that 'marriage is not instituted merely for procreation' and that 'the family is a kind of school of abundant humanity', whilst reiterating the traditional view that 'it is not lawful to regulate procreation by embarking on ways which the Church's teaching authority condemns'.[21] The view that married inter-course could still take place in the woman's 'safe period' if pregnancy was to be avoided was still regarded as the 'natural' escape mechanism for those desiring intercourse but not chil-dren. It was rarely noticed that, logically, 'nature' cannot have structured sexual intercourse for the supreme 'end' of procrea-tion if 'nature' provides an escape mechanism and if 'nature' aborts great numbers of fertilized ova in the normal course of the woman's life.

The Theological Commission reported in 1968. A majority favoured a major revision of the traditional teaching, so that the supreme 'end' of marriage be no longer seen solely as the procreative one. The 'end' of producing marital union, the 'one flesh' (to use the biblical term), was equally significant; therefore it was legitimate to 'plan' a family (but not willingly to avoid having children at all); therefore contraception could have a role in Christian marriage. The minority of the commission opposed this conclusion, arguing that it was a radical departure from the traditional teaching.[22] But the papal encyclical *Humanæ Vitae* settled the matter at the end of 1968. The traditional teaching was upheld, and thus the minority view of the Commission. Contraception was pronounced yet again to be illicit and against nature. This has not convinced great numbers of Catholics. 'The official teaching of the Roman Catholic Church condemns artificial contraception, but dissent from such official teaching is, in my view, both justifiable and widespread in Roman Catholi-cism,' writes a leading ethicist.[23]

The Anglican communion had never been so committed to a rigid view of marriage based upon natural law teaching. Successive Lambeth Conferences dealt with the matter incon-clusively until in 1958 the Report *The Family in Contemporary Society* was presented, and its major conclusions endorsed. This made two main points: that 'a new value is ascribed to coitus, which, as the specific and consummating act of marriage, is seen to be no mere means to generation, but an act of positive importance for the marriage union and for the perfecting of husband and wife', and that 'a conscientious decision to use contraceptives would in certain circumstances be justified'.[24] This led to the significant resolution No. 115 which said, 'This Conference believes that the responsibility for deciding upon the number and frequency of children has been laid by God upon the consciences of parents everywhere: that this planning, in such ways as are mutually acceptable to husband and wife in Christian conscience, is a right and important factor in Christian family life and should be the result of positive choice before God. Such responsible parenthood, built on obedience to all the duties of marriage, requires a wise stewardship of the resources and abilities of the family as well as a thoughtful consideration of the varying population needs and problems of society and the claims of future generations.'

Other church bodies had been arguing to the same end, whilst major theologians had been at work to interpret sexuality in fresh relational ways. Thus Sherwin Bailey (highly influential at the 1958 Lambeth Conference) had argued for an understanding of marriage that was based upon the biblical theme of the 'one flesh' union;[25] Helmut Thielicke had shown that modern understanding of sexuality could be fruitfully expressed within the traditional Lutheran concept of the 'orders', and had stressed that these are orders of creation and that man transcends nature and should therefore, responsibly, improve or develop or modify the 'natural' processes, so that contraception in an over-populated world can be required by God;[26] Karl Barth had discussed the four options open to the married (complete abstinence, the 'safe period', *coitus interruptus* and contraception) and could see no way out but to choose one of them, the fourth being less objectionable than the others.[27] But it was not until the 1970s when marriage was being described in much more clearly relational terms that this sense of grudgingness was removed from Protestant discussion of contraception; this leads us to the next section.

3. The pressures for contraception, the new awareness of sexuality and the rising tide of divorce all pushed Christians towards a redefinition of marriage and reappraisal of the possibility of divorce. It became clearer that some Christian marriages do indeed break down, and there was no virtue in trying to hide from that unpalatable fact. As Monica Furlong put

it: 'The Christian is someone who should be more ready to admit to failure than the next man . . . it is the recognition of his essential poverty which is his passport to the Kingdom. Divorce should in a sense be easier for him than for the next man . . . He knows that man is a poor thing, and that he makes mistakes, but that in God's goodness they can still become part of a creative process.'[28] But if marriage is a rigidly permanent institution, an 'estate', then of course divorce remains inconceivable, as it does on Catholic teaching in which marriage is a special sacramental bonding which, once applied, cannot be un-applied. It also became clearer that to talk of an 'estate' (which Anglican theology often did) was unsatisfactory because rigid and too legalistic.

The conviction that marriage is primarily an 'estate', a fixed order, an institution, was firmly held at the turn of the century. It could be put hilariously by authors like G. K. Chesterton, who wrote a scintillating essay entitled 'The Sentimentalism of Divorce', pouring withering scorn on all who talk glibly about divorce, taunting them with a picture of a 'fashionable divorce' in which perhaps a frosted divorce-cake is provided for the congratulatory guests, and, in military circles, cut by the co-respondent's sword. He said, 'Marriage is an institution like any other, set up deliberately to have certain functions and limitations: it is an institution like private property, or conscription, or the legal liberties of the subject. To talk as if it were made or melted with certain changing moods is a waste of words . . . A farm cannot simply float away from a farmer in proportion as his interest in it grows fainter than it was . . . The new sentimentalists . . . must not suggest that an institution can be actually identical with an emotion.'[29] But the Chesterton hard line would not do: it undervalued the emotional and conative elements in the marriage bond. If a couple do not *will* to be together, and if they have no tender feelings whatever for each other, what creative meaning is left in the assertion that they are in the married state?

Whilst the theologians continued to explore more personal and relational ways of understanding marriage, the Church of England found itself obliged to take a fresh look at the divorce laws. Pressure for reform was become overwhelming. English divorce law was based upon the notion of the matrimonial offence; if one party could successfully sue the other for having committed an offence against the marriage (e.g. adultery), then the marriage could be terminated and one party would appear in the end to be 'innocent' and the other 'guilty'. Was that satisfactory? An Anglican commission reported in 1966 – *Putting Asunder* – that the basis should be changed.[30] Instead of the courts having to adjudicate on whether or not some 'offence' had been proven, they should determine whether or not there was 'irretrievable breakdown' in the marriage. This led to the Divorce Reform Act of 1969 (later consolidated into the Matrimonial Causes Act of 1973) which is based upon the principle of irretrievable breakdown and enables a divorce to be granted in certain cases even against the wish of one of the parties. The issue here was the secular law, but the approach made in *Putting Asunder* showed that marriage was no longer being understood as an institution that must be preserved whatever the feeling of those living within it; in effect, the church was beginning to talk of marriage as a special sort of human relationship. Inevitably that church would have to re-think its marriage doctrine.

A Commission reported in 1971 in *Marriage, Divorce and the Church* that the doctrine should be revised; marriage should be understood as primarily a unique human relationship intended by God to be permanent. 'A marriage which grows and deepens so that it attains fully to its nature, "becomes what it is", a lifelong union. Just as it is possible for any organism to wither and die before it has grown into its full nature, so too marriage may break down before it has grown into what it should become.'[31] Therefore it should be reluctantly accepted that some Christian marriages do not become what they are and could be; they break down. Therefore provision for this should be made in the church's discipline and liturgy. A minority opposed all these conclusions, arguing on traditional catholic lines that marriage was sacramentally indissoluble, and a fairly vigorous argument followed.[32] But the General Synod was reluctant to accept the Report; it commissioned another one, which reported in 1978 and reached the same basic conclusions by an almost identical process of reasons.[33] This too did not gain sufficient support for church practice to be altered; but it showed that the theology of marriage had changed, whether or not the church liked the implications.

Opposition to this steady but deliberate shifting of the theology of marriage comes from two directions. There is still a small Protestant minority wanting the indissolubilist position to be maintained.[34] But there is also a conservative biblical argument, that Jesus taught marriage to be unbreakable and divorce to be tantamount to adultery, so that it must be maintained as a permanent union even if circumstances oblige the couple to separate and live apart. That is permissible, but divorce and remarriage is contrary to New Testament teaching.[35]

Roman Catholic practice, having rejected the general developments in Protestant doctrine, has had to resort to a rapid development in the concept of nullity in order to respond to the huge pressure for divorce from its members. When a marriage is declared null it means that the church is saying that it never was a 'sacramental union' in the first place, was not therefore indissoluble, and can now be regarded as never having been at all. If the union was never consummated by sexual intercourse, it never became a sacramental union. If the parties did not give full consent, if one of them was not at the time a baptized Christian, if there was mistaken identity, then it was not an indissoluble union. It can be annulled. But that sort of attempt to invalidate the original promises can, of course, open very wide doors. This has occurred. If one party (at the time of the consent expressed in the original marriage service) had a 'divorce mentality' – i.e. believed that in some circumstances divorce might be legitimate – that can be held to show that 'full consent' was not given, so the marriage never was. Thus the concept of nullity has been turned into a convenient device for invalidating marriages, some of which may for many years have had the true marks and signs of marriage. The Church of England explored this way out of the 'divorce dilemma' as far back as 1955 and set its face against it.[36] Arguably, secular law is more realistic than Roman Catholic law in this matter; the former enquires into the present state of the marriage when assessing breakdown, but the latter focusses its enquiry on the state of the parties and their mentality when consent was given (which could have been twenty, thirty or forty years ago).

The reformulation of the basis, purpose and character of marriage that has occurred within Protestant churches especially can best be seen in their marriage liturgies. The 1980 Alternative Service Book states that marriage is given that husband and wife may find comfort and help each other, living faithfully together in need and in plenty, in sorrow and in joy. It is given that with delight and tenderness they may know each other in love, and, through the joy of their bodily union, may strengthen the union of their hearts and lives. It is given, that they may have children and be blessed in caring for them and bringing them up in accordance with God's will, to his praise and glory. The 1975 Methodist Service Book states that marriage is the life-long union in body, mind and spirit, of one man and one woman. It is his will that in marriage the love of man and woman should be fulfilled in the wholeness of their life together, in mutual companionship, helpfulness and care . . . such marriage is the foundation of true family life, and, when blessed with the gift of children, is God's chosen way for the continuance of mankind . . . The 1979 United Reformed Church service states that God has provided (marriage) for the companionship of honour and comfort in mutual care, so that husband and wife may live faithfully together. God has provided it for the fulfilling of human love in mutual honour so that husband and wife may know each other with delight. God has provided it for the birth and nurture of children so that they may find the security of love and grow up in the heritage of the faith. God has provided it for the enrichment of society, so that husband and wife being joined together may enter into the life of the community as a new creation.

4. The determined assertion of the rights and status of women has injected a wholly new and creative element into the debate about the nature of sexuality. It is really *very* new. The women's emancipation movements early in the century had mainly a political objective – the vote. But in 1963 a new force was released when Betty Friedan's work was published[37], and the National Organization of Women was formed (NOW). Mrs Friedan had set out to study the domesticated American family woman who was being repeatedly told by advertisements and women's magazines that she could fulfil herself totally in being a good mother and home-maker. The study revealed the enormous frustrations that result, and released a pent-up surge of violent emotion. Women claimed the right to pattern their own lives for themselves, without having to copy the male stereotype or to fit into places in society which he allocated to them. They claimed that their sexuality was quite distinct from the male's and had its own rights; nor was the role of 'good mother and homemaker' adequate any longer. The movement has been a protest, a howl of anger, a plea for rights.

Amongst Christians this has resulted in three main developments: a sad confession of the way in which the Christian tradition has treated women, with a constant querying as to why this should have been so; a strong protest at the ways in which women have been denied leadership in the church and refused ordination to the presbyterate (by many churches, but not all); a plea that our theology should make serious attempts to stress the feminine as well as the masculine attributes of the Godhead. Whilst this has sometimes been at the level of strident protest at the male-ness of so much liturgy and hymnody, with its incipient sexism, the grounds have been the nature of the Godhead: God is both Father and Mother of the human race. The general result has undoubtedly been a new respect for woman, but it is doubtful if it has had any direct impact upon the theology of sexuality and marriage. Its influence is more apparent by the 1980s in the heightened sensitivity with which marriage is discussed.[38]

This development has been resisted by Anglo-Catholics, for whom the thought of women seeking ordination to the priesthood has been anathema and for whom this is the major issue. It has also been resisted by biblical conservatives. For them the key question to be asked about a marriage is not, 'What is the nature of human sexuality and how can it be fulfilled by the marriage union?' (the question which has largely dominated most Protestant theology), but, 'What is the nature of the God-appointed authority structure that should prevail between male and female, and how can marriage fulfil it?' This writing has seen the recent wave of divorce as a breakdown in authority, and has thus over-simplified it; the result is to find an over-simple answer – we must re-assert the God-appointed authority of the male.[39]

5. The pleas for the homosexual. Traditional Christianity found homosexuality quite abhorrent, 'unnatural', condemned in both Old and New Testaments, and to be regarded as a sign of corruption in society (as with Sodom and Gomorrah). It also condemned masturbation as 'self-abuse', an act liable to promote later impotence and all sorts of horrors. But the advent of the first Kinsey Report in 1948 drew attention to the latent homosexuality in almost all men, and to the unpalatable fact that about 5% of men never felt any sexual attraction to the opposite sex and were to be regarded as wholly homosexual. Ever since, there have been inconclusive arguments concerning the causes of homosexuality and therefore the cures for it. Is it caused by

some sort of emotional deprivation during infancy? Or due to
some lack of hormones? Or some other basically physical factor
in the make-up of the person? Or to some traumatic sexual
encounters in childhood? Or to all of these together? It remains
a mystery.[40] In Britain the Wolfenden Commission reported in
1957 that homosexual acts between consenting adults in private
should no longer be regarded as criminal offences; this sparked
off a huge debate about the function of the law as well as the right
way to respond to homosexuality. It resulted in the Sexual
Offences Act of 1969, which carried out the Wolfenden proposals, and helped pave the way for homosexuals to 'come out', to
declare themselves in public and to champion their rights and
demand an end to the superstitious horror with which they had
previously been treated in society. Numerous societies were
formed to promote their interests, including the Gay Christian
Movement and the Open Church Group.

The response of Christians has inevitably been varied.[41] First,
there has been total opposition to any reassessment of the
homosexual's state on the grounds that it is 'unnatural'. Human
sexuality is designed within the natural law to effect procreation;
any use of it for other ends is essentially immoral. A person
claiming to be wholly homosexual must in some way be
orientated contrary to God's will; the only course for him is to
sublimate his sexuality totally. The *Declaration on Certain
Questions concerning Sexual Ethics* issued by the Vatican in
December 1975 stated this position firmly: 'homosexual acts are
intrinsically disordered and can in no case be approved of'.
Many Catholic moral theologians have found this position
intolerable, especially since they wish to work with a much more
dynamic notion of the 'natural law', or because they want to
work with a more comprehensive and considerate understanding of the human person, or both.[42]

Second, some Christians have wanted to retain the traditional
Protestant abhorrence, but mainly upon scriptural grounds.
They do not accept the general thrust of much recent biblical
scholarship which doubts whether the repudiation of the
homosexual was as absolute as it has been held to be, or that
Paul's strictures can be held to be binding upon us today since he
did not know what we now know about the condition, or that the
primitive understanding of sexuality is to be determinative for
us. For them an acceptance of homosexuality by Christians is a
denial of biblical authority.[43] Some biblical conservatives have,

however, started with the traditional view, gone fresh to the scriptures, and emerged with different conclusions altogether, to their surprise. They have even gone so far as to argue that a permanent homosexual union is entirely valid.[44]

Third, there are many Christians who have come to accept that some people, through no apparent fault of their own, are permanently homosexual. But like all God's children, they are created to find fulfilment in love, including inter-personal sexual love. That being so, their morality must be judged on precisely the same criteria as that of heterosexual behaviour. The homosexual is not somehow so different that acts of loving have to be judged on a different basis altogether. There is inevitably, then, a case for 'homosexual marriage', although many of the writers in this field are somewhat reluctant to investigate it. The most open acceptance of this position occurs in the work of Norman Pittenger, who in *Time for Consent* outlined an ethic for homosexuals thus:[45]

1. No-one should accept his homosexuality without questioning it.
2. If he recognizes that he is a homosexual, then he should gladly accept it as his condition, unless he wishes to change it.
3. God will help the homosexual to be the best that he can be; so seek God's help.
4. Do not try to make others homosexual if they are not; exercise strong self-control in sexual advances to others.
5. Make friends in the same ways as do all others.
6. If a homosexual is in love, it must be tested by the normal criteria, and may only take physical expression in a truly 'loving' relationship.

Church reports have rarely gone as far as this, but have certainly argued on similar lines. Thus a Report presented to the Methodist Conference in 1979 and 1981 argued this position, but was not endorsed by that church.[46] An Anglican report entitled *Homosexual Relationships*, again not endorsed, argued a similar case but suggested that clergy must be a special consideration.[47] What these reports showed was that Christian bodies were prepared to debate the issue openly, even if the full logic of an 'acceptance' position was too hard at first to face up to. The debates have certainly helped to have a much more enlightened view of the issues in Christian circles.

Fourth, there is a tiny minority of Christian homosexuals who have felt that their condition is one to glory in, that God has made them thus by positive intention, and that they should practise love-making in a thankful and open manner. Since this apparently carefree position is not held by the mainstream churches they have felt impelled to found their own – the Metropolitan Church. There is a spirit of crusading about the whole position, vigorously expressed in the autobiography of the founder, Troy Perry.[48]

6. The widespread eroticism within modern culture. It has been argued powerfully by historians that there have been waves of eroticism within European culture at certain periods, but that the wave which became noticeable in Western culture by the end of the 1950s has been the most momentous and powerful, and shows no signs of abating.[49] There may be a variety of reasons for this. In a depersonalized but alerted world, the one area of life which is essentially private and in which personal meaning can be found is the sexual. To put it crudely, the young person who is unemployed and unskilled and apparently unwanted by society, can find both gratification and a limited amount of meaning in intimate sexual relationships. At that point he or she may become a 'person', treasured and wanted. Again, a society geared to mass consumerism must employ extensive titillation to sell its goods, so that advertising must stress the sexual and the hedonistic. One could go on seeking explanations for this current state of affairs; how do Christians reckon to offer moral guidance? On the whole, the traditional arguments for sexual restraint and in condemnation of fornication or adultery now appear somewhat threadbare. Widespread contraception, easily available abortion, modern treatments for venereal disease, appear to weaken them almost to the point of making them irrelevant.

The position has been confounded because whilst trying to respond to the powerful challenge presented at this point by modern culture, Christians have at the same time been embroiled in the ongoing debate amongst themselves about the nature of Christian morality and how it is to be taught and presented to this generation. Is Christian morality expressed best by a clear and easily memorable set of commandments, such as 'Thou shalt not commit fornication nor adultery', or is it more subtle than that, an assertion of positive values such as 'Thou shalt always act in a fully loving and respectful way to others'? If it is the former, it is easy to teach, and it is easy to spot when people have gone wrong; if it is the latter, it has to be taught differently, by providing lots of illustrations and by considerable debate and discussion. There may always be a fuzzy area of uncertainty about much of it; if someone has transgressed it is more difficult to be aware of it; it assumes a moral maturity on behalf of the people trying to live by it. The 'situation ethics' debate has inevitably featured much of this discussion, especially since that debate has mainly used sexual morality as its standard example. The first occasion on which this debate surfaced into official church life was when the British Council of Churches asked a group to prepare a satisfactory statement of sexual morality for this generation. The report, entitled *Sex and Morality*,[50] argued firmly and cogently for a re-statement of traditional morality in terms of the more positive injunction upon Christians to love and respect others. It would not accept that Christian morality could be encapsulated in crisp, negative commandments. The Report could not be endorsed by the BCC; its presentation to that body showed the deep division between Christians on the nature of Christian morality, let alone the nature of sexual morality.

Two sensitive writers who have struggled hard to redeem the Christian sex ethic from its apparently insensitive and negative ethos deserve honourable mention. The first, a Protestant student chaplain working in the USA and keenly aware both of students' attitudes and of current sexual research, is Richard Hettlinger. He deplored the pious nonsense talked in the past about what the church regarded as wicked sexual behaviour, and argued an ethic based upon profound respect for the other person, and for the deep capacity of sexuality to convey meanings of belonging, commitment and the desire for creativity between a couple. On this basis he argued that 'if the full meaning of sex is discovered in personal relationships, the ultimate intimacy of intercourse should be preserved until the ultimate commitment to another person, which is represented by marriage.'[51] As for engaged couples having intercourse together prior to marriage, he could quite accept that in some responsible cases 'it it quite possible that the act will be little different in its significance for them than if it precedes marriage', and quotes with approval Canon Bryan Green's advice to 'thank God for the experience and ask forgiveness for the lack of discipline'.[52]

The other is a Roman Catholic, Jack Dominian, who has written widely in the field of marriage, marriage breakdown and Christian morality. He wants to uphold the profound character of love and to advocate morality in terms of that which will promote the full loving, and therefore enhancement, of others; sexual intercourse has a particularly significant 'symbolic' value, expressing caring, commitment and appreciation of the other. It is a 'language' of gratitude, hope, reconciliation, sexual identity, mutual acceptance and equality. He is sharply critical of the nuances in *Humanae Vitae* and argues that a sexual ethic must be grounded in 'a positive acceptance of human sexuality' which is 'directed to the enlargement of the human potential'. 'Man, reflecting the image of God, fulfils this most completely when the starting point of his growth is to consider himself as a sexual person in relationships of love with other sexual persons.'[53]

Questions for Discussion

(a) What is there of permanent value in the biblical teaching concerning sexuality?

(b) Outline a sexual ethic for Christians to live by today.

Chapter 7

Theories Many

In Chapter 1 I referred to the ways in which LeRoy Long attempted a rough classification of the various types of Christian approach towards an ethical system or framework of ethical concepts. He divided these approaches up into two main groups, those which stressed the ends and those which stressed the means. In the former one might encounter a major stress (or, in his terms, 'motif') upon the deliberative (which particularly stresses reason), the prescriptive (which stresses what has been laid down or commanded by authority), or the relational (which stresses devotion to or dependence upon Christ). In the latter group one would especially encounter the motif of the institutional (where the stress is upon the need for order and the restraint of sin and evil), or the operational (where the stress is upon influencing the centres of power) or the intentional (stressing the creation of the dedicated society, however small). Long is in effect warning us against the assumption that Christians are likely to be agreed about either ends or means in matters of ethics.

But there are yet more complications, yet more opportunities for variety and the tensions introduced by rival theories, since Christian ethics does not exist in a cosy little vacuum unaffected by the influences of the wider intellectual world. Moral theories abound in that world today, as they have always done, and there is a wide-ranging disagreement about the nature and purpose of all ethical thought and talk. Moral philosophy, with all its intricate arguments, is a constant background to all Christian moral and ethical theorizing.[1]

Moral philosophers have always been intrigued by the basic questions as to the source of mankind's concern about morals and the nature of the moral judgments we are always making. Four schools of thought illustrate the types of positions that have been adopted in modern British moral philosophy.

1. *Naturalism* asserts that ethics is an aspect of some science or other. So, if a statement like 'one should always be honest' is taken to mean, 'the majority of humans find that honesty is in practice desirable', ethics has become a matter of determining what most people actually desire, which is an aspect of psychology. If it has a more historical bent, ethics could almost become an aspect of anthropology. Again, if 'one should always be honest' means 'in the evolution of the human race the process is aided by human honesty', ethics has now become an aspect of biology. If it means 'human society is more stable when honesty is practised', then ethics has become an aspect of sociology, of what makes human societies function as they do. It is not unusual for scientists in any of the fields just cited to hold the view that their discipline embraces lots of others, and often they like to sweep ethics into their area of study; they often do not raise in any serious way the question as to whether or not this is legitimate.

There are obvious advantages about this general view. It becomes possible to keep ethics in clear bounds, and to base it upon 'scientific' observation and measurement. Like all science, it becomes independent of the particular views or values of the observer. But against this it is held that in practice we simply do not come to ethical conclusions by treating ethical issues as if they were the outcome of scientific enquiries. Moreover in practice we often seem to have a deep down conviction that some things are 'right' even if the majority of others do not think so; that is, in practice we act again and again on the actual assumption that what is 'right' is grounded somewhere else than merely within general human awareness. Further, on this account of ethics the implicit assumption is that one can deduce what 'ought to be' from what 'is'.

This introduces us to an argument which has raged since the beginning of this century when G. E. Moore wrote a major book entitled *Principia Ethica*, which was largely an all-out attack on all forms of naturalism. He coined a famous phrase 'the naturalistic fallacy', by which he meant the assumption that one could define 'good' in any way whatever, and also the assumption that one could define it in some natural way by reference to some non-ethical characteristic (e.g. observable and measurable qualities, or theological concepts). To him, 'good' was quite indefinable, and therein lies the real 'fallacy' against which he inveighed. He pointed out that one could not define 'yellow', even though there are certain characteristics which go with yellow light (e.g. the wavelength of that light); one simply has to see 'yellow' in order to know what it is like. In the same way one has to 'see' what is 'good' and one cannot define it by comparison or likeness to anything else. One cannot deduce what 'ought to be' from what 'is'.

2. *Intuitionism*, is the conviction that we know by intuition what is 'good' and what is not, for there is no other way of grasping at the 'good', which is indefinable. This general approach seemed fairly attractive to moral philosophers for a brief period early in this century, but soon began to appear increasingly flawed. For instance, if we know by intuition, how is it that different people seem to 'know' quite different versions of the 'good' so that, in the end, they disagree about it? Further, does it do justice to much of our experience, where we find that several 'goods' present themselves to us and we are confused as to which of them is to be reckoned of the greatest value? Intuition does not seem to solve such a problem. Thus a family trying to resolve whether or not to send grannie into an old peoples' home may feel very deeply and certainly that she ought to be looked after by them; but equally she ought not to disrupt the family and take the energy which the children ought to receive from their parents. How can one sort out such a tension? In the end, whichever way the decision goes, those making it may feel a troubled conscience, aware that they have not done the 'good' or the 'right' and aware that from within their own intuitive moral awareness there was no faculty for resolving the matter satisfactorily. Yet there are strengths in the intuitionist position. It recognizes that ethics is distinctive, using its own special ways of discourse and procedure, not to be regarded as an element in some other science or discipline.

3. *Emotivism* asserts that moral statements are mainly ones that express the attitudes of the speaker and attempt to produce the same attitudes or emotions in the hearer. If I say that every married person should stay faithful to his or her partner I am not actually saying something that describes some quality of the permanence-of-marriage which is built into the universe and is obvious to anyone thinking about it. I am saying how I personally feel about marriage and how I want everyone else

to think about it. My remark says nothing about the universe in general or the nature of reality; it tells others about my feelings. One of the protagonists of this view – A. J. Ayer – goes a little bit further still, because he says that some such statements also imply an element of command in them. I am almost commanding other people to stay faithful in their marriages.

Again, 'naturalism' is being denied. The great interest, however, is the uses to which moral talk can be put, what purpose it fulfils in our everyday speech. The emotivists generally say that the main purpose is to influence other people. They then became interested in the circumstances in which we usually use such talk and what we hope to gain by doing so, and whether or not there is a certain amount of description present in the statements. If I say 'this apple is good' I may of course be saying that I feel very attracted by the apple and want to eat it, so that I am here expressing my feelings. But maybe I am also saying something about the apple: that I have good grounds for commending it to other people also, that it has some special qualities. This concentration upon the usage to which the moral talk is being put was especially acceptable in the general climate of the linguistic analysis upon which so much general philosophy was concentrating especially in the 1950s and 1960s.

4. *Prescriptivism* holds that there is some distinct moral obligation carried within moral discourse. Words like 'good' or 'best' are not merely expressing how we feel about the subjects which these words are used to describe, they are impelling us to have a disposition to act in a certain manner. If we say that it is 'good' to keep promises, we are actually trying to encourage our hearers to keep promises; we are not just describing how we happen to feel upon the matter. So morality becomes quite definitely a matter of our choosing certain values, and not just recognizing that they exist in the descriptions offered by others. Most theorists within this approach (e.g. R. M. Hare) claim further that for a statement to be 'moral' (and therefore in some sense putting the hearer under moral obligation) its basic maxim must be universalizable. It must apply to all others in like conditions. This gives to morality a grounding in reason and saves it from being purely arbitrary or subjective, which is an obvious weakness in emotivism. It has given much more compulsion to moral

words than emotivism was expressing.

All of this theorizing can appear to be of mere academic interest. Worse, it can appear to belittle the whole business of ethics, since the moral philosophers are particuarly careful in their discussions to avoid committing themselves to firm moral opinions or stances, and use somewhat trivial examples about which they might argue. This is odd, because many of them (e.g. Bertrand Russell) were prepared to enter the fray of public and political controversy and to appear to revel in it, championing some very unpopular causes quite fervently. An especially clear and lucid account of recent work ends up by bemoaning the fact that 'ethics as a serious subject has been left further and further behind', but also ventures the guess that 'the most boring days are over'.[2]

If the moral philosophers have been generally chary of telling us what to do, is that the case with all ethical discussion? Obviously not. There are great numbers of thinkers who engage in ethical discussion of one sort or another and are desperately anxious to tell us what to do. We can call these the 'ethical system-makers' as distinct from the moral philosophers, although the sharp distinction between the two may be somewhat unfair at times; they can overlap and the divisions be blurred. In practice Christians, and everyone else, are more likely to be affected by the 'system-makers' who only incidentally concern themselves with worries about the nature of ethical judgments and the functions served by ethical language. Their main concern is undoubtedly to get us to behave as they think fit, and thereby to get the world improved in the directions they think desirable. They can indeed become propagandists in their cause and can introduce a passion into the discussion which the moral philosophers would eschew on the grounds that passion does not produce a better understanding. True – but passion may help to produce action, which is the more dominant interest with the system-makers. They want to change the world. There are at least four main 'systems' which one encounters regularly and commonly today, all of which have in one way or another affected most of us.

1. *Humanism*. This is a vague term, and there are many forms of belief in man which become included under this umbrella, but the common element is the belief that man is of intrinsic value and can know and realize what is 'good' with-

out reliance upon any sources or values outside himself. Humanism inevitably has a very high view of man, of human beings, and generally holds this to be self-evident. It also tends either to repudiate some transcendent source of value (such as belief in God) or else to maintain a detached agnosticism which amounts to saying, 'If there is a God, which there may possibly be, then that God is not one that makes any difference to human existence as we experience it.' It is clear that there may be very noble and lofty brands of humanism, in which the dignity and grandeur of man is maintained against all sorts of odds.

Humanism has been a feature of European life, especially since the great days of Greco-Roman culture, and has often flowered in periods of widespread general acceptance of Christianity, such as the Middle Ages; however, more recently it has acquired an anti-Christian flavour, so that some of its forms are belligerently secularist and sharply critical of the role of organized religion in promoting what it sees as corrupted morality. Nevertheless Christians have become increasingly reluctant to let go of the word, since it represents a lofty view of man despite all the tendencies in the modern world to dehumanize him, to reduce him to a cog in a huge machine, or to make him into a fairly useful beast. Christians, too, want to speak up for the inherent dignity of man. They do so usually on the grounds that man is made in the image of God, is redeemed in Christ and destined for eternal life; the hard-core humanists who repudiate all religion are driven to claim that man's goodness and value are self-evident. Thus there is much common ground, covering much of the current protest against oppression and the denial of human rights, the resort to violence in all its forms, the practice of torture, or any action which devalues humanity.

But there is also a different basis for humanist and Christian moralities. The latter holds that human value derives from God's grace; the former is bound to claim that it lies within man himself. One notices the difference when asking questions like, 'Why bother to keep a hopelessly handicapped baby alive?' The latter replies, 'Because it is a child of God, loved and valued by God, and therefore possessing an inherent claim upon our loving and caring', the former has considerable difficulty in pointing to that within the handicapped person which can be claimed to be of any great value, great enough to warrant a lot of care and the spending of resources upon it. The humanist may also be trenchant in his criticism of the Christian's habit of talking about God and then deriving some moral obligation from such talk. He may dismiss this as the naturalistic fallacy again. But meanwhile humanism as a system has considerable difficulty in upholding the dignity of man in the face of the appalling evils which men do to one another and the degree of tragedy within human existence. Nevertheless it produces its moral heroes.

2. *Utilitarianism* often overlaps with humanism, but not necessarily so. It is tempting to class this as yet another moral theory, but it is probably more than that and offers virtually a complete system. It affirms that moral good is that which promotes the greatest degree of human well-being. A form of this theory (hedonistic utilitarianism), not now so common amongst moral philosophers, saw this more crudely in terms of happiness. But to the former, idealistic type, the good will also promote the greatest diminution in human pain and misery. There is inevitably a stress upon calculation. What will produce the greatest good for the greatest number? But that does not quite resolve the moral problems, because the 'greatest good' still needs definition. In practice many utilitarians are humanists, and here would answer in terms of the development of human personality and potentiality. This means a basic problem which all forms of humanism must experience: how to define what is 'good' for human beings, what goals or standards should be set for human development. Phrases like 'the fully rounded human personality' are regrettably vague even when supported by psychological terms like 'balanced', 'self-realized', 'self-actualized', etc. Another criticism locates the weakness of this general theory in its inability to cater adequately for the concept of justice. Suppose a great deal of pleasure is obtained by some hunters by the killing of animals which primitive tribes need for food? How does one calculate the pros and cons on either side? Or, to state the issue very crudely, suppose three sadists derive great pleasure from torturing one hapless victim, does the amount of pleasure quite over-ride the injustice involved?

There has usually been a strong element of utilitarianism in English moral thinking; sometimes, as mentioned above, the 'good' being defined solely in terms of pleasure. That is 'good' which promotes the greatest pleasure for the greatest number.

One can sense this, for example, in John Locke. But most utilitarians now, prefer 'ideal utilitarianism', and the 'good' may be seen in terms of love and friendship, or knowledge, or aesthetic experience. There may even be a place for some of the conventional rules against lying, cheating, stealing, etc. The most significant figures have probably been Jeremy Bentham (1748–1832) and John Stuart Mill (1806–1873); the latter's championing of the individual against the powers of the state and other collectives has found a strong echo in much contemporary protest, and is noticeable in the work of a body like the National Council for Civil Liberties, which could almost be regarded as having Mill's essay *On Liberty* (1859) as its charter.

The great strengths of utilitarianism in practice are its plain universalism and a common-sense style about much of its arguments, especially when being critical of established authorities such as church or state and the pretensions which often cloak their self-interest, to the detriment of the individual. Thus the happiness of a Bantu peasant is reckoned to be just as important as the happiness of a Boer overlord; the happiness of a factory worker matters as much as that of his master, but one should beware because the master may have a lot of conventional middle-class and established morality on his side which may be a cloak for his self-interest. However, not only is there the basic problem of defining the 'good', but utilitarians have often ended up with a prudential ethic which seems to ignore many of the heights and depths of human experience and possibility. They have also tended to ignore the rather special obligations which we acquire by virtue of social life, such as duties to children or family or parents.

3. *Communism*. Communist ethics, derived from Karl Marx, are theoretically very simple indeed. That is right which furthers the end of the revolution, the creation of the classless society in which the means of production will be owned by all and no class will be alienated by having to sell its labour to others. Communist ethics are plainly teleological (that is, determined almost totally by the 'end' to which all acts are related, viz., the revolution). Anything whatever is 'good' if it furthers that end – murder, lying, anarchy, etc., – which is why those who have sharply different ethical systems often look askance at communists and suggest that they have 'no ethics' or else claim that they are notoriously inconsistent. A classic instance occurred in

the Second World War. To begin with, when it was a conflict between the Allies and Germany, communists regarded it as a conflict between two sets of capitalist systems and taught that therefore it imposed no obligations whatever upon them. However, when Hitler's Germany attacked Russia, which most observers regarded as an inevitable extension of a war designed to satisfy German expansion, communists suddenly announced that it was no longer a capitalist war at all and therefore every communist must fight in it. Overnight, the war suddenly changed its character!

Communism aims to produce a 'new man', who will not only be freed from the oppression under which the working classes previously laboured, but will be imbued with a profound sense of solidarity with working men everywhere and be passionately concerned to promote communism, having an uncompromising attitude to all its enemies and an unflinching resolve for peace, equality and the freedom of nations. In this cause he will make the most tremendous sacrifices. The solidarity will of course put men and women on an equal footing, and will totally ignore racial divisions and distinctions. When communism is in an early stage of development, as with many Eastern European nations today, this will involve a great stress on virtues which sound almost Puritan in their origin – on sobriety, hard work, stable family life, simple life-styles, obedience to authority and submission to the state.

There is a strand of humanism running through most communist ethics. The well-being of man is regarded as a self-evident good, but it is understood to involve man's freedom from exploitation in his labour and from all forms of 'superstition', of which religion is one of the most insidious. Thus it is often possible for communist theorists to claim that communism can have 'a human face', or be expressed in ways that show its fundamental concern for human beings and human good. But inevitably one then encounters the deep paradox that dominates communist ethics, for communism as it has developed in Europe holds a very high view of the state. The state is that collective which holds together all the 'property' of all, which owns everything, which has a right to claim the allegiance of all its members and their daily toil, which is ethically the supreme good. Thus the individual does not have 'rights' over against the state; all such presumed rights are the product of the liberal-bourgeois mentality or the corruptions which religion introduces. Only the state has rights, and it divides them out to the individuals composing it as may be deemed fit, or else it may withhold them if that serves the final good of the state better.

From this doctrine of the supremacy of the state springs the quite astonishing cruelty and repressiveness which seems to characterize every communist society. Lenin himself was reluctant to give democratic power to the workers, holding that the Communist Party alone must be the disciplined cadre of true revolutionaries in whom power must rest; from this step it is inevitable that the Party becomes the new power élite, taking privileges and wealth to itself; from this it is almost inevitable that the new Party replaces the old aristocracy and behaves as inhumanly towards its opponents. The totalitarian state results, not infrequently given to the same ideological prejudices as its sworn enemies, the Fascists – viz. antisemitism. The habit of making scapegoats out of the Jews is now a depressing feature of modern Russia.

The great strength of communist ethics is first and foremost its moral seriousness. Marxism is not a theory to enable one to understand the world, but to change it. To be a Marxist is to be enlisted on the side of the historical process which is leading surely and certainly to the abolition of classes and the inauguration of the ideal society in which 'from each according to his ability; to each according to his need' will be the rule. Thus it expresses LeRoy Long's 'operational' motif with tremendous passion; it is not at all surprising that it has enormous appeal to backward societies struggling to escape from serfdom. Its other strength is its sharp analysis of the moralities and ideologies which prevail on all sides; Marxism shows how deeply these are related to the economic self-interest of the groups concerned. Of course the middle and upper classes will always treat social revolution with abhorrence and preach a docile submission to the social order – it is comfortably within their own interests that it should remain undisturbed.

But there are severe problems in Marxist ethics. One is the general disinterest in ethical theorizing itself, which tends to obscure the seriousness mentioned above. However, the basic assumption within Marxism is that certain values are implicit within the historical process itself and that a correct ('scientific') understanding of this process will indicate those values, which have of course an objective validity. Yet, on the other hand, all moral values are relative to the interests of social groups. If the latter statement is true then it is impossible to stand outside the historical process in some lofty and undetermined manner (labelled 'scientific') and evaluate rival moralities. But this point may sound like some philosophic pedantry, for the main problem which Christians encounter with Marxist ethics is that they are integrally related to the Marxist understanding of history and, in the end, of all reality. Is human history an inevitable process which can be adequately comprehended in atheistic terms, or is it the outworking of the love of God which is mediated to man through Jesus Christ? This produces a fundamental level of disagreement, even from those Christians who are sympathetic to Marxism and deeply indebted to its social analysis. Thus a most appreciative Christian is bound in the end to write thus: 'Features like class- struggle, the dictatorship of the proletariat or the role of the Communist Party are in part a piece of analytic theory which, with all due correction and revision, have to play a part in a Christian's articulation of his love-seeking-for-justice. But they are also ideological slogans which bear the mark of a conception of man and history which the Christian cannot fully accept . . . It is important to emphasize that the source of this criticism is not a rejection of Marxism as social theory but a radical questioning of the philosophical foundation of its ethos – the rejection of the Triune God of love.'[3]

4. *Existentialism* and its many subtle variations have a remarkable appeal. Existentialism denies any validity whatever to our normal *mores*, rules and moral systems. There is no such thing as 'human nature' which ought to conform to prescribed patterns, or to ways of behaviour ordered by some external authority. All human existence is to be understood as the opportunity to become something new, to step into the future and help create it by making free decisions. One can only become one's true self by exercising such freedom; if one acts by conformity to rules or expected roles it is actually 'bad faith', one is not being an 'authentic' self. Therefore existentialists make an annoying habit of not telling us what to do, on the grounds that it is fundamentally impossible. No one person can tell another what the other's freedom should result in, or it would no longer be genuine freedom at all. This

means that an extreme individualism runs right through this style of thinking. The only way in which the existence of others seems to be taken seriously into account is in the general ethical maxim that one should so act as to let others be free whilst oneself remaining free. This maxim is odd; whence, on existentialist theory, comes any obligation such as this?

Existentialism is not inevitably anti-Christian nor atheistic. Many Christians have contributed to its development (notably the Danish Søren Kierkegaard, 1813–1855) and more recently thinkers like Bultmann (1884–1978) or an English theologian like John Macquarrie. Most recent Christian existentialists have seen in it a very significant way of understanding human existence and have wanted to relate it to the Christian understanding of how man may become 'authentic' through the preaching of the gospel, the response of faith and the grace of Christ. But existentialism can also appear in stark aesthetic form, as in the thought of the French philosopher Jean-Paul Sartre.

The contribution of existentialism to moral thinking has been considerable. It has laid great stress upon the making of decisions and their significance in the emergence of the personality. It has stressed the freedom of the person, and been adamant in opposition to all the dehumanizing influences of the modern mass media and the claims of the technologists to 'engineer' human beings. It has raised searching questions about traditional moralities and whether or not they serve to enhance the human person or to keep him in old chains and servitudes. It has posed constant questions about the traditional roles which we play, and queried whether this can ever be appropriate for the free person. But on the other hand it has been intensely individualistic; it cannot handle the moral questions posed by our membership of, and obligations towards, groups. Whilst it has helped us to be open towards the future, it has often scorned the wisdom and experience of the past and the way that is expressed in moral rules and roles. This produces an almost fantasy view of the world, with isolated individuals behaving in a supposedly 'free' way that bears little relation to what normal life is always like. As Dorothy Emmet remarked: 'It is only in extreme Existentialist literature that people can live just as "Outsiders" or pure individuals, with no interest but one of contempt for role morality, with no awareness of problems arising out of possible conflicts between their roles, and with no institutional loyalties.'[4] This also means that in the end it has made little contribution to social morality; its atomistic view of human existence makes that virtually impossible.

Three Christian schemes

Granted the general climate of moral theories as indicated by the sketches just offered, what schemes are nowadays suggested for Christians in their making of moral decisions? By a 'scheme' is meant a coherent system of principles and methods which will give Christians appropriate procedures. Undoubtedly the scheme which has attracted the most attention during the last twenty years has been that known as 'situation ethics'. Its most persuasive exponent has been the American ethicist Joseph Fletcher, whose book entitled *Situation Ethics* was first published in Britain in 1966.[5] A similar, but not identical, position was adopted by Bishop John Robinson in the books which caused such a furore in that same period – in *Honest to God* and then *Christian Morals Today*[6] – but Fletcher is the more systematic and consistent advocate. Whilst this scheme roused much passion at the time, not least because Fletcher subtitled it 'the new morality', the criticisms by other Christian ethicists have been thorough and somewhat damning, as we shall see. However, this scheme has such immediate simplicity and attractiveness that it has entered fairly considerably into the general consciousness of Christians, especially the young. The many critiques, mainly to be found in other books and scholarly circles, are of course not as widely known as the main Fletcher thesis, so it is quite widely accepted in many Christian circles.

Fletcher wrote in a rumbustious, knock-about style that makes interesting reading. He held that the choice of moral schemes was fairly simple: either you adopt legalism of one sort or another, finding morality summed up in a complex mass of moral laws, or you are a complete antinomian, denying that any scheme exists and making moral decisions in a haphazard manner tantamount to moral anarchy, or else you opt for the only viable and acceptable alternative. This, for enlightened modern Christians, must be 'situationism'. Many readers will feel that to be far too simple as an introductory

description of morality, but even so this does not really affect
the value of the scheme he advocates.

By 'situationism' Fletcher means six affirmations. Only
'love' is intrinsically good, nothing else; the ruling norm of
Christian decision is love, nothing else; love and justice are
the same, since justice is love distributed; love wills the neighbour's good, whether we like him or not; only the end justifies
the means, nothing else; love's decisions are made situation-
ally, not prescriptively. He infers that every situation we face
is unique, so that we can never have enough moral laws or
rules to cover each conceivable occasion. In each situation the
Christian has to ask one fundamental question: what does love
require of me? No other question matters as much, for there
is only one norm or guide, that of love. By love he means
active goodwill in partnership with reason, only seeking the
neighbour's good, and he holds that this is what the New
Testament calls agape. Further, the New Testament writers
understood this to be the one supreme and binding injunction
upon all Christians, the way of Jesus and the way taught by
Paul. The Christian will have to calculate what love requires,
for it is not always obvious, but reason is the God-given tool
to enable that calculation to occur.

It is rather important to see what Fletcher does not say. He
does not say that 'anything goes' and thereby encourage what
is loosely termed 'permissiveness'. His opponents have often
misunderstood him at this point; the love which he advocates
is a most demanding requirement, involving immense capacity
for self-sacrifice and a very high view of the value of other
human beings. He does not completely ignore the centuries of
Christian teaching; he has a limited respect for it, but only it
seems as far as it illuminates what agape-love is like. He is
most definitely not a hedonist, arguing for the supremacy of
pleasure. He is not indifferent to the authority of the Bible,
but claims that his position is grounded in it. He is, however,
a most trenchant anti-legalist. Again and again he quotes instances of moral laws (such as those condemning killing, or
adultery) which may have to be flouted in the cause of love; to
follow them would mean an obvious moral failure.

Because this scheme was being propounded at a time when
Christians were beginning a worried search for new styles of
sexual morality, Fletcher's work became one element in that
debate. There was a further reason, in that he used illus-

trations from sexual morality more frequently than from any other realm. He denied that adultery was intrinsically, always wrong, or that fornication was. These acts could only be wrong if they were not wholly 'loving' in the situations concerned, and he used considerable ingenuity in describing possible situations in which either might be right. His critics often failed to note that although these situations were decidedly bizarre, the one who was upheld for breaking the old established rules was almost always one for whom that meant great sacrifice and often courage. Personal pleasure was never put forward as an acceptable end for Christians.

Is this scheme a good one? There is much to say in its favour. It is refreshingly simple in its main thesis, and rescues the Christian ethic from the obscure, the dogmatic, and from an elaborate string of moral laws. It provides a guideline for a complex situation in which many values seem to compete for loyalty, and one cannot be satisfied without over-riding another. It upholds the supreme value of persons, which is especially important in a highly technological age in which machines and systems and vast institutions seem to be crushing the individual. It embodies a compassion which has often appeared to be lacking from much Christian ethics and, more particularly, church practice. It recovers some significant New Testament insights.

Nevertheless, it is open to severe criticism. It appears to be woefully naive about the usual way in which we make moral decisions. We simply do not have time to assess all the facts, sort out priorities, ask 'What does love require here?' and then proceed as if we have never been in a situation quite like this before. Instead, we need a system of general rules which have been so ingrained into us that they are almost part of our sub-conscious, and which have come to us via the church and the experience of centuries of other Christians. We need not imagine that each situation is especially unique; it usually won't be, and the inherited rules will almost certainly cover it. Moreover, we are all sinners and we rarely want to love totally, so we shall not calculate out in some dispassionate and pure way what love will require. We are more likely to let our own deep-seated self-interest decide what we should do, and it will not coincide with 'love'. If we live by rules, we shall be saved from that self-deception.[7]

Further, it implies that 'love' is somewhat unpredictable if its actions are not usually expressed in reliable rules. But does not agape have a constant structure about it? The witness of the Bible is adamant that this is so, hence the frequent refrain that God is a covenant God and is always 'faithful'.[8] It is not quite accurate to sum up all New Testament teaching by the term 'love' since, as was described in Chapter 2, there are many other forms of moral injunction to be found there.[9] Again, the system gives one no clear guide as to what the 'situation' is meant to include. What are its boundaries? If, for example, one is involved in a situation involving a man taking from his work something which does not belong to him, does one consider only the man? Or his family and home problems also? And the firm and its practices? And the man's union and its practices? And his mates and their concerns? And the law of the land? And the national position if this goes unchecked? And the views of rival political parties? So one could go on. But Fletcher's usual practice seems to be to include only the immediate participants in his reckonings. This inevitably leads to a further criticism.

Paul Ramsey warns that situationism is intensely personal and unable to cope with the large and corporate issues of social morality. 'No social morality ever was founded, or ever will be founded, upon a situational ethic', he writes.[10] John Macquarrie concurs, and goes on to say that 'much of this discussion has been pitiably irrelevant to the major ethical issues of our time'.[11] Fletcher has, of course, read Reinhold Niebuhr and claims him as virtually a situationist. Put against him, Fletcher holds in a somewhat perfectionist way that of course 'love' is immediately applicable to all situations. Therefore it is quite wrong to follow the course which Niebuhr and most social ethics adopts, of seeking justice in the social order, that being the appropriate approximation to love. He announces brashly that these 'gambits have completely muddied the waters of all ethics, Christian and non-Christian', which seems somewhat extreme.[12] Deeper down, it is doubtful if Fletcher quite understands why the Niebuhr-Brunner-Temple tradition adopts its position concerning justice, and this makes for the fatal flaw in situationism's capacity to contribute a social ethic. If a Christian politician is caught up in some highly complicated tussle for power between rival groups it is not pertinent to say to him, 'Do what love demands', but it is appropriate to tell him to seek justice between all the rival claimants, and to strengthen those social agencies which can promote it all round. Fletcher does not see this apparently; the many examples with which his book is replete are not drawn from this general 'social' area of ethics. In the current jargon, Fletcher does not seem to be a 'political animal' at all.

One more comment is needed about the perfectionism which seems to run through Fletcher's writing. He expects Christians to be able to know what 'love' requires, and to be able then to do it. This assumption often occurs in Protestant ethics. In its most crass form it occurs in those Christians who seem to believe that they have a personal and utterly reliable hot-line to God, and who can then speak with sublime certainty about 'what God wants'. That certainty is one of the most dangerous presumptions Christians can ever live with. It is one against which the biblical writers are constantly warning us. 'My thoughts are not your thoughts,' says the Lord. His ways and his nature are an ultimate glorious mystery far beyond our comprehension. Our understanding of his truth is always partial, muddled and smeared by our self-interest. When we seek to discover God's will we must always go to the church, seek wider reflection and the perspectives of other Christians. Most especially, we must never claim complete certainty, or we shall inevitably slither into self-righteousness, the arrogance of those who are sublimely confident that they are doing what God requires. It is only too clear in the Gospels that the greatest sin, against which Jesus warns us over and over again, is not lust or avarice or envy – but self-righteousness. That is of the devil, even though it is cloaked in beautiful religious garb. Is Fletcher alert enough to the dangers in his perfectionism?

But similar dangers occur in other Christian ethicists, and one has to keep asking of them the simple question, 'How do you expect me to have this remarkable capacity to know what is good, or right, or required by God?' One gets the feeling that some Christians presume that we have a facility whereby we will get a 'holy hunch' as to what is right. John Robinson talks about love as being a 'built-in moral compass' always pointing us to the right.[13] Others share a similar confidence, but expressed in different terminology. Thus Paul Lehmann advocates a system which is in many ways similar to Fletcher's, a system he calls 'contextual ethics'.[14] He says that the basic question Christians have to ask is, 'What is God doing in this situation?', and this will provide the key for Christian morality. Christians must act in a way that promotes the activity which God is already contributing within that situation. If one asks the 64,000 dollar question,

'How does one *know* what God is doing?', Lehmann replies, 'He is making life more human', but then finds it difficult to give a more precise formulation to that rather generalized statement. In the end Lehmann, too, seems to expect us to have a holy hunch which will push us into a certain direction intuitively. Is this position open to the objections, then, which intuitionism always involves? It appears so.

A wholly different style of scheme from that offered by Fletcher, is described as a 'framework for Christian morality' in a book by a Roman Catholic moralist, Gerard Hughes.[15] It would be quite unfair to expect in this small book anything as detailed as that in Fletcher. Indeed, Father Hughes has not set out to present an elaborate or systematic account. He has contented himself with a brief outline of the main dilemmas in Christian moral thinking, and then in about twenty pages has offered a thumb-nail sketch of a system. He begins by stating that the moral life is one of 'fulfilment' in discovering God's plan for our existence. This only comes about when we discover what are our true needs; our wants give us a start here, but some are good and some are not, so we need a way of assessing them and this requires some overall pattern for our wants. This will properly involve us in self-criticism and 'moral integrity' and requires emotional maturity. But then we have to balance our wants against those of others, so that we have to become sensitive to the requirements of justice.

What procedures should Christians follow, then? It would seem that these should go something like the following: ask what we want in the situation, then ask for as much further information about the situation as we can get, then try to put our wants into some sort of sequence of priorities, then ask if action upon them is going to satisfy the needs of as many people as possible. If not, then we must re-evaluate those priorities until the cause of other people (= justice) is more satisfactorily met. Then, we should do what, in the light of these procedures so far, we now feel that we 'want'. To be sure, Gerard Hughes is carefully tentative about this, but he spends a little time on outlining two fictional instances where decisions come to be made in this manner.

One's first reaction is that this seems to be a different sort of discussion altogether from that of Fletcher. The whole approach, the terms and concepts and considerations, are different. There is something very refreshing about it because

Hughes seems to be writing for normal ordinary people engaged in normal ordinary living and coming at life in a normal human way. One can identify very easily with the person whom Hughes is trying to help; indeed, there is rarely any special moral language that has to be utilized. Christians and non-Christians could say, 'Yes, that is what it feels like in practice, and I can see myself doing what Hughes suggests.' The starting point is normal human nature and its wants, and it is regarded as wholly legitimate to try to meet them as simply as possible.

The first major problem concerns how Christian this procedure is. As has already been observed, anyone can go ahead on these lines. But Hughes, who is a traditional Catholic at this point, is at pains to begin by saying that as our true end as human beings is with God, our true 'wants' will only be satisfied when we encounter and seek after God, the God who is Father of our Lord Jesus Christ. This want (the want for God) is so deeply implanted in us all that it can be taken to be one of the constituent elements in human nature, according to Catholic theology. But if that is so, one would expect that supreme 'want' to feature more prominently at the point where Hughes says that we must organize our wants according to a pattern of priorities. One would also expect God's calling to us in Christ to be more apparent when discussing the way we can learn some 'wants' and learn to discard others. Thus the whole scheme appears to be too loosely related to God's activity on our behalf in and through Jesus. It is not christological enough.

Next, it seems to ignore the centuries of Christian experience and the way in which all sorts of general rules have come down to us. They don't feature in the scheme, although in one of the illustrations at the end (involving the break-up of a marriage) Hughes is at pains to argue that Jesus' teaching on marriage and divorce must be taken as an 'ideal'. The relation of this 'ideal' to our own practice is not made clear; one gets the feeling that, being an 'ideal', it can fairly readily be given a slight nod of approval and then, for all practical purposes, ignored. Finally, Hughes mentions two of the great snags. There are great numbers of people for whom talk of 'fulfilment' is somewhat hollow because they have suffered sickness, or severe deprivation, or some tragedy or other. This is a lasting mystery for which the goal of 'fulfilment' does indeed seem to be utopian. But then there is the problem of how, towards the end of the scheme, one handles the issue of justice. Hughes frankly admits that 'our moral theory is at this point inadequate'.[16]

Summing up, it is important for Protestants to read Hughes carefully, since he can be a clear educator into the apparently different style of Catholic teaching. He makes the moral life seem so much more natural and understandable, but at the cost of taking from it much of the challenge which Protestants usually expect to find in the whole struggle to be obedient to Christ. Maybe Hughes makes the moral life deceptively easy. But perhaps Catholics especially ought to read Fletcher. In the 1950s, before Fletcher had ever been heard of, the Pope condemned 'situation ethics' as being basically unprincipled and ignoring the 'moral law', but not all of that harsh dismissal is totally fair to Fletcher's system; moreover, some of Fletcher's castigation of Christian legalism is important for both Protestant and Catholic to hear, since both have shown regrettable tendencies to lapse into harsh legalisms.

As a third example of a Christian moral system, we look at a wholly different approach, that cautiously presented by an American Protestant, Philip Wogaman, in a book entitled *A Christian Method of Moral Judgment*.[17] Wogaman writes fluently, making constant reference to current issues, and gives one the immediate impression of being extremely alert to modern dilemmas. But he is also deeply concerned to reflect as a Christian with a proper grounding in doctrine. This appears early in the book, where he lays out four criteria for an adequate Christian method (or 'system' as I have been calling it in this chapter). These are:

1. It must be tentative, always allowing for the possibility that our particular judgments may be mistaken.

2. It must be faithful to the central affirmations of Christian faith.

3. It must provide a basis for investing judgments with whole-hearted commitment and seriousness without abandoning tentativeness (that is, moral judgment, even if accepted as fallible, will not end up in a haze so that our wills are paralysed and we become so scrupulous or super-critical that we do nothing whatever).

4. It must provide a basis for clarifying moral dialogue (or, put in other words, it must allow a thorough-going moral debate to

be carried on, without foreclosing the matter of silencing any group of Christians).

Having set out these criteria, Wogaman then suggests that the method of 'moral presumption' is the most adequate. That is, Christians will normally have a whole set of assumptions about what is moral and what is not, and they should start off their moral assessments by assuming that their initial intentions are legitimate, but that then they should be measured, or tested, against some special 'presumptions'. These 'presumptions' may only be over-ridden if there is an extremely good case for doing so (as, in many a serious or extreme instance, there may be), but only with reluctance and very good reason. He points out that a similar process often happens in legal cases, or indeed in the just war tradition (where Christians assumed war to be wrong unless it met the seven criteria, which it rarely did). There are four major positive 'presumptions', thus:

1. The goodness of created existence.
2. The value of individual life.
3. The unity of the human family in God.
4. The equality of persons in God.

The first presumption would normally make an act of suicide morally doubtful, likewise euthanasia, or preparation for nuclear war; the second would normally make genocide, slavery, the use of dangerous drugs in medical experiments, capital punishment, the cheapening of human life during war, or the dismissal of the humanity of opponents, all morally suspect; the third puts queries against racism and some forms of nationalism; the fourth would presumably pose questions against sexism or a caste system in society (but Wogaman does not explicitly say so). By this method of 'presumption' Wogaman is not saying that, for example, some act implying racism can never be right and must be intrinsically wrong in all possible circumstances; he is saying that there must be very strong and overwhelming reasons for such an act, since Christians hold to the unity of the human family as a strong and major element in their understanding of what God wills for his children. He does not actually guess at what those reasons might be, but leaves open the possibility that in this complex world there might conceivably be some.

But Wogaman follows these positive presumptions with two negative ones. A burden of proof falls upon anyone who neglects human finitude, and human sinfulness. Whenever these two are ignored, there is grave doubt that the result will be a Christian judgment. So, for example, Wogaman warns those who go too easily along with the Marxist notions of the general infallibility of the revolutionary classes. They too are fallible, however good their cause, noble their lives, or just their claims. Likewise he warns against the moral claims of the powerful; those claims will always be mixed up with self-interest because we are all sinners, and therefore he argues for a presumption of the cause of the weak against that of the powerful. The powerful, after all, even if they are deeply Christian, will always be engaged in subtle attempts to retain their power, as is the normal way with sinful human beings.

So far, so good. There are six presumptions against which we must not normally act, save in instances where we can find an overwhelmingly good case and can provide the necessary burden of proof. Wogaman goes on to cite five other considerations of a slightly different character. He is intrigued by the old Greek ethical thinking which presented the moral life as a careful avoidance of extremes, and which introduced the term 'the golden mean' into popular ethics. He coins the phrase 'polar opposites' to argue that certain extremes must be avoided. Christian moral judgment will never normally go down heavily on either end of these pairs:

1. The individual/social nature of man.
2. Freedom/responsibility.
3. Subsidiarity/universality.
4. Conservation/innovation.
5. Optimism/pessimism.

Thus any action which implies that man is an individual without any corporate nature (the first extreme in the first polarity cited above) is morally suspect. So is one which seems to ignore the uniqueness of the individual and treats man as a mass (which is the other polarity). Any act which seems to treat freedom as an ultimate good, or any, on the other hand, which treats responsibility as an ultimate, is likewise suspect. The third polarity uses a term which has become commonplace in recent Catholic social thinking – subsidiarity. This means the citing of decision-making at the lowest possible level of the social structure, as near the grass roots as possible. Universality, the other pole, implies that the decisions can appertain as far as possible from everyone (and must therefore be made by the representatives of everyone, who will need to be high up the social structure). The fourth polarity expresses the tension between encouraging the new and creative and innovative, yet conserving the values of the past; neither extreme must become absolute, neither the quest for the new nor the respect for the old. The fifth attempts to express the middle road between too much hopefulness, which can be dangerously naive, and the cynicism which saps away all moral effort.

Although Wogaman does not put all these 'presumptions' together and outline what they add up to as a method, one assumes that when making moral judgments the Christian must in his view go through a process which involves asking a series of questions. In the light of later chapters in the book they would seem to be something like this:

1. What would the community of faith (i.e. the church) teach?
2. What does the Christian tradition teach?
3. What data is provided by factual evidence and relevant technical expertise?
4. What does the custom of the land (including civil law of course) indicate?

Using (presumably) one's reason, one sorts out an initial response using these four initial authorities, and then has to test this against the presumptions, so this will lead to the following series of questions:

5. Have any of these following presumptions been over-ridden and, if so, is there grave reason to justify doing so: the goodness of creation, the value of individual life, the unity of the human family in God, the equality of persons in God?
6. Have any of these presumptions been ignored, and, if so, is there sufficient grave reason for doing so: the finitude of human judgment, the sinfulness of human intention and reasoning?
7. Have any of these polarities been carried to such an extreme that the opposite pole has been ignored – the individual and social nature of man, freedom and responsibility, subsidiarity and universality, conservation and innovation, optimism and pessimism?

This sequence is very different from Fletcher's method (which, of course, was rather vaguely presented by him) and very different from that of Hughes. It is patently Christian, with a profound respect for Christian theology and perspectives and doctrine. It is realistic, and raises the sort of questions that help to throw most useful light on morality. It avoids some of the stale debates that have been occasioned by situation ethics and the place for rules or laws or guidelines, and instead offers us a different terminology and a different way of approach to moral problems. It operates with a fundamental awareness that many moral issues are corporate ones, so that the 'system' or method needs to be applicable to both individuals and to groups. Thus Wogaman's illustrations are drawn as much from social and political life as from the sphere of inter-personal morality.[18]

However, there are also snags. The method appears, rightly or wrongly, to be quite complicated when it is set out as a series of questions, as above. It is so elaborate that one cannot imagine Christians often wanting to resort to it, save with major matters that are going to involve considerable times for reflection. It assumes a fair level of competence on the part of those doing it. It is perhaps instructive to note that although the writer outlines all these issues he never then does what is suggested above – i.e. list all the questions that appear to be indicated by the 'method' and thus describe the actual procedures to be followed. Had he done so, the rather cumbrous result would have been more apparent. Finally, whilst his rationale for the method of moral presumption was convincing, and the four positive and two negative presumptions appear very adequate, the rationale offered for the 'polar opposites' was less convincing, less grounded in Christian theology, and not so well illustrated. One is left wondering whether this latter theme was an after-thought.

The three chosen 'methods' or 'systems' – those of Fletcher, Hughes and Wogaman – remind us of some of the constant notes being struck in this study. They remind us that there is no standard method for Christians to use in the making of moral judgments, no standard vocabulary to describe the method or methods, no easy little list of considerations which can be taught tomorrow in every Sunday School and which will then cover all the usual problems in ethics for tomorrow's Christians. Nor is there certainty for the Christian when a decision has been taken; he or she cannot be utterly and absolutely assured for ever that it was perfectly right. The

Christian moral life simply is not like that. In ethics, as in all discipleship, one lives by faith and not by sight.

Questions for Discussion

(*a*) Which of the ethical 'systems' outlined here seems to you to be the most convincing? Why?

(*b*) If a young Christian believes 'situation ethics' to be the appropriate form of the Christian ethic, what would you advise him or her regarding its adequacy?

Chapter 8

Ethics and the Churches Today

IN Chapter 4 an outline was given of the general development of Christian social ethics down through the centuries, and brief sketches of some of the major positions and thinkers. Generally speaking, the main Christian voices were concerned to legitimize the social order, the possession of private property and the basic status of the family. Moral theology was designed to assist the priest in the confessional, so that he knew how to assess sins and the appropriate penalties. It was not primarily designed to teach the lay Christian how to make mature judgments on everyday ethical issues. Of course the Reformation challenged that role for moral theology very profoundly; the Reformers were deeply concerned to provide guidance and instruction for the lay Christian, so that he could make responsible Christian judgments for himself. It did not, however, offer a fundamental critique of the social order; its criticisms were mainly directed at tyrannical rulers or those who were opposed to granting Protestants their religious freedom.

The main wracking of the Christian conscience came in England with the discovery of poverty in the new vulgar cities created by the industrial revolution. It was the nineteenth century which saw this appalling deprivation spread through the length and breadth of the land and which woke the churches, particularly as the century drew to its close. It was a terrible eye-opening to discover that in the heyday of the British Empire, when the whole mood of the ruling classes was one of optimistic expansion and 'progress', the majority of the people in the cities were living in degrading squalor. The main response of the churches was to organize charitable relief – soup kitchens, labour yards, educational provision, clubs, hostels, holidays by the sea, settlements, temperance crusades, food parcels at Christmas, clothing stores, etc. In a study of West Ham, David

Sheppard comments of all this good work that, 'Relief, temperance and provision of clubs and settlements did not change the society which caused the wounds. They only put ointment on them.' He goes on to note that 'Fear has prevented the Christian Church from supporting the aspirations of the poor or of working class people. It still does.'[1]

But how was the Christian voice sounded? Up until the present century it was to be heard mainly in the pronouncements of bishops (in the established church) and in the oratory of the preacher (especially in the non-conformist churches). The theologian such as Maurice was mainly influential on those who read theology, which was a small educated élite in the churches. The populace in general, and the ordinary churchgoer, would look to the bishops or the great preachers. The bishop's pastoral letter was often regarded as indicating what the 'church' as a body thought or was meant to think; the roar of the preacher was an equal indicator, and a formidable force in moulding public opinion. '"The pulpit leads the world." Few would dare to advance this claim today, but it would not have sounded an exaggeration in the last century.'[2] Men like Hugh Price Hughes, John Clifford and R. W. Dale had such powerful sway that governments took careful note of their opinions. F. W. Robertson of Brighton could sway the most influential people in the land.[3]

The twentieth century has eroded the authority of the individual thinker, church leader or preacher; whilst many have deplored this tendency and keep asking the longing question, 'Where are the great names today?', we should note that this tendency makes way for the authority of the church as a whole to be rediscovered. This century has therefore seen all the churches trying to establish organs through which they can formulate a common mind on the crucial ethical issues (as well as other matters, of course) and by which they can speak to their own members and to the world at large. In the sphere of ethics a milestone in this whole process was the Conference on Christian Politics, Economics and Citizenship (usually referred to as COPEC) held in Birmingham in April 1924. The First World War had cruelly exposed the inadequacy of Christian social thinking; in its aftermath the churches felt called to help rebuild the country and point the way towards a better society. They felt called to give more specific information as well as guidance to their members. They knew that they could not do this any more from the restricted base of any one denomination.

COPEC was thoroughly prepared. Twelve reports were published beforehand for all delegates and others, the first dealing with theology (the nature of God and his purpose for the world), nine on specific issues (e.g. education, housing), one on the social function of the church, and one on historical illustrations of the social effects of Christianity. A big effort was made to enlist competent laity as well as church leaders. In the event the theology was hardly discussed at all, but the specific issues had a good airing and the conference had a stern warning from Charles Gore: 'This Conference will be judged by its practical work, and for that I tremble. We need tremendous courage to ask ourselves whether we are really prepared to accept those fundamental principles and to apply them whatever the effect upon our party politics.' However, the greatest inspirer for the conference was also its chairman – William Temple – and he both guided it serenely through and helped in planning its successor (Malvern, 1941). At Malvern, Temple made a comment which helps us to see the value of such conferences:

> It is said that gatherings of Christians have said similar things for a very long time, and nothing happens. My answer would be that a great deal happens . . . Between the wars three great changes took place in England: the whole penal system was reformed in a wholly Christian direction; there was a vast extension of secondary education; and the proper housing of the people was at last undertaken on a great scale. I call that a good deal to happen in twenty years. It is true that no one can say just how much the Church or specifically Christian principles had to do with it. But the Church was solidly behind all these reforms.[4]

But whilst Christians were thus discovering nationally that they desperately needed each other and could not hazard useful judgments on ethical and social matters without the fullest consultation with both the experts and their fellow Christians in other traditions, this same discovery was happening on the wider world scene. In 1925 the first world conference on Life and Work was held in Stockholm. The ecumenical movement was then in its infancy, so that this gathering was largely of the European and American church leaders. Only six delegates from the younger churches were present. Ecumenism at the time was constantly using the slogan 'service unites, doctrine divides', being under the impression that social and ethical matters and common policies for helping the poor and needy would raise no fundamental theological disagreements. On the other hand the discussion of doctrine was bound to do so, so was promoted through another ecumenical agency, Faith and Order. That slogan could not last long, for obvious reasons. If all the 'service' of the churches was done without any reference to the theological rationale, then it would soon become direction-less. If doctrine was assumed to be divisive that would dampen any efforts to have serious doctrinal discussion.

Fortunately the slogan was soon lost sight of, and especially as the result of the major effort made by Life and Work to mount a conference in Oxford in 1937. The avowed purpose of the Universal Christian Conference on Life and Work was: 'to concentrate the mind of Christendom upon the mind of Christ as revealed in the Gospels towards those great social, industrial and international questions which are so acutely urgent in our civilization', but the theological ground upon which it worked was actually much more extensive than the phrase 'the mind of Christ as revealed in the Gospels' indicated. This became apparent in the extensive reports which paved the way for the Oxford conference on Church, Community and State, in which more than 300 people collaborated.

Oxford was planned largely through the genius of a layman, J. H. Oldham, who knew the ecumenical scene better than almost anyone else (he was Secretary of the International Missionary Council) and who knew where the experts were. It was a period of national rebuilding amidst constant economic insecurity; a time when the most alert could sense the creeping tide of secularism and materialism which was affecting the industrialized nations; but, ominously, it was the time when the new Nazi state was beginning to threaten the foundation of the church. Hitler was insisting that only pure Aryans could be members of the church in Germany, and that the state should exercise oversight over appointments. The small Confessing Church was struggling to assert itself as the true voice of German Protestantism in defiance of Hitler, and strengthened by the resolute voice of Karl Barth from nearby Switzerland. The documents were remarkably perceptive in their analysis of the current threats to the dignity of man and the role of the church. The final report has later been described as 'the most comprehensive ecumenical statement on problems of church and society ever produced'.[5] Throughout the conference there ran the watchword 'Let the Church be the Church', which was not a pious tautology but a constant plea that the church be seen as the divine society, the gift and calling of God, which must be able to stand in prophetic relationship to the state and, most urgently, to the totalitarian state.

The Oxford discussions made careful use of the concept of 'middle axioms', not least because Temple was again one of the major contributors.[6] A later commentator, Ronald Preston, remarks that he can think of at least eight advantages of this concept, one of which is that they 'help the church to take some purchase over events and not lag far behind with an irrelevant message';[7] he also notes three criticisms which have later emerged in ecumenical circles: the method is élitist, it ignores the ideological differences which colour the way all Christians approach issues, it implies a rather static concept of Christian doctrine – but Preston is not convinced by these.[8] There was also a properly Christian visionary and inspirational element in the work of Oxford, as can be sensed in this small extract from the final report:

> There is no legal, political, or economic system so bad or so good as to absolve individuals from the responsibility to transcend its requirements by acts of Christian charity. Institutional requirements necessarily prescribe only the minimum. Even in the best possible social system they can only achieve general standards in which the selfishness of the human heart is taken for granted and presupposed. But the man who is in Christ knows a higher obligation, which transcends the requirements of justice – the obligation of a love which is the fulfilling of the law.[9]

In 1948 the two main strands of the young ecumenical movement – Life and Work, Faith and Order – came powerfully together to form the World Council of Churches. The first assembly in Amsterdam ushered in a great range of shared concerns and studies, not least the common desire to help a war-torn world to be rebuilt and to channel a massive amount of Christian help to the most needy. The WCC in its infancy was especially dominated by Europeans and Americans from the middle-of-the-road Protestant circles. Its social ethic was primarily directed towards what it termed 'The Responsible

Society'. But it was the organ through which Christians were rapidly learning how to share concern and vision and action, how to consult with and learn from each other, how to develop a world view that was no longer restricted by denomination or nationality. In the twenty years that folowed, all sorts of very significant developments began to take place. Many young churches began to assert themselves and make their voices heard, so that the old Euro-American dominance was eroded. The Roman Catholics arrived as very active and influential 'observers'. Some Pentecostalists joined in. The range of studies and concerns grew, and the expertise developed. Very importantly, the Orthodox came to play an active role.

Prior to this, most Western Christians knew nothing about the ancient traditions of either Russian or Eastern Orthodoxy. That changed quickly. The Orthodox were able to explain over and over again that to them the church and the state are two aspects of one essential reality – man's social character. The church's task is to enable man to participate in the liturgy whereby he is constantly renewed by the vision of heaven and the self-giving of Christ. The state is to serve man's material and social needs as a sort of 'deacon' on behalf of God in which task it has the church's explicit blessing. By the two agencies acting in harmony the world is to be steadily 'divinized', permeated by the spiritual power of God. The individual Christian is to be helped to practise agape, creative suffering and self-emptying or kenosis (as in the famous passage in Phil. 2.1–13). This meant that in Orthodox circles there was a wholly different style of reflection upon Christian ethics and far more emphasis upon participation in the liturgy and man's solidarity with all fellowmen and with the natural order. But the Orthodox also had much to learn, for they were to be exposed to the prophetic task of the church, especially in its relations to the state, at a time when their own bitter experiences of ruthless communist governments was making them reconsider the bland assumptions they had traditionally made about the state as deacon to the nation's needs.

Two major events in the 1960s served to change the character of ecumenical ethics significantly. The first was the Second Vatican Council (1961–1965) which was such an explosive force in Roman Catholicism. That, and the course of Roman Catholic ethics, is discussed below. The second event was a conference called by the WCC in Geneva in July 1966, a world conference on Church and Society sub-titled 'Christians in the Technical and Social Revolutions of Our Time'. The WCC had for many years had a programme of studies on how the churches were to respond to the recent phenomenon of rapid social change; this conference was carefully planned as a result of those studies. Four major sets of essays were first published – *Christian Social Ethics in a Changing World, Responsible Government in a Revolutionary World, Economic Growth in World Perspective* and *Man in Community*[10] – then it was decided that this event should enable the assembled group to speak *to* the WCC rather than *for* it. This meant a far greater number of participants from the Third World, and far fewer church leaders, since it was the emerging Christian voice that was wanted in preference to the 'official' voice. Of the 338 participants nominated by the churches, 180 were laymen (including 50 politicians and civil servants); there were 30 youth participants and 38 observers. Undoubtedly it was this conference that enabled the young churches to speak loudly about their major concerns, to force the issues of revolution and violence on to the consciousness of Western Christians, to clamour for a more adequate understanding of their needs, to seek a more dynamic theology to inform the Christian churches and provide the basis for more adequate action and teaching.

The Report from the Geneva Conference to the churches spoke of the four great concerns which had been dominant: modern technology, the need for accelerated development in many continents, the struggle for world peace (and the growing cruelties to which the world was being exposed), and the problem of a just political and social order. It noted that in the past Christians had usually worked to transform society quietly, working through established institutions according to their rules. Now many Christians were seeking 'a more radical or revolutionary position', and, 'It is important to recognize that this radical position has a solid foundation in Christian tradition.'[11]

Geneva caused one American observer to protest. Paul Ramsey wrote a book which was sharply critical of the methodology and outcome of the conference.[12] He disliked the fervour which had apparently gripped the delegates and made them direct some powerful denunciatory rhetoric against the American government in its handling of the Vietnam war, but he also raised two fundamental questions. The first concerned the status of the final Report and the other documents emerging as a result of the conference. What authority did they possess, he asked? The delegates were not mandated by the churches to express certain viewpoints, so that the conference could not speak for the churches, yet it had appeared to do so and the media had certainly assumed that it was doing so. That outraged Ramsey. He argued that the delegates there could only speak for themselves, and that the procedures of such a conference were not well designed for even that to happen properly. If one throws together 400 people from all parts of the world, most of whom have never met before, and then hastily assembles some rapidly-devised papers, and gets people to raise their hands in agreement, what does it mean? To an expert in Christian ethics, it meant a charade as far as the value of the judgments thus arrived at. But more importantly he argued that the conference had gone far too far in its making of specific recommendations to governments. It may be legitimate for Christians to express some general perspectives which affect their judgments of what should be done in certain cases; it is not appropriate for Christians to go further and advocate specific or detailed policies. They do not know enough of the relevant facts of the case to justify immediate policy statements or to advocate specific courses of action; in many cases involving social ethics, only governments possess sufficient 'facts' to produce policies for immediate implementation. Sometimes even they cannot do so, but must wait until they possess more data. A gathering of Christians meeting for ten days certainly cannot master the technical data relevant to specific situations. This criticism was shared by many others equally expert in the matter, as for example in this dictum by Alan Booth: 'The task of the churches is to deepen debate on such issues, not to attempt itself to conclude it.'[13] One of the architects of Geneva admitted that on this point, 'he had a strong case'.[14]

Geneva, and the criticisms of Ramsey, helped the churches in their discovery of how to formulate Christian judgments and approaches; there was a noticeable breadth of approach afterwards, in which one can sense both the share being taken by the Orthodox and that of the younger churches caught up in a much more revolutionary theology. But also there has been a deeper respect for the facts of the case, and for the extreme difficulty of knowing how one gets from the present state of affairs (which may be highly and dangerously unsatisfactory) to a more satisfactory one for which a term like 'just' may be more appropriate. There may be several ways of getting from the 'here' to the 'there', and there may not always be much to choose between those ways; Christian judgment must accept this. It must also accept that sometimes the choice of ways depends on technical factors, and not noticeably on 'Christian' grounds at all. Thus the desirable end of helping under-developed countries (as they used to be called in the 1960s) may lead to the choice between several immediate means, that choice being dependent mainly on economic or geographical or technological factors which could be regarded as religiously or ideologically neutral.

The debate amongst Christians as to what sort of society we should be working and aiming for was affected in the late 1960s and the early 1970s by four concerns. The first was the population explosion. Christians, along with others, became alerted to the enormous implications of a world in which the population was doubling every thirty years and would soon be doubling at much less than that.[15] Can such vast numbers be fed? Will there be room for them on this small planet? The second was the dawning awareness of the ambiguity built into all technology. Previously mankind had had a fascinated confidence in technology, which could produce such marvels, harness all the forces of nature to benefit everyone, and thereby usher in the Brave New World. But that confidence was being eroded rapidly; technology was introducing some of the most terrible threats to the human race through the nuclear bomb; it would make for a dehumanized world; it might even enable an élite to control everyone else and thus make the majority of people into serfs all over again. The doubts became the very stuff of which the hippy revolution was produced.[16] The third was the sudden awareness that maybe the earth's resources would soon be exhausted, an unpleasant thought to which the so-called 'Club of Rome' had contributed an apparently scientific and accurate prophecy of imminent doom.[17] The fourth was the disturbing discovery that economic aid granted by the rich to the poor was not going to improve the lot of the latter in the end, because the world trading and financial system was so constructed as to guarantee that the rich would stay rich. The whole social structure carries an in-built disposition towards injustice. The phrase 'structures of injustice' began to appear, and it became increasingly clear that a wholesale restructuring would be needed if current massive social inequalities were to be removed, and the voice of the poor to be heard.

Christian thinking came to terms with these unpalatable new truths as quickly as everyone else's. It meant rethinking the previously accepted social aims. So the 'responsible society', which had been the objective in 1948 when the WCC was born, had to be reconsidered. The WCC came up with the clumsy phrase 'the just, sustainable and participatory society'. The shift which this entailed can be most clearly seen if one writes out the original definition of the responsible society and adds (in italics) the new clauses that are needed if the recent developments are accepted, thus:

> A responsible society is one where freedom is the freedom of men who acknowledge *and help create the necessary new structures enabling them to carry* responsibility for justice *for all men, in all social, economic and political, national and international structures, where* public order *is the embodiment of constructive institutional change*, where those who hold *or aspire to* political authority or economic power *or managerial function*, feel responsible for its exercise to God and *are accountable* to the people, *the nations and mankind as a whole*, whose welfare is affected by (it), *through appropriate organs of society.*[18]

However, to redefine the Christian objectives for society does not remove some of the inherent contradictions that may still lurk within the redefinitions. Paul Abrecht, the Director of the WCC Department on Church and Society since 1954, pointed out in 1981 that there were three basic snags within the new objectives: Can one reconcile a sustainable society with a just one? Is there conflict between a participatory society and the essential role for expertise and technical knowledge within a 'sustainable' one? What stand does one take if further scientific and technological advance can only be made at the cost of unacceptable risk?[19]

These developments were not without their critics. In England the most publicized criticism was uttered by Edward Norman in 1978 when giving the Reith Lectures on *Christianity and the World Order*, broadcast by the BBC. His theme was the steady 'politicization' that had recently happened amongst the Christian leadership, and especially through the agencies of the WCC. By this he meant the 'internal transformation of the faith itself, so that it comes to be defined by political values',[20] whereas it ought to be seen as 'a sense of the ultimate worthlessness of human expectations of a better life on earth'. 'The prevailing emphasis upon the transformation of the material world has robbed men of their bridge to eternity.'[21] Norman held that trendy WCC-style theologians, deeply imbued with a Marxist brand of Third World liberation theology, were the main culprits. A riposte to his book, published soon after, made the major criticism that Norman had lost his grip upon biblical faith and, in the words of one contributor, David Jenkins, simply did not hold to a belief in the sort of God witnessed to by the Bible.[22] It is indeed difficult to divorce the passion for justice and righteousness, to be practised here on earth now and tomorrow, from the God about whom the prophets spoke.

A similar attack was made in the USA by Ernest Lefever.[23] The WCC had become Marxist orientated, and the clearest sign of its selective ideological stance was in the notorious Programme to Combat Racism (PCR), which had given large sums of money to African liberation movements who had practised some of the most vile and cruel acts of terrorism. Little protest had ever been made by the WCC against the villainies of communist regimes; instead it had become the uncritical mouthpiece of the Third World. But Lefever also reiterated Paul Ramsey's criticisms and wanted the WCC to become more 'democratic' so as to reflect accurately the opinions of most of its member Christians. The PCR had come under sharp criticism in England also, especially within the Anglican Church, as a result of which the British Council of Churches had published a careful evaluation of its aims and work mainly to reassure opinion within the Church of England.[24] The PCR was regularly used by critics as a sign of WCC selective political slantings, but also of its doubtful social ethics. How can a Christian support violent revolutionary terrorist movements? The same critics rarely noticed that traditional Christian ethics had found little difficulty in supporting régimes that practised violence – that is, they often failed to see that one is supporting violence and often cruelty when supporting many modern (or ancient) régimes which may have the trappings of established respectability.

Officially the PCR had wanted to assist the racially oppressed in educational and humanitarian work; inevitably the racially oppressed were often the colonially oppressed who were struggling to gain independence by violent means (just as the colonial power was using violent means to restrain them). The issues became very blurred, more especially because the grants, given for humanitarian purposes, could be argued as support for the purchase of guns, and support for the policies of the bodies assisted. In the general muddle of argument these distinctions were only too easily forgotten, especially since a hostile Western press was waiting to condemn the WCC in any case. The WCC did not improve its image by rather poor publicity and little awareness of the outrage it would cause by the grants. This whole matter is a good example of how easy it is to misunderstand a complex ethical issue, or to misrepresent it, unless it is presented very clearly indeed and with scrupulous concern for the sensitivities of all those affected.[25]

Roman Catholic developments

The moral teaching of the Roman Catholic church is expressed mainly through the encyclical letters of the Popes, through their solemn utterances, and through the teaching of national hierarchies. The first – the encyclicals – are normally regarded as the most authoritative source and as the best guide to the teaching office of the church, the magisterium. The second is normally held to be consistent with the first, although papal pronouncements may not carry within them the same degree of prior consultation. The third is meant to be a local interpretation and application of the principles set out in the first two. None of these sources is regarded as infallible; infallibility only pertains to a papal statement made *ex cathedra* (i.e. from the 'chair') when pertaining to a matter which is central to the faith; moral matters do not come under this general heading. Nevertheless, there is a very strong authority given to official and especially papal moral teaching, an authority which is usually difficult to define. Thus the *Dogmatic Constitution on the Church* ch. 3, (the crucial document on this matter from Vatican II) states that, 'In matters of faith and morals, submission of will and of mind must be shown in a special way to the authentic teaching authority of the Roman Pontiff', and that his supreme magisterium can be sensed in the character of the documents, from frequent repetition of the same doctrine, or from his manner of speaking. This provides one rather fortunate escape-clause for any papal pronouncement subsequently found to be embarrassingly inadequate or wrong; if it is not repeated later by others then it can be held to be less and less authoritative on the grounds of 'infrequency'. The general authority probably cannot be defined any closer, then, than the following vague statement: 'The Church's authority is valid only when stating the good principles on which society must be built and judging the means society uses to its ends in the light of those principles'.[26] There is a constant duty upon each Christian to know what the church teaches, to assent to it with the will and thus obey it with a good conscience; but in the last resort each Christian must still act according to the dictates of his own conscience.

In matters of social morality the Popes have issued a long string of significant encyclicals, through which the steadily developing mind of the church can be fairly easily traced. They are regarded by Catholics and Protestants as the main source for determining what the magisterium is saying. The social teaching that responded to the new conditions of the industrialized world was ushered in originally by the epoch-making *Rerum Novarum* of 1891. There, for the first time, a Pope showed awareness of the misery and squalor of the working classes and argued for the workers' right to associate together for a just wage. He implicitly ceded that there is a right to strike, and that the state must try to regulate working agreements. But 'socialism' was condemned, since the Pope believed it to be inherently atheistic and wanting to abolish private property. He based the legitimacy of private property on the duty of man to work, and his need of a reward for this work; this is confirmed by civil and Divine Law, where the tenth commandment was quoted.

The series was continued in 1931 when, forty years later, *Quadragesimo Anno* appeared. It is more sophisticated in its understanding of socialism, although this still seems to be a term which would more accurately denote communism. It is not envisaged, for example, that there could be a profoundly Christian type of socialism, or that socialism is not inherently atheistic and materialistic. There is a noticeable development in the understanding of property, which is now seen to have a twofold character, individual and social, thus enabling a more helpful understanding of the importance of communally owned property. The encyclical was mainly salutary for its obvious welcome for a wholly radical re-ordering of the social structure. No longer could it be said that catholic ethics merely justified the social status quo; there was a distinctly revolutionary flavour to much of the letter. The same Pope – Pius XI – followed this in 1937, however, with the most explicit denunciation of communism in the encyclical *Divini Redemptoris*; here 'communism' was identified and condemned as lawless and atheistic (the term 'socialism' having dropped out of use), and much encouragement was given to the lay movement known as Catholic Action, as the true apostolate in family and civil society. This letter was to have unforeseen consequences for the church after the Second World War, when Eastern Europe became communist. 'The feelings of hostility were mutual. Seen through communist eyes the pronouncements of the Vatican confirmed the reactionary nature of a church which had never condemned Nazis and Fascists with equal vigour.'[27]

In 1961 the great reforming Pope, John XXIII, contributed to the series in *Mater et Magistra*, or 'New Light on Social Problems'. This acknowledged the vast complexity of social problems, with the nations all being caught up in a web of economic and other forces, so that the call for justice has to have many aspects. The Pope conceded more obviously here that there is a need for state intervention in many of the affairs of man's social life; he was noticeably milder in attacks on communism. He followed this in 1963 with *Pacem in Terris* (Peace on Earth), which was an open appeal to all men of goodwill, and which never mentioned the wickedness of communists. It was part of the great thaw which the urgent desire for world peace had produced in the old stale Cold War; maybe it contributed to that thaw. Certainly it was an important element in the sudden change of relations between the Vatican and the European communist governments. It was very clearly based upon a rather elaborate doctrine of the natural law and those extensive human rights and duties that can be deduced from it. It argued that these rights must be honoured at four general levels of social life including the international, which meant that international relations were given a much more specific place in the teaching. This led to straightforward support for the United Nations, but also to an interesting and fairly new notion, that of 'subsidiarity', which is the principle that decisions should always be taken at the lowest practicable level in the social order, thereby ensuring the greatest degree of public participation.

This encyclical showed especially the strengths and weaknesses of basing a teaching upon the doctrine of natural law. The main strength is that it is thus possible to find much common ground with all men of goodwill, and to stand alongside them in their hopes and aspirations. But there are serious weaknesses. If our moral obligation is imbued in everyone by nature, then the Christian revelation can be held to carry it a bit further, to be a topping put on to the 'natural' foundation. This means that the foundation is not subject to the thorough criticism which prophetic religion directs to all human aspiration, believing that mankind has a solidarity not only of general aspiration but also in sin. Natural law thinking does not recognize adequately the tensions, the alienation, the conflicts which are inherent in man's make-up. It is somewhat bland. It also tends to stress the conservative and to play down the urgency for dynamic social change; it loses sight of the ultimate judgment of God upon all human societies and pretensions, a judgment which will appear at the last day.[28] Paul Tillich reluctantly refused to share in the general adulation greeting the encyclical, since it simply did not recognize the basic 'ambiguity' in man and was therefore naive about human nature and failed to distinguish between genuine hope and utopian expectations.[29]

The work of Vatican II produced one major document in social ethics which broke with that tradition and made clear attempts to base itself upon a more biblical perspective upon man. The church was seen as the 'people of God' on their pilgrimage through history, experiencing salvation and being always called forward. It made occasional references to show that the traditional doctrine of natural law was not totally forgotten. The document was obviously attempting to reflect upon and respond to the great pressures of the era, and was actually the longest produced by the Council. Entitled *Gaudium et Spes* (Joy and Hope), it was subtitled 'Pastoral Constitution on the Church in the World of Today'. It acknowledged the inherent tensions in all human nature. It talked about the Christian life as one in which man discovers his 'true humanity', which it identified clearly with the life in Christ. It reiterated many familiar notes, yet set within a much more realistic and dynamic picture of the social order, and made clear the various sorts of 'dialogue' which have to be developed between different groups of men.

Pope Paul VI issued one epoch-making encyclical in 1967 – *Populorum Progressio* (On the Progress of Peoples). He tackled the great matters of the chronic disparity between the rich and the poor nations, all the tensions that that introduces into international affairs, and the inequalities also present within each nation. It was issued at a time when men still fondly believed that good will and steady changes in the economic order could produce the new and just world; perhaps this letter was the most noble expression of that hope. It made a moving appeal to the rich to give extensive aid to the poor, and saw this as a precondition for a world of peace. 'Development is the new word for peace,' it said. For the first time a papal letter cited other authorities than merely previous Popes or biblical texts. It called for a massive world development fund, and conceded in one paragraph the possible right of violent revolution (see p. 106). It produced a euphoria in many areas of the Catholic church, which the Vatican was later to go to enormous pains to damp down. Two illustrations suffice. It enabled the WCC and the Vatican to share together in establishing Sodepax, a joint agency to promote the study of development and peace issues. Soon Sodepax began to issue radical and challenging documents;[30] mysteriously, by the end of the 1970s this agency was quietly dissolved. Second, it had profound effect upon the emerging social consciousness of some of the leaders of Catholic social thought in Latin America. Its most immediate result was the remarkable *Pastoral from the Third World* issued in 1967 by seventeen bishops, mainly Brazilian. It was social dynamite in countries in which the Catholic Church was still largely identified with the ruling and oppressive rich families, and in which the majority of bishops and priests were still supporters of the old order. It asserted that, 'Christians have a duty to show that true socialism is the fullest way of living Christianity, with a just distribution of goods and equality for all. Far from being distressed by it, we must be happy to recognize and support a new form of social life that is better suited to the times we live in and more in conformity with the spirit of the gospel.'[31] It helped to prepare for the major conference of Catholic bishops at Medellin in 1968 when the hierarchies were substantially influenced into much more radical postures.

To return to the general series of social encyclicals, Pope Paul VI continued these in *Octo Adveniens* (Eighty Years On), a fairly general letter which eschewed Marxism but was not wholly condemnatory as in the past, pointed to the ambiguity in all social systems (Tillich's point being taken?), and laid great stress on human rights. It condemned racialism and appealed for Christian involvement in politics. The series has been further continued by the present Pope, John Paul II, in 1981 in *Laborem Exercens* (The Exercise of Work), one of the longest of these letters. It states that 'human work is a key, probably the essential key, to the whole social question', and bases itself on biblical teaching and reference to other relevant disciplines (i.e. no longer does natural law provide the sole basis). It argues for a just wage, for the right to be a member of a union, for the right to strike. It also states firmly that 'the right to private property is subordinated to the right to common use, to the fact that goods are meant for everyone', it advocates worker participation in the ownership of the means of production, and it denounces 'economism' (which seems to mean 'monetarism').

Whilst the, series of letters on the general issue of the structuring of human society has proceeded in this matter, other encyclicals have also been issued on moral matters, especially on sexual morality. These have all been restatements of what is affirmed to be the church's traditional teaching, as in *Casti Connubii* (Christian Marriage) in 1930, or *Humanae Vitae* (On Human Life) in 1968. In these two instances the basis in natural law was strongly affirmed; indeed, in the latter case, woodenly argued. This was in noticeable contrast to *Gaudium et Spes*, which was suggesting other ways of understanding sexuality, and was thus implicitly repudiated in 1968. The 1976 *Declaration on Certain Questions concerning Sexual Ethics* was again a reiteration; we are thus faced with the curious situation that the Popes have always seen the need for constant development in their social teaching, but no development whatever in relation to sexuality.

It was previously mentioned that there is a third source of Catholic moral teaching, the occasional pastoral letters of the national hierarchies. Thus in England the bishops issued *Abortion and the Right to Live* in 1980.[32] This was a short, readable statement of the traditional position, designed for parish teaching. Because the encyclicals are designed mainly for priests and those who are highly literate, there is always an important place for more popular presentations. But hierarchies will sometimes issue very much more extensive studies if they feel that the national need demands it and if there is no direct statement available from the magisterium. An extremely important example is the long letter on *War and Peace in a Nuclear Age* issued by the US bishops at a time when President Reagan's policy was stepping up the tempo of the arms race.[33] The bishops made a major study of the basic moral issues, coming to the conclusion that the use of nuclear weapons was immoral, the development of the arms trade likewise, and that the major emphasis of government policy must be on ways and means of disarmament and the creation of a more powerful international peace-keeping agency. The letter cut sharply across government policy and was immediately denounced by the White House (a sign that it was being heeded); although the Pope had said to the United Nations on 11 June 1982 that 'deterrence based on balance – not as an end in itself but as a step on the way to progressive disarmament – may still be judged to be morally acceptable', the bishops put a decidedly different nuance on to Catholic teaching, so that it could not appear to justify the policy of ever-increasing deterrence as practised by the super-powers.

The British churches

Prior to the Second World War the only church which had an effective body reflecting on its behalf upon the most pressing moral and social issues was the Church of Scotland through its Church and Nation Committee. This brought regular reports to the Assembly; because that body represents the nationhood of Scotland in a unique way not parallelled at all in England or Wales or Ireland, those reports were widely publicized and served to express Christian opinion both to the church membership and the people at large. The Committee's reports still serve that purpose; they carry considerable authority by virtue of the Church of Scotland's established and dominant position, and in a country which is characterized by moral seriousness related to a strong public sense.[34]

By the late 1940s the English churches were aware of an urgent need for their members to be better informed and for their general witness to society to be clearer and more obviously Christian. They had learnt something of the complexity of the moral-social issues, and their own experience from COPEC onwards had demonstrated the need to act together and to draw heavily upon the expertise of lay people. In the Church of England these considerations led to the creation of the Board for Social Responsibility. This has brought a long string of reports to the General Synod on a wide range of issues; the Synod has debated them and usually commended them for study; the reports then carry the authority of the Board together with a rather vague sense of general approval from the synod and thus the church as a whole. Sometimes the reports would not even carry that somewhat indefinable aura of approval, but be published later as reports that were 'presented' to synod; in extreme cases a report might not even carry the full approval of the Board, let alone the synod, and yet be published later. This happened in 1979 with a highly controversial report on *Homosexual Relationships*, which expressed a limited approval of them but within a stringent framework of 'love'. The report was published with a disclaimer from some members of the Board, and was sub-titled 'A Contribution to Discussion'.[35]

The work of the Board has instituted a new style of ethical reflection within the Church of England. Previously it was left to bishops to speak to their own dioceses, and for the Archbishops to appoint a special working party when a major matter arose (e.g. reform of the divorce law). Now there is a better mechanism for asking small working parties to work for a long time on complex matters, to utilize the skills of experts as well as moral theologians, and to submit their results to a body (the Board) for scrutiny before submission to the governing body of the church (the General Synod). The final report may be entitled 'a survey', 'a comment', 'a Christian perspective', 'an ethical discussion', 'an ethical enquiry', 'a Christian examination', 'an Anglican contribution to the debate', or sometimes merely 'a report'. The intention is fairly clear – to promote informed Christian ethical reflection, under the general approval of the Church of England and with an ethical method which is held to be widely acceptable, but not to profess to represent in any definitive way the church's mind or explicit teaching on the subject.

The cynic wants to know what good all these reports do. Has any one of them ever produced a change in policy by a government, for example? Not necessarily. 'Good' may simply reside in the way that some areas of Christian opinion have become better informed, clearer about the ethical implications of the faith, and more able to make an effective Christian contribution to the common life. In some cases there has undoubtedly been a wider consequence. Thus in 1970 a report was issued for use during European Conservation Year entitled *Man in his Living Environment* (An Ethical Assessment)[36] and advocating what can loosely be described as 'the ecological attitude'. Soon afterwards a major debate took place in the House of Lords and the government set up the permanent Royal Commission on Environmental Pollution, and an Advisory

Council on Noise; undoubtedly the report was an element in the general pressures leading to that political result. One of the Bishops who had contributed to the report and the House of Lords debate became a member of that Royal Commission (the Bishop of Norwich). One other obvious good is the way such reports have helped to promote Christian reflection in areas which matter profoundly but in which moral theologians have not been noticeably interested – for example, industrial ethics. The Board has had close links with the extensive industrial chaplaincy work carried out mainly by Anglicans in a wide range of industrial settings. The result has been a string of reports in this field, such as *Understanding Closed Shops* and *Work or What?* in 1977, *Work and the Future* in 1979, and *Winters of Discontent* in 1981.[37] No other church has found the means to engage in such well-informed discussion of these matters.

The proliferation of this work, and the many reports, caused the Board to ask its general secretary – Giles Ecclestone – to survey its work and report back in 1980. This was done in *The Church of England and Politics: Reflections on Christian Social Engagement*.[38] The survey covers the many areas of the Board's concerns. It notes the identification of the church with the established order and the 'centre' of most political thinking; it recognizes that in the past the church's influence has been mainly by representations to those in power, and that this has not been difficult for the established church. But that situation is rapidly changing. Moreover recent theology is pressing for the church to regain a sense of 'God's bias towards the poor'; this shift is to be seen as part of a recovery of the perspectives on the Kingdom of God which alone will be able to give adequate over-all direction to the Christian involvements. 'For the Church in England the risk is not, as it may be in Latin America or other parts of the third world, that the Kingdom is identified with the achievement of finite goals of justice; it is that we fail completely to relate our efforts, and the tasks we identify, to the dimensions of the Kingdom.' As a specific instance Ecclestone holds that, 'At the present time what is most needed is discernment to see what in the structure of our welfare society needs actively to be defended and what must be developed if the human impulse which gave rise to it is to find expression in new circumstances.'[39]

The other churches have had fewer resources to devote to sustained social and ethical comment. The United Reformed Church has a Church and Society Department which encourages this work; it has taken a special interest in marriage and divorce problems, including work on services for those who wish to be released from marriage vows; it attracted particular attention in a Report on *Non-violent Action*[40] which was welcomed by the British Council of Churches and recommended by the Roman Catholic Justice and Peace Commission. It does not hold that its reports are binding upon all URC members. Instead, when approved by the annual Assembly, they are indicative of the general mind of the church. This is less true of the statements of the Baptist Union. That body never claims to speak for all its constituent churches; the Union is more like a consultative forum for churches which are independent of each other but all hold to 'Baptist principles'. Its International and Social Responsibility Department includes ethical-social issues in its concerns.

The Methodist Church has a different and more authoritative structure. The Methodist Conference speaks for the church and to the church, and has a long tradition of Declarations and Statements which 'are intended to help those who have a responsibility to expound the social implications of the Christian Faith and to guide the Methodist people in the application of the Gospel to everyday life'.[41] These are prepared by working parties appointed by the Division of Social Responsibility, and have to be adopted by the Conference before they can acquire much authority. The Division was created in 1973 out of the previous Department of Christian Citizenship, which had been formed out of the Temperance and Social Welfare Department in the early 1950s. This change in nomenclature shows the development in the range and scope of the church's concerns. In the early part of the century, right up to the Second World War, the major but not only concern was temperance and 'social welfare'. Afterward it had to be extended to Christian 'citizenship', but that still had a rather narrow connotation;[42] the term 'social responsibility' may have echoes of the WCC's concern for a 'responsible society' but it implies a much wider canvas. This shifting of concern was characteristic of all the Free Churches; beginning the century with the remnants of what was then called the 'non-conformist conscience' and a preoccupation with temperance and gambling, they have rapidly come to share deep concern for all the major ethical issues.

It cannot be said that such an authoritative body as the Methodist Conference has always been consistent in its views or its methods of arriving at them. In 1961 it condemned abortion as 'destruction of human life'; in 1966 it accepted abortion as legitimate in certain cases; in 1976 it implied that a foetus could hardly be termed a 'person', but said that there was never a time when it 'totally lacks human significance.[43] The grounds for the discussion were noticeably different in each of the three cases. That is partly because the people involved in the discussion and drafting were different, and partly because the Free Churches seem to lay less stress on continuity than most other churches. It is also because there is no accepted tradition of how to go about the formulation of such statements, so that each one may have a quite different style of argument and may bear little relation to the methodology employed in other cases. This would apply not only to Methodist statements, but also those of other Protestant churches, as would Giles Ecclestone's comment cited above.

The British churches have had in the British Council of Churches a useful forum to which to submit matters of common ethical concern, but have tended to use it mainly for international issues and major strategical problems, such as those associated with the development of nuclear weapons. Its handling of the issues related to nuclear war has shown both the lack of an overall acceptable methodology and the difficulty of either making a statement too remote from everyday politics or too detailed, erring through assuming too much political wisdom. The first major report, entitled *The Era of Atomic Power*, appeared in 1946 and seemed to be too immediately positive about atomic power, largely because it saw it as the means whereby 'democracy' could be defended. One of the few purely Anglican statements followed soon afterwards, *The Church and the Atom* (1948), which was critical of the previous BCC statement for being facile about 'democracy', judged the dropping of the atomic bombs to have been immoral, but could see a moral case for the policy of deterrence. Its arguments were based on a strong assertion of the notion of a natural moral law and paid careful attention to the just war doctrine, but argued that some situations of 'necessity' may require the threat of atomic weapons, a position later echoed by the Pope in 1982. By 1959 it was becoming clear that the West was prepared to use atomic weapons first, due to the alleged disparity between their conventional forces and those of the Russians. The BCC reacted by *Christians and Atomic War* which argued for general restraint and a toning down of the Cold War polemics. This was fairly soon followed by *The Valley of Decision* in 1961 which stated that pacifism and the Campaign for Nuclear Disarmament were mistaken, that there is a place for enlightened self-interest in Christian morality, and that deterrence offered the best chance for the avoidance of all-out nuclear war (by this time the development and deployment of the H-bomb had caused 'atomic' war to be entitled 'nuclear'). It saw the distinctive Christian doctrine that is most relevant to be that of providence, the belief that God will somehow use the wrath of sinful man to praise him and serve good ends.[44]

In 1961 the WCC had issued a major study, *Christians and the Prevention of War in an Atomic Age*, which asserted that to the Christian all war must be regarded as having strict limits, one being that armaments should only be used to repel an aggressor, another being that the H-bomb, being indiscriminate, could not be used even in retaliation. The document did not deal very carefully with the deterrence arguments and was open to the criticism of saying that one could possess H-bombs as long as one never used them. By this time CND was very strong in England, and the first Test Ban Treaty had been under negotiation. The BCC issued *The British Nuclear Deterrent*, a report which generally supported current government policy. Its great weakness was that it did not seem to have any specifically Christian insights at all,[45] a failing also evident in the 1972 *Search for Security* report which was largely taken up with accurate description of the nature of the weapons being developed and the nature of the decisions to be taken. This became a mildly supportive view of current government policy again, and lacked those distinctive Christian perspectives. Perhaps its gravest weakness was the presupposition that the search for national security, which must dominate a politician's attitudes, must also dominate the Christian's approach (see also p. 101).

Since this time the position of the BCC has slightly shifted away from support for deterrence policies and towards disarmament as the first priority. This may be because by the end of the 1970s more and more Christians began to believe that the arms race is inherently wrong when one considers the magnitude of the risks it involves. This is not a reversion to some pacifist position, since these Christians usually argue that conventional forces must be increased and defence treaties like NATO be maintained. In 1983 the BCC recognized that it needed to pay much more careful attention to the whole issue, and so a 'peace desk' was set up, enabling a permanent secretariat to monitor the arguments and assist in formulating a consensus Christian judgment if possible.

In all this moral debate the pacifist case was constantly noted, but pacifists have never been anything but a tiny minority in most British churches. The style of argument used in the reports has changed considerably from time to time, with less desire to make use of the old just war tradition. Some Christians have felt the BCC to be an inadequate forum for Christian ethical reflection on this issue, and so the Christian Council for Approaches to Defence and Disarmament was founded in London in 1961 to promote detailed and up-to-date study without prior commitment to general church acceptability. It has tended not to subject the deterrence doctrine to intense analysis, a failure also noticeable in BCC reports, and to be inclined to suggest policy directions which are not too far from existing political thought. It has been noticeably opposed to unilateral disarmament.

The BCC ventured into the field of sexual ethics in the 1966 document on *Sex and Morality* discussed previously, but made a substantial effort to try to produce a more adequate and comprehensive view of what Christians should be working for in the whole of national life when it issued *Britain Today and Tomorrow* in 1978.[46] This report made little attempt to lay out the groundwork of a social ethic which might be acceptable to most Christians, nor did it enter into much discussion about the nature of social ethics. It tended to be descriptive of the current scene and to suggest the directions in which social policy ought to move. It inevitably lacked much sharp critique and, because each section was produced by a different working party, there was some inconsistency.

Whilst the BCC has not been used extensively by the churches for the formulation of social objectives or social strategy acceptable to the mainstream churches, a wide range of smaller agencies has been set up to represent or stimulate Christian opinion on specific matters. Many of these agencies (e.g. the World Development Movement) have close links with the mainstream churches and are funded by them, but others are not (e.g. the World Disarmament Campaign). Sometimes the need for such agencies passes and they are disbanded or subsumed into something else. An interesting instance is the Churches Council on Gambling. In the late nineteenth century much Free Church and Anglican opinion became shocked by the damage being done amongst the poor by widespread gambling practices.

That opinion, as a sort of gut reaction, saw gambling as inherently wrong, whereas the Roman Catholic tradition (shared by many Anglicans) saw it as a matter of 'indifference' – that is, only wrong in excess, depending upon the proportion of the particular instance. Those who saw gambling as inherently wrong cast about for a whole variety of arguments to justify that stance, arguments widely accepted amongst them until the late 1960s. The Churches Council on Gambling was a moral watch-dog body set up to obtain detailed information on gambling and to pressurize the government of the day into restrictive legislation. However, by the 1970s the inadequacy of most of the moral arguments being utilized was only too apparent. The Council became more of an information body than a moral watch-dog; when in 1982 it was clear that current legislation was on the whole both fair and effective in keeping gambling within bounds and providing protection for both the punter and the gambling industry, it became obvious that a different sort of body was needed to keep a watchful eye on gambling. The Churches' Council was wound up, and the National Council on Gambling replaced it, being a body representing all the interests involved, including the churches.

Catholic and Protestant

It is clear that there have been very substantial differences in the ways in which Catholics and Protestants have formulated ethical judgments. Catholics have tended to look to the magisterium, Protestants to the Bible along with other sources. Catholics have based much of their individual ethics upon a view of human nature as seeking to attain certain ends, ends which need to be related to the moral law; supernatural grace can produce those special Christian virtues which relate the person to the whole purpose of God as seen in Jesus Christ. Protestants have viewed all human nature as fallen, including the human will; the new life in grace is that which results from justification and is a radical renewal of the whole person. Catholic social ethics has tended to be built from a doctrine of the natural law; Protestant from a doctrine of the two kingdoms, or of the 'responsible society' or some such picture of the social good. Catholic moral theology has been designed for the benefit of the priest; Protestant ethics has attemped to guide the believer. Catholics seem to have been excessively rigid over some matters (e.g. contraception) and lax over others (e.g. drinking to excess); Protestants appear to have been rigid over quite different matters (e.g. gambling) and tolerant over others (e.g. abortion). The terminologies have been different.

It is quite clear that for a wide variety of reasons these two positions have drawn increasingly closer during the period immediately preceding and then after the Vatican II Council, which finished in 1965. A general study of the main contrasts between the two great systems, made by James Gustafson in 1978, describes the traditional characteristics and remarks that, 'It is fair to say . . . that a major difference in the two traditions historically has been the place of Scripture in ethical thought. Indeed, this has been *the* major difference.'[47] He concludes by noting the 'polarities' that always exist in ethical thinking, so that one theme always needs to be held in tension with a partner; traditionally the two contrasting systems tended to put too much weight on one partner, to the neglect of the other. 'Reconstructive or revisionist proposals made by Roman Catholic and Protestant moral theorists address explicitly or implicitly the following traditional and persistent polarities: being and becoming, structure and process, order and dynamics, continuity and change, determination and freedom, nature and history, nature and grace, law and gospel,'[48] and Catholic writers now generally attempt to stress the second term (whereas in the past they stressed the first), whilst Protestants do the opposite. Thus both sides are extremely sensitive to the other and learning from each other, and inevitably growing closer together and developing much mutual respect.

Both sides tend, too, to be growing together and developing mutual respect because they increasingly find themselves sharing in both reflection and action upon the same social issues. Kenneth Leech suggests that this is especially noticeable in Britain in three areas – war and peace, homelessness and racial justice – and claims that this is partly based upon 'the clear evidence of a convergence of positions on social justice and the theological basis of Christian social action'.[49] He hints that Catholics are increasingly willing to contribute to public debate on such issues and thus emerge from the minority position they have previously held in public life and general Christian witness. In Ireland, on the other hand, where traditionally Catholicism has had such a significant voice and the Protestant minority has related to it with heated polemics and misunderstandings, there has grown up a steady process of mutual consultation on social issues despite the appalling horrors of internal strife within Ulster. A symbol of this, and the degree of consensus now found to be possible, is the Council of Churches/Roman Catholic Joint Group on Social Questions which has issued a string of reports on crucial social issues: on Drug Abuse (1972), Housing in Northern Ireland (1973), Teenage Drinking (1974), Underdevelopment in Rural Ireland (1976), Violence in Ireland (1976). This last report included a historical account which provided a consensus on the development of the conflict, an account not agreed without considerable 'travail of conscience' on the part of both Catholic and Protestant participants.[50]

Roman Catholics have never been official members of the WCC or the BCC, but the case for their fuller participation in the latter has grown stronger with the years. However, one of the hesitations on the part of Roman Catholics has been the degree to which they would be bound by any moral statements issued by the BCC if they had become members. A Liaison Committee was appointed to examine that issue. Its report was published in 1978 and went into a careful study of the different methods adopted by the two traditions and the different concepts of authority which flavour any statements or documents produced. But it concluded that, 'we do not believe that differences on the question of authority constitute a serious obstacle to co-operation between the churches on moral issues' and that there is 'a clear case for a more economic use of our resources and a pooling of the available advice',[51] a judgment later accepted by both the BCC and the Roman Catholic Bishops' Conference. Thus the trend towards a common approach to moral issues continues, and makes it more and more possible to expect the major churches to be able to share in agreed responses.

Questions for Discussion

(a) Has the work of the WCC been a help or a hindrance, and in what ways, to Christian moral thinking?

(b) On what issues do you think the churches have done too little or too much public protest or teaching?

Chapter 9

Some Current Problems

Human rights

In most disciplines there come times when a new mood grips the participants, or a new range of ideas becomes widely disseminated, or new styles of working are introduced, and a new vocabulary is required. It is not that the old style is necessarily wrong, but that the new style demands fresh words and concepts. To a certain extent this has happened over the last forty years in ethics. A new range of methods and terms has arrived on the scene and has attracted a wide degree of acceptance by the general public, all based on the notion of 'human rights'. Strictly speaking this is not a wholly new notion; what is new is the extent to which it has become used, and its widespread value in many areas of ethical concern, from politics to medical ethics. The talk about human rights is talk, then, about ethical problems that are as old as the hills, but now utilizing a different sort of argument or claim, couched in a slightly different language.

John Locke (1632–1704) had held that certain 'rights' were inherent in our human nature. All men are equal in that they possess rights which originate in them and are prior to any which are granted them by society. Society has no authority to take them away. although in some cases (e.g. criminals shut up in prison) it may suspend them for a limited period. Those 'rights' still remain as an attribute of the person, even though some of them cannot be fully expressed for the moment; they remain because it is impossible to be a 'person' without possessing them. The language of human rights became common currency in the world of politics when these concepts became enshrined in 1776 in the Declaration of American Independence which states:

'Everyone has the right to life, liberty, and the pursuit of happiness' and affirms that 'these truths are self-evident'.

The French Revolution brought these ideas vividly on to the European scene, yet these 'truths' were not so easily regarded as being 'self-evident' to most thinking men. It is difficult to know how presumed 'rights' can exist prior to there being any government and system of law to uphold and grant them; maybe the connection between inalienable 'rights' and society (or government) is not as simple as Locke had argued. John Stuart Mill (1808–1873) did not accept Locke's argument, but concentrated on showing how the power of the majority must be prepared to give way to the wishes of the minority if society as a whole is to benefit. On grounds of general utility and expediency he argued that the individual's initiative would otherwise be thwarted, and so society as a whole would suffer, unless there was a large area of 'liberty'. The majority must of course restrict this liberty if individuals threaten the fabric of the social order, but not otherwise. This can at times sound like an argument in favour of 'human rights', but it is of a different type altogether. It is mainly designed to restrain government and give the individual room to develop, rather than a plea for the assertion of fundamental rights. The result of the wide dissemination of these ideas was that they entered into the whole bloodstream of American and European politics.

On 6 January 1941 President Roosevelt issued his famous Four Freedoms, sensing that the Western powers needed a simple but convincing statement of their political goals as they were drawn increasingly into the desperate struggles of a world war. These four were: freedom of speech and expression; freedom to worship God as one chooses; freedom from want; freedom from fear. In the Atlantic Charter signed later that summer with Churchill as a statement of Allied war aims, the last two were again cited. This meant that when the war was drawing to its close, and the Allies recognized that some sort of international agency would be needed for keeping the peace and carrying forward the Allied cause, attention was already being given to some sort of statement of universal human rights to which the nations should be pledged when the world was being rebuilt. The young WCC co-operated extensively in this task, and was probably the most significant non-political agency involved. There was a hopeful exuberance about the UN's work at this stage, as can be sensed in this account from a Lebanese Christian (Charles Habib Malik) intimately involved:

> We were fully conscious of the fact that we were embarked upon something unprecedented and historic . . . For we believed that nothing was more needful in a world that had just emerged from a most devastating war . . . than to reaffirm the full integrity of man. We loved man and thought him to be wonderful, and we wanted him to be fully himself, enjoying his inherent dignity and freedom . . . [1]

On 10 December 1948 the General Assembly of the United Nations, meeting in Paris, formally adopted the Universal Declaration of Human Rights. This has thirty articles, of which the first is: 'All human beings are born free and equal in dignity and rights. They are endowed with reason and conscience and should act towards one another in a spirit of brotherhood.' The Declaration is a standard towards which all the member nations should be aiming, and is to be regarded as universal, applicable to all men everywhere. Nevertheless, although forty-eight nations voted for the Declaration (which also became enshrined in the Charter) and none voted against, eight abstained. These included South Africa and Saudi Arabia, but also Russia and Eastern European nations.

There is noticeably 'Western' flavour to the Declaration. It states that 'No one shall be subject to torture or to cruel, inhuman or degrading treatment or punishment' (article 5); 'no one shall be subject to arbitrary arrest, detention or exile' (article 9); 'everyone has the right to own property' (article 17); 'everyone has the right to freedom of thought, conscience and religion' (article 18); 'the will of the people shall be the basis of the authority of the government; this will shall be expressed in periodic and genuine elections' (article 21.3). Not only is there a Western flavour, but sometimes an affluent one also: 'Everyone has the right to rest and leisure, including reasonable limitation of working hours and periodic holidays with pay' (article 24). At such points the Declaration seems not only to be a standard towards which all should work, but a utopian dream so far from reality as to be quite useless for immediate practicable policies. Indeed, how can one talk of 'holidays with pay' when every country in the world suffers from chronic unemployment?

The signing of the Declaration obscured the fundamental ideological rift between the Eastern and Western nations. To the West, human rights are inherent in the individual person; it is the duty of the state to sustain them, and only to impose such limitations as are necessary in order to safeguard the equal rights of others. To the communist East that is fundamentally wrong, since it makes the individual supreme in significance, and the state secondary. Instead, the state must be regarded as the supreme social reality and source of authority. It is then incumbent upon the state to grant rights to persons according to the over-all needs of the state. Thus to the East rights derive from the state; to the West they derive from the essence of human personhood. For this reason the Eastern bloc countries abstained from the vote for the Declaration. They did not do so because they wished to deny what rights are outlined there, but because they understand the whole question from a different perspective. Moreover, they would hold that the Declaration does not go far enough. It makes no mention of the major forces that enslave persons and repress their rights, which are primarily economic ones, most obvious in the exploitative capitalist systems which make the workers into tools.

Others might well feel that there is confusion within all systems of 'rights'. To what does the right to life refer if the human community has not been able to arrange for a fair distribution of food, so that many millions are doomed to perish from famine each year? Or, equally serious, how can one talk so glibly of some of these rights when a country is being torn apart by civil war or, worse, terrorism? Is there not a duty which the state must exercise of maintaining a general standard of law and order when some aggrieved minority is practising terrorism against the majority? Can it do so without suspending some of the rights of some, if not all, its citizens? These objections are really saying that human rights talk is all too apt to be profoundly unrealistic, and therefore very unsatisfactory for the guidance of politicians, since politics is the art of the possible. Nevertheless, they establish standards which almost all nations now claim to be pursuing, and therefore human rights talk gives some immediate leverage upon situations of gross violation of the dignity of the human person.[2]

In 1966 the UN extended its attempt to define human rights by two further 'covenants' on Civil and Political Rights, and on Economic, Social and Cultural Rights. The former ran to thirty-one articles and was mainly an elaboration of the Universal Declaration; the latter went further by proposing a Human Rights committee to act as a watch-dog over those countries prepared to accept its jurisdiction in this field. This paved the way for the establishment later of the European Commission on Human Rights, since most European nations signed the International Covenant. It also paved the way for the various monitoring groups set up to check on human rights violations in Europe, resulting from the Helsinki agreements signed by the world super-powers in 1977, when both Russia and America were pursuing detente vigorously.

The development of these various concepts of human rights has led to the widespread use of human rights language in many areas of moral concern. The Women's Liberation movement has championed women's rights as one way of expressing its cause. Sometimes, in some circles, this may appear to have over-reached itself. Thus a body known as 'Women's Right to Choose' (formerly the Abortion Law Reform Association)[3] claims that the choice of whether or not to continue a pregnancy should be the woman's alone, on the grounds that it is a woman's right to control her own body and fertility, and a woman's right to make the moral decision concerning abortion, without interference from any other party. Neither of these two 'rights' is cited in the 1949 Declaration, of course, which showed no interest in medical issues. Neither of these two presumed rights is expressed in a context which acknowledges any 'rights' that there may be pertaining to the foetus. Thus human rights language is here used as a convenient device for asserting one side (the mother's) in a situation which is far more complex, morally, than the language suggests. This is not to say that this is a wrong use of such language, nor that there may not be a very strong moral case for abortion, but that this style of language, if pressed sharply and exclusively, may bring considerable distortion to a moral consideration of the case. The use of the language of rights in other more political contexts is different and clearly much more obviously appropriate. Thus all sorts of 'Rights' offices and agencies have opened to advise the general public of their entitlements to benefits in the welfare state under the complex tangle of regulations now operative. These are attempting to explain the character of civil legislation, telling people what the law has already prescribed for them. Here the language is of course appropriate, in that it is referring to legal 'right'.

The most publicized agency for promoting human rights is probably Amnesty International, devoting itself mainly to the rights of conscience of the individual, the right to be treated as a human being and not subject to degrading torture, and the international campaign to outlaw the death penalty.[4] Amnesty constantly refers to the Universal Declaration, and challenges states to abide by those rights in their dealings with persons who hold minority opinions, but have not committed criminal acts, and not to impose arbitrary imprisonment, etc. Similarly, the International Commission of Jurists has been concerned with observance of human rights throughout the legal processes employed by modern states, with an especial eye upon the practices in one-party states.[5] Other agencies have been active in collecting information concerning the violations of rights of minority groups of one sort or another, such as the Minority Rights Group.[6]

How have Christians responded to this new style of moral talk? From the first, Christians have found it possible to talk about 'human rights', since that talk is related to a way of expressing the dignity of man. But it is not a way that is followed, for example, in the biblical traditions. No biblical writer claims that man has rights; instead, man is constantly reminded that he has duties to God and to neighbour. The early church is nowhere encouraged to stand up for its 'rights', but to endure under oppression. It was never seriously suggested by any of the great founding fathers of Christian ethics that the individual Christian should either claim 'rights' for himself, or champion them for others. The result has been that Christians have found themselves drawn willy-nilly into human rights discussion without having a long tradition behind them. This talk has been especially easy to promote, however, in circles where the concept of natural law has been prominent. Thus the encyclical *Pacem in Terris* (1963) began by stating: 'Any well-regulated and profitable association of men in society demands the acceptance of one fundamental principle: that each individual man is truly a person. He is a nature, that is, endowed with intelligence and free will. As such he has rights and duties, which together flow as a direct consequence from his nature. These rights and duties are universal and inviolable, and therefore altogether inalienable.'[7] The letter goes on to enumerate these rights before discussing duties; it begins with the right to life, and ends with the right to the legal protection of man's rights, and is fairly clearly indebted to the Universal Declaration.

But as we have seen previously, most Protestants do not find the doctrine of a natural law to be satisfactory. Does this also invalidate for them any notions of human rights? Not necessarily. In 1950 Paul Ramsey had concluded a major work on Christian ethics with what he termed a 'full-length illustration' of Christian love in search of a social policy, in which he showed how the assertion that man has basic human rights can be taken into the primary Christian convictions about man upon which Christian ethics builds. But it will mean that there will be a radical shift of emphasis with regard to 'rights', because when man is most aware that he stands in the image of God he is least concerned about his own personal value. 'A Christian doctrine of rights . . . follows primarily from man's service of God, and not from man's nature as man. Personality and its rights are in Christian ethics read, as it were, backward from Christ into man . . . To be in the image of God means to do the work of love in valuing one's neighbour'.[8] Ramsey goes on to stress that man's primary relationship to others in a community is one of service towards them and not a business of claiming rights from them; his approach tends to suggest that 'rights' are only aspects of the community's wish to permit persons to be as free as possible. However, he ends by saying that the use of 'rights' helps us to avoid the softness of much sentimental liberalism, and so presumably it will sharpen up the questions of justice in society.

In 1974, in preparation for a WCC consultation, David Jenkins suggested that Christians should see in human rights talk what he terms a 'disturbing notion' rather than a distinctive reference to some specific entities that can be entitled 'rights'; whenever injustice is being practised it is wholly necessary for it to be 'disturbed' by the Great Disturber (God), using if need be the language of rights. 'Theologically speaking, any phrase claiming that "so-and-so is a human right" can best be understood as a disturbing notion . . . One is thus concerned with injustice, deprivation and counting; not with rights and justice as if they were positive notions.'[9] Later in 1975 the General Synod of the Netherlands Reformed Church regarded human rights as a way of talking about our relationships to our neighbours (since we must uphold their human rights and seek their liberation if these are being denied to them). 'Human rights are not abstract principles which are ours because of our birth and which "cling" to us as individuals. Human rights consist basically of the living space we are prepared to allow each other.'[10]

In 1977 a report was presented to the General Synod of the Church of England which regarded the notion of human rights as more firmly grounded than the two previous quotations would suggest; it is 'a new view of familiar features of the moral landscape'. It argued that the biblical theme of man as being made in God's image was the foundation to work from in this connection:

> This is the basis upon which as Christians we ground our understanding of the inherent dignity of man. And while it does not entitle us to develop a theory of rights against God, it represents the surest foundation for regarding men and women as persons having infinite worth . . . Inherent or inalienable rights can be established on the basis of the doctrine of the image of God when we consider those human characteristics which are both distinctively human and shared with God, e.g. intellectual, moral and spiritual consciousness, and a capacity for personal relationships.[11]

The WCC has all along been deeply concerned to promote human rights. It has also been embroiled in the question of religious liberty and the human 'rights' related to it. In 1948, at the inaugural assembly in Amsterdam, it defined that liberty as follows:

1. Every person has the right to determine his own faith and creed.

2. Every person has the right to express his religious beliefs in worship, teaching and practice, and to proclaim the implications of his beliefs for relationships in a social or political community.

3. Every person has the right to associate with others and to organize with them for religious purposes.

4. Every religious organization formed or maintained by action in accordance with the rights of individual persons, has the right to determine its policies and practices for the accomplishment of its chosen purposes.

This definition was very 'Western' in its ethos. It is highly doubtful whether any communist government could cede items 2. or 4., which imply that religious liberty has a higher authority than does the state. It is highly doubtful whether most Western governments could actually agree with item 4.; suppose some sect arose claiming that one should not pay taxes (as has happened often enough)? No government could permit it freedom to 'practise' that belief. Moreover, this statement did not explicitly grant the right to every person to change his religion (although it is implicit perhaps in item 1.); does it give one the right to have no religion at all? Probably not.

The UN Declaration was much more specific at this point. Article 18 states: 'Every person has the right to freedom of thought, conscience and religion; this right includes freedom to change his religion or belief . . . ', but it does not cite freedom to unbelief. By 1961 the WCC had become much clearer as to the implications of religious liberty, and stated that: 'Religious liberty includes freedom to change one's religion or belief without consequent social, economic and political disabilities. Implicit in this right is the right freely to maintain one's belief or disbelief without external coercion or disability.'[12] The Roman Catholic Church had come along a similar road; in the past her great concern had been to claim liberty for Catholics, but later on for all Christians, and then, finally, for all religions. Thus the Vatican II Decree on Religious Liberty (*Dignitae Humanae*, 1965) affirms in paragraph 13 that: 'The Christian faithful, in common with all other men, possess the civil right not to be hindered in leading their lives in accordance with their conscience. Therefore a harmony exists between the freedom of the church and the religious freedom which is to be recognized as the right of all men . . . ' In August 1976 the Central Committee of the WCC decided to set up an Advisory Group on Human Rights to promote ecumenical study, awareness of human rights violations, and appropriate action by the churches. Thus human rights concerns have become extremely important in Christian circles.

Can one extend the notion of human rights to include, for example, animals? Do they have 'rights' also? Does nature have rights? The recent discussions about ecological responsibility have at times encouraged some participants to talk as if 'nature' is personal, and therefore has 'rights' as do persons. But this is not how the biblical traditions view it. Nature is indeed marvellous, but because it is created by a loving God; we revere it not for its own sake, not because it is to be worshipped, but because it is God's handiwork and the worship is directed to him. As one theologian puts it: 'I do not think our human consciousness is sufficiently analogous to the life of nature to justify applying our term "rights", with its societal and metaphysical overtones, to the natural world. This does not mean, of course, that nature does not have the worth . . . (it) is to be respected without being feared, to be served on its own terms without contempt, to be studied and managed by men without doing violence to its essential structure.'[13]

Medical ethics

The medical profession has always needed ethical codes to direct and guide its work. For centuries the 'Hippocratic Oath' served those purposes admirably, deriving from Greek ethics maybe from long before Christ; until recently it was widely assumed to be the basis for medical ethics. There were four elements in the oath which bear upon medical practice most significantly:

1. The regimen I shall adopt shall be for the benefit of the patients according to my ability and judgment, and not for their hurt or for any wrong.
2. I will give no deadly drug to any, though it be asked of me, nor will I counsel such.
3. I will not aid a woman to procure abortion.
4. Whatsoever things I see or hear concerning the life of men . . . which ought not to be noised abroad, I will keep silence thereon, counting such things to be as sacred secrets.

All of these four raise considerable problems in medical practice today and, many would hold, require so many exceptions that the original statement needs complete revision. Thus the first may rule out all types of experimentation (upon which, it is held, so much medical advance depends). The second appears to foreclose any act which verges upon 'mercy-killing' and maybe even the use of morphia when a patient is in extreme pain. The third can only be maintained with difficulty today, since therapeutic abortion is in many cases permitted by law. The fourth may not be possible to maintain in an absolutist sense; again the law may require doctors to give evidence or reveal information even against the wishes of the patient. Thus the Oath needs revision not merely because of its quaint language but because medical practice has moved on from the simple relationships between doctor and patient and the simple range and types of treatment available until recently.

The World Medical Association attempts to formulate appropriate codes of practice; at its formation in 1947 it straightway set about that task, which led to the Declaration of Geneva upon which an International Code of Medical Ethics was based. The Declaration includes such statements as 'I solemnly pledge myself to consecrate my life to the service of humanity . . . The health of my patient will be my first consideration . . . I will retain the utmost respect for human life from the time of conception; even under threat, I will not use my medical knowledge contrary to the laws of humanity.' Subsequently the WMA has issued Statements on Human Experimentation (1964, revised 1975), Death (1968, known as the Declaration of Sydney), Therapeutic Abortion (1970, the Declaration of Oslo), Discrimination in Medicine (1973), Medical Secrecy (1973), Computers in Medicine (1973), Torture or other cruel, inhumane or degrading treatment of punishment (1975), and has thus begun a steady development of ethical concern and reflection. The various national Medical Associations have also pursued this concern; this led to the British Medical Association publishing its own *Handbook of Medical Ethics*, which first appeared in 1980, and was the first time that the general public could purchase an official statement on the subject.

Because medical practice grew up in Europe in a Christian context, with centuries of medicine being promoted and, to a certain extent, supervised by the church, the result has been a long development of ethical reflection upon medical problems, particularly in the Catholic tradition. This stream of reflection has faced unprecedented issues recently, due to the advances made in medicine and the related disciplines; but also medical practice today is exercised in a different cultural context, and therefore its traditional codes and norms must be acceptable both to those who accept Christian or Jewish theology and those who do not. Nevertheless that stream of development has brought along with it many highly significant concepts which retain their value in this different cultural setting. Take, for example, the distinction made in mediaeval ethics between 'ordinary' and 'extraordinary' means. The former refers to whatever a patient can obtain and undergo without thereby imposing an excessive burden upon himself or others. The latter has been defined as 'whatever here and now is very costly or very unusual or very painful or very difficult or very dangerous, if the good effects that can be expected from its use are not proportionate to the difficulty and inconvenience that are entailed'.[14] Extraordinary means are to be severely questioned; ordinary means are undoubtedly morally acceptable. This distinction is still a most useful one.

A concept which has become more and more significant in medical ethics recently is the simple one of 'respect for persons', that is, respect for the individuality of each patient, the unique value of each patient, the right of each patient to the best available advice and treatment, and the necessity for all treatment to proceed only with that patient's full and free consent. This concept is widely accepted in social work, it is clearly acceptable to those who utilize the terminology of human rights, and is fairly generally acceptable to most religions and many ethical positions such as humanism or utilitarianism. Some Christian moralists, such as Paul Ramsey, see it as a very satisfactory guiding principle to which Christians can give such whole-hearted assent that it can virtually convey almost all that Christian perspectives will offer in this field.[15] But others are doubtful. Stanley Hauerwas, for example, an American who has devoted much attention to medical ethics, is critical on several grounds. He holds that 'respect' for a person does not convey as much profound meaning as does 'love' as Christians understand it; it may enable us to be satisfied with administering a lot of 'technological care' to a patient and neglect the fuller human dimensions of the sort of care that assumes that God is intimately involved; most dangerous, it may enable us to neglect those who hardly qualify for the term 'person', such as the severely retarded child or the senile reduced to a semi-vegetable ex- istence. In reference to the latter Hauerwas wrote a sharp little essay entitled 'Must a Patient be a Person to be a Patient? Or, My Uncle Charlie is Not Much of a Person But He is Still My Uncle Charlie.'[16] The theme was that Uncle Charlie may be a patient in an advanced state of decline such that most definitions of 'person' (e.g. 'rational; able to relate to others') would not quite apply. Yet he is still Uncle Charlie, someone who has a human story behind him and who should be loved because of that human background, whether or not he fulfils an adequate definition of 'person'. As for the former, Hauerwas wants retarded and apparently hopeless children to be viewed as highly significant members of the human family, and of their own family, even if the fine word 'person' cannot quite be applied to them in their present plight; he is aware that we can all too easily refuse them that designation because actually we are frightened or embarrassed by them and we want justification for 'putting them away' or letting them die, and to be determined by whether or not they are 'persons' may provide an all-too-easy escape route for us in such moral dilemmas. He keeps on reiterating that medicine must be viewed as a tragic profession because it is shot through and through with such problems, with human failures and inadequacies and, in the end, with death.[17]

The debate about whether or not the title 'person' is appropriate constantly recurs in the discussions about the morality of abortion. Can the foetus be regarded as a 'person'? If so, to abort it is tantamount to murder. Roman Catholic theology has asserted such a status for the foetus in a quite uncompromising manner. The Pope declared in 1930 that, 'The infliction of death, whether upon mother or upon child, is against the commandment of God and the voice of nature: "Thou shalt not kill!" The lives of both are equally sacred' (this was in a context in which 'child' meant 'unborn child'). In 1951 a papal declaration said: 'Even the unborn child is "man" to the same degree and by the same title as the mother' (*Marriage and the Moral Law*). In the 1974 Declaration on Procured Abortion the foetus was said to be regarded as 'life from the moment of fertilization of the ovum'. This means that even to abort a fertilized egg which has not yet become lodged in the wall of the womb is murder, and is the basis for condemnation of the 'morning after' pill which prevents such lodgment (technically called 'nidation'). Thus the basis is established for what appears to be an intransigent attitude towards all abortion. This basis has several serious moral problems associated with it, however. If in the normal course large numbers of fertilized eggs are aborted and nidation does not occur – and some guesses put the proportion as high as forty per cent – is 'nature' automatically abortion-prone? If so, can it be 'against nature' to assist this prone-ness? Or again, if all fertilized eggs are to be regarded as 'persons', should we not hold some sort of funeral for them if they have been aborted?[18]

However, although the Roman Catholic position is adamant in seeing the fertilized egg and the foetus as 'persons',[19] and legitimately refers to them as 'innocent', it is still licit in certain circumstances to permit an operation upon a pregnant woman which may indirectly cause an abortion. This can be justified on the important moral principle known as 'double effect'. This states that an action which has both a bad and a good effect may be performed if the good effect accomplished is greater than the evil effect and if, in addition, at least four other considerations are met. These are: the act must be either good or indifferent; the agent's intentions must be right; the evil effect must not be the means to the good effect; there must be a proportionately grave reason for doing such an act, since there is a general obligation to avoid evil so far as possible. Thus supposing a pregnant woman is suffering from some disease of the womb or other condition which imposes a critical risk to her life, it is legitimate to operate so as to save her life, even though a side-effect of the operation may mean the death of the unborn child.

If the title 'person' cannot be applied to the foetus this does not, of course, mean that the foetus is said to have no moral value whatever. It does not degrade the status of the foetus to that of, say, an unwelcome tumour which needs to be cut out of the body as quickly as possible. A foetus can have moral worth, and can be regarded as a 'potential person'. However, the consequence is almost certainly to be a less rigorist attitude towards abortion which goes some, if not all, of the way to support the 1967 Abortion Act which permits abortion when the mother's life is threatened; when there is a strong possibility of the birth of a severely handicapped child; when the risk to the mother and family is greater if the abortion is not carried out than if it is. The general abhorrence which Christians have traditionally felt towards abortion does not find, apparently, a full expression in the current Act, nor in its rather liberal practice at present, so that it is not surprising that there have been repeated parliamentary efforts to stiffen it ever since 1967. But here we note an oddity. Whilst most countries have steadily liberalized their abortion laws over the last thirty years, they have also granted the foetus more rights under the law. 'The consistent tendency of the law over the last two decades has been to recognize more and more rights in the unborn child – except (in the oddest of paradoxes) the right to life itself.' American courts especially impute to the foetus a legal personality; the law 'treats the foetus consistently as a person and hence the subject of rights'.[20]

It may be that the problem of abortion should not be approached by asking the question, 'What is the status of the foetus?', but that it should be regarded as yet another of those complex moral issues which centre on a conflict of interests. There is the value of the foetus, which should ideally be enabled to develop into a unique human personality whose attributes have a full opportunity for further growth and development. On the other hand there is the value of the mother and maybe other members of her existing family; their health and well-being are also significant. Indeed, if the mother's health is allowed to be seriously impaired then she and possibly many others will perhaps suffer many forms of deprivation. The basic moral problem is then that of balancing the interests of the foetus against those of the mother and family, rather than one of definition concerning the foetus. That is the implicit approach of the *Abortion, An Ethical Discussion* report presented to the Church of England.[21] This remains one of the most useful discussions yet conducted on this subject by an official church agency.

Discussions on medical ethics often link the problems of abortion with those posed by euthanasia – which means literally 'a good death' – on the grounds that both are concerned with the definition of what is life and when it is to be preserved. Strictly speaking, euthanasia is more concerned with the right of a person to choose to terminate a life deemed to be intolerable, usually because of an incurable and agonizing terminal illness. It is therefore a rather special form of suicide. Christian tradition has always classed suicide as a grave moral evil. In a particularly sensitive discussion of it Bonhoeffer dismisses some of the reasons used to denounce it, points out that it is not always an act without courage, but says, 'Man must not lay hands upon himself, even though he must sacrifice his life for others. But if his earthly life has become a torment for him, he must commit it intact into God's hand, from which it came, and he must not try to break free by his own efforts, for in dying he falls again into the hand of God, which he found too severe while he lived.'[22] Suicide is morally abhorrent, then, because it is a personal denial of personal value, which to a Christian is a denial that God has set a unique value upon our lives. Euthanasia is very nearly the same, although in this case it is more usual to get other (e.g. doctors or nurses) to collaborate by making lethal drugs available or by withholding life-sustaining treatment or apparatus. Despite the recent pressures of the Voluntary Euthanasia Society most medical and legal opinion has been firmly opposed,[23] as has most Christian opinion, and so have been the recent judgments of the churches.[24] But most Christians would agree with most humanists that the ancient maxim attributed to A. H. Clough holds good: 'Thou shalt not kill, but need'st not strive officiously to keep alive.'

There are, however, constant problems over the definition of death. When is someone 'dead'? When the heart has stopped? Or the breathing? Or a whole string of physical functionings such as brain activity? It is obvious that this question depends upon one's view of man. If he is a collection of physiological activities they must be kept up as long as possible; if he has a quality beyond these, a 'human dimension' which may include ability to respond to others, to remember and to pray, then if this has terminated there is no point in prolonging physical existence. Death is not the defeat of medical skill, but the natural end-state God has decreed for us all in his mercy.

Turning now to developments in the sexual realm, it is all too obvious that these have introduced unprecedented challenges to traditional Christian ethics in this century. The advent of the pill has revolutionized sexual behaviour; for the first time in the history of the human race sexual intercourse is possible for a fertile couple without the likelihood of pregnancy resulting. But other developments pose special problems also. It is now possible to take sperm from the husband and use it to fertilize an egg in a wife's womb in cases where normal intercourse proves impossible – Artificial Insemination by Husband. There can hardly be moral objection to such a practice. A baby resulting from this may not have been conceived in the normal way by sexual intercourse, but it is genetically no different from one conceived normally by the husband and wife. However, problems arise in the case of AID (Artificial Insemination by Donor), where the sperm has been donated by an anonymous person. Whilst this can hardly be argued as equivalent to adultery, it can obviously cause marital distress if done without the husband's consent. But if he approves? Here Christians become very chary about expressing definitive judgments. Thus a BCC report concedes many problems in AID but could not condemn it outright; Norman Anderson seems to regard it as 'distinctly questionable' but finds it hard to say exactly why it should be classed as morally wrong; John Atkinson says that despite the moral complexities 'we should hesitate long before ruling AID out of court'.[25]

This wariness gets substantially more negative when one considers the other developments in what is now termed genetic engineering. It is now possible for a woman to contribute an egg to be fertilized by sperm from any donor male and then placed in some other woman's womb for purposes of incubation and growth and birth. Whose baby is this? If, of course, it proves possible for such a fertilized egg to be incubated in an artificial womb the question remains, plus all sorts of questions about nurturing the embryo in a non-human setting so as to deny it that prenatal human caring. Most Christians agree that here the linkage at present provided by our sexuality, whereby human life is conceived in a human context and nurtured by at least one of the humans initially involved (i.e. the mother), is an essential element in our humanity. Right from the beginning, we are conceived and nurtured in a setting of human relatedness; if that is denied us, then a crucial aspect of personhood is denied and we are less than properly human. So there is almost unanimous dread at the prospect of such stunted human beings being deliberately produced; it is morally abhorrent. This abhorrence becomes even more pronounced when Christians consider the possibility of cloning – that is, reproducing 'persons' with identical genetic make-up to a chosen donor from whom the basic genetic material is taken. There would be a number of radical differences between clones and, say, identical twins. 'Of these, the paramount one would undoubtedly be that the members of a clone had been produced in order to resemble the characteristics of somebody else . . . They would not be brought into the world in order to develop as unique individuals and to be themselves.'[26] Thus an artificial element would feature in their whole existence as persons, or as imitation persons.

This very negative reaction might imply that Christians are fundamentally opposed to recent developments in genetics. This would be unbalanced, for genetics is a science which has the ambiguities of all science. It can be used to discover the inner mechanisms of our genetic construction so as to produce techniques which can bring much legitimate release and relief to persons suffering from various disabilities (e.g. infertility). It can possibly help in the whole task of restricting the unhealthy genes in the general human gene 'pool'. It can improve knowledge, which is inherently a good. It may enable us to find ways of countering genetic defects.[27] So it is fundamentally true that 'between the geneticist and the theologian there is no essential ground of conflict'.[28] But there is an urgency about providing the geneticist with adequate guidelines and moral signposts for his work.

Of the several other emerging areas of moral perplexity in the practice of medicine there is only space to mention two others, which lead on from the previous one. The first is the question of experiments with human beings. There was a universal sense of horror when the Second World War was over and it was discovered that some Nazi doctors had conducted inhumane and degrading experiments upon prisoners, sometimes involving much suffering. The WMA's work resulted in the Helsinki Declaration of 1975 which had elaborated Article 7 of the International Covenant on Civil Rights adopted by the UN in 1966. The WMA code is quite elaborate, offering guidelines for such matters as adequately qualified staff, adequate supervision by civil authority, careful evaluation of risks, the avoidance of unnecessary suffering, and especially the securing of full consent from the patient. The literature on this matter has tended to concentrate upon this last item, especially because of unpleasant stories of mental patients or prisoners from deprived minority groups being the subjects of experiments without their knowledge. However, Charles Curran especially wants the code to be developed further so as to ensure that in the whole conduct of the experimenting the patient is fully involved in both an awareness of the risks (so as to give adequate consent) and an on-going sharing concerning the research. 'The subject should be treated as a participant and not merely as a quarry supplying the material necessary for the research.'[29]

The second is the practice of 'spare-part surgery' or transplants. It has aroused wide publicity and excitement, and has of course attracted a large proportion of the resources available for medical research and development. It is highly questionable whether it should have gained so much access to scarce resources, but that is basically a political decision which helps to direct the course of medical practice in a specific way (and thereby to rule out other possible options such as the extensive development of 'community medicine'). The question which faces the Christian moralist is whether or not it is legitimate to give to a person the spare organs of another, or even of an animal. Is this a somewhat brutal assault upon the essence of a human personality? Most Christians do not feel so. The graft of someone else's cornea does not infringe upon the essential personality of the recipient; it simply means that he or she can see better if the operation succeeds. Similarly a heart or kidney transplant enables the recipient to experience a fuller life, but the personality is not somehow altered by the arrival in the body of someone else's heart or kidney. But is there a limit to all this? G. R. Dunstan thinks so. He feels free to see 'no theological or

ethical problem inherent in the transplanting of merely functional organs, like heart, kidney or liver, but to see problems
loom around the transplanting of gonads, or of the brain if that
became feasible – for these carry some of the constituents of
what we call "personality", and it is "persons" who "relate".[30]
Thus, not surprisingly, we are back to that dominant concept
again, the nature and value of the human 'person', which in
previous generations was often talked of in terms of the 'soul' or
the 'sacredness of the human'. Here we have discovered that
that concept cannot be wholly separated from concern for the
body, and that there are some parts of this which must be
considered as somehow sacrosanct or irreplaceable.

Technology

It is a truism, constantly mouthed by preachers and pundits, that
technological and scientific competence have grown apace in the
modern world, whilst our capacity to control and manage these
powers has not. Mankind does not seem to have grown more
morally mature. Scientific skill outstrips moral skill. The truism
is not, however, particularly helpful, or profound. Scientific skill
involves ability to determine how things actually work by
specially controlled observation; this depends first on the ability
to postulate how perhaps things work, and thus to mount the
appropriate experiments. That may involve talents such as
imagination, the art of thinking about old problems in quite
fresh ways, the knack of spotting subtle and hitherto unnoticed
connections between one set of data and another, and the rare
gift of being able to put all these elements together into a
passable 'theory'. The scientific enterprise, in so far as it is this
insatiable curiosity into how things work, can hardly be regarded
as somehow unworthy or 'un-Christian' or evil, even when it is
asking the most fundamental questions about the structure of
the universe. The scientist is learning to 'think God's thoughts
after him' and, as Christians understand it, to explore the
richness of creation on the assumption that it is orderly.

Two things happen to the work and thought of the scientist. It
is often put into some over-arching view of the world, and made
to sustain and justify it. Thus seventeenth-century scientific
ideas were later set within a view which saw the world making an
almost irresistible progress; it was hardly the fault of the
scientists, but that shifting in attitudes was to have extraordinary

influence upon Europe.[31] Only fairly recently has it begun to occur to large numbers of people to question the apparent connection between 'more scientific knowledge' and 'human progress'. But secondly, science is made to serve a political purpose. It is set to work to attain goals determined by 'politics' in the widest sense – by politicians, by commerce and industry, and by the hope of being able to meet some popular need which may indeed have been engineered by commerce and advertising, or may have simply welled up into people's expectations (like the hope of finding a miracle cure for cancer). It is in the realm of 'politics' in this widest sense that highly significant decisions are taken, values are selected and goals determined – and where, therefore, the ethical character of the decisions can be evaluated. This is where ethical scrutiny and assessment become relevant. It was, after all, a political decision to pour resources into getting an American on to the moon first, rather than developing new means of rebuilding the decaying inner cities or of concentrating on new types of low-cost technology for the poorer nations. Politics decided on the priorities involved and then set in motion the frenzied effort which achieved the goal; it arranged also for the bills to be paid. The scientists were able to satisfy some of their insatiable curiosity, which may well have seemed 'good' to them, but politics set the goal.

The persons who put scientific knowledge to work – the technologists and engineers of all sorts – are the servants of 'politics' in the sense outlined above. They are usually instructed to find the cheapest and most workable way of effecting a project which is determined by politics. Theoretically there is little ethical difficulty at stake, but in practice there is. The distinction between the 'politician' and the 'engineer' soon blurs. The 'engineer' claims that there is only one satisfactory way of achieving the goal others have set for him, but he may often doctor the evidence to suit his personal preferences or his own scale of values; he may be quite unaware that he is doing so. Moreover, he may be highly competent in an extremely restricted area of ability; he may have no skill or imagination outside it. He may be quite unaware of the wider implications of what he proposes, as when a fertilizer is proposed for farming purposes and the consultant has no concern about what happens to the rivers into which it will later be swilled. The engineer often has a deep urge to show that he can do something unprecedented (e.g. construct tall buildings cheaply); he then can hardly resist the temptation to persuade the politician that it ought to be done, that people will like it and want it. All this means that the most careful checks and balances are needed upon all 'politics', so that it is constantly being evaluated, but also that all sorts of controls need to be developed upon technology and what it wants to do next. The business of ethics has, however, become swallowed up very obviously in the business of politics. If we were to revert to the original truism, we need to work much harder on developing these structures of control and evaluation at almost all levels of society and in every sphere in which human knowledge is constantly extending itself. Our political wit and political institutions need to mature along with our scientific skill.

Apart from the ethical issues already cited (e.g. the issue within medical ethics concerning the nature of the human person), does modern technology throw up any fresh ethical issues? It probably highlights some issues which were previously present but not very important; now they have become prominent. Three in particular stand out. The first concerns the quality of human life, and is not unrelated to that recurring problem in medical ethics concerning persons. Is it legitimate and desirable and ethical to work for some patterns of human community which are now possible but which may be both enhancing in some respects yet diminishing to the human person in others? Would it be 'right' to produce a community in which everyone lived in neat boxes in perhaps huge complexes (like files in a cabinet), all food and energy needs were supplied at the press of a button and all 'work' reduced to a minimum, normal health worries taken care of by constant monitoring of the human body, and efficient education and information services provided so that nobody became too disruptive and anti-social? It is of course a scenario envisaged in science fiction and futuristic speculation. Would it actually diminish the essential human stuff of life, that which makes life into a worthwhile adventure, or would it be an appalling diminution? Would the quality of human experience in such a context be in some ways better or worse than the quality of life of the average person in our sort of society? It is immensely difficult to answer because one does not instinctively know what criteria to utilize. Moreover, if such a scenario also involved continuing massive population growth and a gobbling up of the earth's resources, these future humans may suddenly find themselves in a huge desert and may then die of inevitable starvation. The 'quality of life' discussion, then, is inextricably linked with discussion about population, resources, ecology. As a WCC study put it in 1970, 'the future of man and the earth as man's natural environment are inextricably bound together and cannot be considered separately. Man and the earth have a common history; such an holistic vision is needed if we are to face the challenges of the future.'[32]

The second emerging issue is that of time-scale, and how to think responsibly now so as to promote the welfare of future generations as well as our own. Much of ethics has been able to speculate about the problem of 'means' and 'ends' with a rather reassuring assumption as the basis of the whole discussion – the assumption that when we choose certain 'means' to effect our objectives, the outcome can be predicted confidently, and it will be one whose effects are mainly directed upon us, upon this generation, this group of people engaged in the discussion. Possibly they will affect our children, but if so, that is still immediately important to us and we can 'feel' the importance because of a sense of immediate personal links with the next generations. But supposing we are suddenly asked, as we now are, to evaluate some problems (e.g. the disposal of nuclear waste) as they will affect people in thousands of years time? It is a feat of the imagination to conjure up a genuine concern for such far-distant mortals. John Habgood argues that 'the full consequence of some of these decisions may have to be considered on a time-scale longer than that of recorded history. In such a society the bequest which each generation makes to its successors has to be evaluated as a balanced whole', but he does not give many hints as to how one does this.[33] Hugh Montefiore claims that the Christian perspectives on eternity are utterly essential in approaching such ethical problems and chastizes those theologians who, in their desire to espouse the 'secular', become incapable of thinking properly about the future at all. 'If there is no perspective of eternity, man is bound to exploit this world to the full, and he will find good reasons for attempting an ever higher material standard of living . . .'[34] but again he finds it hard to state precisely how one evaluates long-term concerns over against short-term ones.

The third issue is that of risk. Many of the emerging ethical issues revolve around the evaluation of risk, and involve determining what is acceptable risk and what is not. How does one do that? Risk is, after all, inherent to life in this sort of world. Presumably God, desiring to create a world in which human beings can freely find him, lets it be as it now is, in the old-fashioned phrase, a 'vale of soul-making', or as modern theologians would have it, the sort of setting in which we can find out how to love and how to grow in love.[35] Security, in the sense of exemption from risks, is virtually denounced in the Bible as a form of idolatry. Some risks are noble; the climber who insists on going up the rock face when a storm is brewing is absurd. But in both those cases the person who will suffer is the person who is taking the risk. What about the designer who must get someone else to be the test pilot for a revolutionary new aircraft? There it becomes more tricky, for he must build every possible safeguard into the initial flight – and then risk it, thereby risking someone else's skin. He may, however, be in such a new scientific territory that he does not quite know how to evaluate the risks or reduce them to a minimum. Yet the persons who may possibly suffer are still very few, so the risks may well seem commensurate. It becomes far more difficult to determine the morality of exposing future innocent generations to possible risk. As one ethicist puts it, referring to the risks from radio-active waste: 'My mind boggles when I try to multiply present risks by thousands, as I must do to grasp the problem, then to project it over the next century.'[36]

Thus in this matter of facing up to risks, one is driven back to some basic criteria. The risk must be freely accepted by those concerned, who must have the fullest possible data made available to them. The risk must be commensurate with the possible good to be achieved (which is a variant of the constant theme in Christian ethics concerning proportion). The risk must be reduced to the minimum possible. But exactly how to stretch all these criteria to cover future generations (who cannot freely accept them) is immensely difficult, and Christian ethics has not yet found out how to get an adequate leverage on to that problem.

Life-style

A large number of disturbing factors, put together, have caused a very considerable prompting of the Christian conscience in the last few years. Before that it was fairly widely assumed, in the gentle and genial and tolerant way in which English Christianity proceeds, that the appropriate pattern of life for the Christian was one of honesty in business, diligence and hard work, good-natured concern for others, stable family life, regularity at church and the means of grace, and the general avoidance of ostentation by living decently but without extravagance, as well as giving generously to good causes. Political enthusiasm was an acceptable extra, provided that it did not distract from faithful attendance at church, and did not lead into those shrill extremes which one notices in political fanatics.

The disturbances have come because that rosy picture assumes a fairly stable world in which everyone has a reasonable chance to practise the sort of virtues being upheld: honesty, probity, charity, comfortable simplicity, etc. But the chances are no longer to be regarded as reasonable, nor the world to be stable. One quarter of the world's population lives in unparalleled prosperity, steadily become richer every year. One quarter lives in appalling poverty, with no hope of relief. The rest live in an uneasy middle condition, subject to vast forces over which they have little control, likely to be able to exist on the happier edge of the poverty trap but unable to sample the full delights of the rich. The settled pattern of life in the affluent countries looks more and more blasphemous. Moreover, the culture that characterizes them seems more and more shallow, superficial and rootless. Its values look absurd, and its status symbols become every more tawdry. Those Christians who have sensed all this most keenly, especially the young, have come to realize that a different set of virtues seems to be required if one is to be faithful to Christ in such a setting. A pattern of life which is distinctly different from normal genteel middle-class Christianity seems to be demanded, yet it must not be shrill and arrogant and holier-than-thou; it must have a fairly humble tolerance and advocate itself quietly. As Edward Patey puts it: 'Whatever else may be the distinguishing mark of the Christian it is certainly not an intolerance of all those who have come to different conclusions about the practical road by which they travel as followers of the Lord Jesus.'[37]

But in that case what should it be like? Here a new term has been coined. Nobody refers to Luther's phrase about 'the obedience of the Christian man' any more, or the traditional Catholic 'practice of the virtues', or the non-conformist term 'Christian citizenship'. Instead, 'life-style' has become the new phrase to express this practice of the Christian life. There seem to have been four common convictions running through all the various attempts to discover this appropriate life-style for today's Christians.

1. 'Nature' must be respected. Man has dominion over the natural order; indeed, but he must be a good steward of it, caring for nature and lovingly tending it. He must not exploit nature recklessly, must not destroy its resources in some wanton manner, must not idly exterminate species of animal or plant, for he too has his being rooted in the natural order. It is his home; it does not have an infinite capacity to absorb all man's folly; it can be ruined.[38] So advocates of 'life-style' tend to be fervent supporters of the Friends of the Earth, firmly opposed to the careless development of new chemicals to improve quick crops, deeply concerned about the varieties of animal, bird and plant life, conservationists who may well have a little silage tin round by the back door so that waste products can be recycled and put back into the garden.

2. Human solidarity must be demonstrated. We are all part of the one great family of mankind. Therefore all that denies that solidarity must be repudiated – all snobbery, all racism, all extreme nationalism, all class-consciousness, all sexist dis-crimination. Especially one must respect the poor and, as far as possible, stand alongside them. All men are to be honoured because they are God's children; compassion and acceptance must determine our dealings with others; we must have a special alertness towards the weak, the powerless, the poor, the needy. So advocates of 'life-style' tend to be internationalist in their attitudes, keen to support the UN and its agencies, quick to champion human rights, supporters of Christian Aid and the World Development Movement.

3. We must express a different spirit in relation to material goods and the endless stream of gadgets produced by consumer societies and then held to be 'essential' to the good life. We must sit lightly to them all, for whilst many are an undeniable asset (e.g. washing machines) and remove much unnecessary drudgery from normal life, the pursuit of bigger and brighter and better ones is a worse enslavement. A German theologian, commenting on the new mood he detected among the young, found himself utilizing words from a radical revolutionary figure of the late 1960s, Daniel Cohn-Bendit, who said: 'The essential thing is to have an experience which breaks completely with the old society,'[39] and advocating that mood for Christians today. Probably that would mean removing the word 'completely' from

the quotation, for most Christians do not see themselves cutting themselves off totally from the undoubted benefits of modern society, but having a fresh attitude towards consumerism. Thus they want to practise the art of distancing themselves from affluence, of careful stewardship, of simplicity in clothes and furniture, of much more general sharing of goods.

4. There is a desire to promote a total change in the economic and political systems, so that the world's resources are shared justly, but again and again the stress is upon non-violence, persuasion, example. Thus these 'life-style' advocates are usually liberal in their general political philosophy, and would be enthusiastic in arguing for the Brandt Report[40] and its successors.

The hungering after such a way of expressing the Christian ethic was noticeably helped by a finely-written little book by John Taylor entitled *Enough is Enough*.[41] This same hunger is apparent in circles which were traditionally conservative-evan-gelical amongst whom the recent combination of Bible-study together with alertness to the realities of the modern world has produced much more concern for social and political action to promote a more just economic order. Thus a most formative little book appeared from that milieu by Ronald J. Sider entitled *Rich Christians in an Age of Hunger*. It asserted fervently that, 'Present economic relationships in the world-wide body of Christ are unbiblical, sinful, a hindrance to evangelism . . . It is a sinful abomination for a small fraction of the world's Christians living in the Northern Hemisphere to grow richer year by year.'[42] This thinking has been taken a stage further in Sider's editing of a symposium entitled *Lifestyle in the Eighties: An Evangelical Commitment to Simple Lifestyle*, which mentions commitment to evangelism, to justice, to good stewardship:

> We intend to re-examine our income and expenditure, in order to manage on less and give away more. We lay down no rules or regulations, for either ourselves or others. Yet we resolve to renounce waste and oppose extravagance in personal living, clothing and housing, travel and church buildings. We also accept the distinction between necessities and luxuries . . .[43]

The hunger can also be sensed in a small, unobtrusive group called 'Lifestyle' which appeared in the 1970s and formulated a commitment which affirms: 'I propose to live more simply that all of us may simply live . . . change my own lifestyle as may be necessary, before demanding that others change theirs . . . give more freely that all of us may be free to give . . . enjoy freedom from . . . the tyranny of possessions.' It mentions the intention to 'be generous without ostentation and hospitable without extravagance' and has that shrewd note of practicality to 'make time . . . for sufficient sleep for good health and temper'.[44] This movement, like John Taylor's book, has consistently encouraged the development of small groups, or cells, which will share the problems and perplexities and opportunities of such different scales of values from those current within society at large. In this whole concern one expects to see much more work being done in the future on the development of a Christian ethic to capture the imagination and support of far more Western Christians.

Questions for Discussion

(a) What rules would you now formulate for a Christian life-style?

(b) What moral issues do you see as becoming more and more important in future? What should the churches do about these?

Chapter 10

Ethics in Church Life

IN one way or another Christian ethics finds Christ to be normative. Therefore the Christian moral life can only be nourished adequately within a community for whom Christ is normative, in which he is remembered and revered, in which his teaching is explained and practised, in which it is acknowledged that he is Lord. Whenever that steady nourishing is happening within the Christian community, then inevitably believers are becoming more alert to the nature of their discipleship and of the resources being offered by the community's whole life and worship. Christian ethics is the behaviour which springs from people formed within that environment, that *koinonia* or fellowship.[1] This is not to suggest that Christ is the only norm, the only possible consideration. As James Gustafson points out: 'There are many factors in most moral choices that have their own stubborn autonomy, and are not readily subsumed under an exclusive source of insight, whether this source be Christ, or love, or anything else. It is neither Christ nor love alone that tells the conscientious youth what his vocation ought to be; it is also his aptitudes, his opportunities, his desire to achieve, his awareness of various purposes, and many more.'[2] Nevertheless Christ is the determinative norm, the norm dominating all others.

But that statement solves few problems, because Christians seem to have a vast range of understandings of Christ and what it means for him to be a norm. There is thus a wide range of understanding within most congregations, even wider between the various types of church. In this respect the ordinary congregation may well reflect something of the diversity within the early church. 'Diversity is as integral to first-century Christianity as unity. In short, there is no single closely defined

Christianity or christology in the New Testament,' writes a biblical scholar.[3] The result is that this same diversity – essential to Christianity if it is a universal and catholic faith – produces different patterns of ethics within the church. One can see this most simply when one contrasts those who see Jesus primarily as the one who comes to bring a new law (a second Moses, as is stressed within the Gospel of Matthew) with those for whom he is primarily the one who creates a new relationship with his fellows ('the man for others', as Bonhoeffer called him), a theme noticeable within the Gospel of Luke. Those who see Jesus as normative in the former manner necessarily lay stress upon his teaching, the new law governing our behaviour, and those elements amongst his sayings which can be regarded as most prescriptive. Those who see Jesus as normative but in regard to his style of living will lay stress upon his ministry and its style, upon his healings, his way of relating to all sorts of needy and often outcast people, his compassion for all sufferers and all who are oppressed. For both groups Jesus is normative, and for both it is the Jesus to which the New Testament bears witness, for which it provides the essential pictures and accounts. The two groups have common reference points, but seem to be looking at them through differently tinted spectacles and therefore receiving different impressions.

The Christian *koinonia*, then, is not likely to be a uniform one in which there is a commonly agreed interpretation of Jesus, or of the nature and form of the Christian life, unless we refer to tiny congregations. There will be disagreement about ethics, tensions on each ethical issue, different conclusions as to what is right or fitting. That is integral to the catholicity of the church. There will be differences in individual members' attitudes towards the simplest moral rules. Some will regard them as of the essence of Christian ethics; others will deplore them and find them restrictive and conducive to legalism. There will be marked differences between what are regarded as the major moral ethics of the day. For some, gambling, smoking, drinking (alcohol), adultery and fornication are the most crucial issues; for others, justice, human rights and human solidarity.

Granted this inevitable (and desirable?) diversity, is it then useful or helpful or desirable for each denomination or ecclesiastical tradition to make pronouncements upon current ethical issues? As was outlined in Chapter 8, within the last fifty years especially there has been a growing tendency for all the major church bodies to make such pronouncements or commentary or teaching. The objections to this are constantly voiced, with the problem of the plurality of church opinion, outlined above, linked to other notes of caution. Many hold that debatable matters such as the ethical should be left completely to the individual consciences of the believers, and that the responsibility of the church is to see that the Word is faithfully preached and the sacraments duly administered. Others regard statements on 'political' matters as outside the competence of church bodies. Others suggest that in these matters church bodies often accept a general attitude towards social life, a viewpoint that is really an ideology, which is accepted too uncritically and perhaps unconsciously and made the basis of church comment; this process merely baptizes such ideologies into a 'Christian' viewpoint all too slickly and glibly, and is to be firmly resisted. Others argue that it is often the ethical pronouncements that tend to alienate Christians who disagree, making them feel that they are being un-churched. But against all these dangers one cannot but note that the New Testament itself gives some fairly detailed teaching on ethical and 'political' matters, as we have seen, that the pre-eminent Christian leaders and thinkers have always done so, and that the believer has a basic right to be helped to work out the ethical implications of the faith or else he is even more at the mercy of all the propaganda and strident moralizing that feature so clamourously in the general whirlpool of modern culture.

If church bodies are to offer ethical teaching, what should it be like? It should not imply that the viewpoint and style of argument being adopted is the only conceivable one for Christians within that tradition. It should not imply that Christians coming up with different conclusions or comments cannot possibly be 'faithful' members of the church. It should not be so generalized as to be nothing more than first principles, or it will appear inoffensive and innocuous and not worth saying (as was noted earlier in the comments about 'middle axioms'). On the other hand it should not be too detailed and specific, or venture too far into territory in which technical judgments are being expressed and where there may be even more room for genuine diversity of opinion. Thus it would be silly for a church to declare that the nation should meet the bulk of future energy needs from the coal industry and not from nuclear power because coal is cheaper and always will be. That is a technical judgment on which Christians and others may well disagree; the church has never been promised some special ability in matters of economics. On the whole, judgments should not depend on debatable technical expert opinion. Further, the authority with which the church regards its statements should be clear, as also the manner in which they have been formulated. Then, quite obviously, there is a constant need for the basic principles to be clearly set out, and for the conclusions to be formulated in a reasonable manner.

Preaching and teaching

There are a few signs that preaching is recovering from the slough of despond into which it was often relegated in the 1960s and 1970s. 'Faith in the sermon as a means of communication may be on the way back' claims a recent observer.[4] That may well be so, even if many sermons are still very boring. What concerns us here, however, is whether or not preaching can train Christians in their ethics. The answer depends greatly upon how one views the preaching office and with what authority one invests it. Thus a recent writer, John Stott, who takes a 'high' view of the authority of the Bible and the preached word, describes the sermon as the unique occasion when, 'The Living God is present, according to his covenant pledge, in the midst of his worshipping people, and has promised to make himself known to them through Word and sacrament. Nothing could ever replace this.'[5] The task of the sermon is to relate this Word, conveyed through the Bible, to the everyday experience of the people. Of course, ethical problems are part of that everyday experience. 'Our task is to enable God's truth to flow out of the Scriptures into the lives of the men and women of today.'[6] On the whole, as Stott sees it, there are few inherent problems in this task as long as the preacher is soaked in the Bible and a knowledge of the events and challenges of the day. It is just as possible, he holds, for that task to be done today with forceful divine authority as ever.

Yet this formulation of the Christian mind becomes 'controversial' as one moves from the central doctrines and convictions into ethics; however, Stott believes that the preacher must not dodge the controversial, but regards this area of preaching as rather special and requiring special duties. He suggests four:

1. It must expound the biblical principles involved.
2. It should summarize the alternative applications which faithful Christians make.
3. It should indicate which position the preacher holds.
4. It should leave the congregation free to make up their own minds.[7]

The difficulty with this is simply that it asks too much from any one sermon. It is too big an undertaking for a twenty-minute discourse from the pulpit. To achieve all this, some other means than the traditional sermon, which is a monologue, must be found. It is also doubtful that this procedure fits into the understanding of preaching which is being presented.

On the other hand, a theologian from a different tradition – John Stacey – finds a large credibility gap between what preaching is meant to do (as the theologians describe it) and what it actually does. He is quite clear that preaching is important. 'There has to be an articulation of the faith by which the community lives,'[8] but this is a task for those who can interpret the theologians, handle the Bible with care, and are attuned to modern life. It is not clear what part ethics should play in this task, but in any event the book ends on a sober note by saying that 'preaching is a modest activity for those who would like to be modest'.[9] One gets the impression that it is not going to get across to the hearers as the indisputable Word of God, and that it cannot be expected to achieve a very great deal at one go. That presumably means that it can and does help to form the Christian's general dispositions (which is vitally important to the moral life), but not that it is likely to help the hearers understand moral problems very much better, and then to formulate responsible judgments upon them. That task, one assumes, must be undertaken in some other way within the church's life.

The result of this brief look at two works, both deeply concerned about preaching but written from different theological standpoints, is that ethics can hardly be taught through preaching. If one takes a 'modest' view that is obvious. If, however, one takes a 'high' view it means outlining a procedure which is virtually impossible with most congregations, and using a method which is educationally very poor indeed since there is little place for questions, for teasing out complicated issues, for comments to be thrown in from fresh viewpoints. Preaching is not an exercise which is geared to that sort of need; it is primarily a way of encouraging the church by re-iterating what she believes and then encouraging many shafts of light to come and illuminate today's experience. It is not mainly an educational exercise, but an inspirational one. It is not designed to produce the 'rounded view', the well-considered and thoroughly well-informed opinion, the careful and responsible judgment. It is designed to do something which is probably more important – to renew vision and to renew confidence in God. Only incidentally will ethics be touched upon.

Then what about those incidental touches? They must occur, since the preaching is to relate to today's experience of discipleship. There are at least five general cautionary comments about them, thus:

1. Don't imply that ethical issues are really very simple, so that one person or party represents the 'good' in pristine purity, and another the 'bad'. One of the easy targets for the unwary preacher is the complex one of strikes. Thus a preacher may be appalled by a major industrial stoppage in a local factory, an event which casts its shadow over the lives of many in the congregation, and assumes that the basic cause is the workers' greed for more money. Aided by the reporting of the event in the press (which is all too prone to lay the blame at once at the workers' door) the preacher duly castigates the workers. But that may ignore the rather obvious fact that management is also concerned to get more money, that shareholders are always wanting better dividends, and that the general pressures running right through industry are fuelled by the desire for more money. It may ignore the possibility that the strike is not about money, but working conditions or insensitive management. Indeed, it may be a very healthy sign, since 'a strike can be, and may well be, a sign and a symbol that the system is working; the right to strike is a fundamental freedom'.[10] Most likely the strike is about a complex of issues, so preachers should make that clear and be restrained in all their comment. They should read carefully the opening article by Michael Taylor in a Christian symposium entitled *Perspectives on Strikes*.[11]

2. Don't imply that the Bible has plain and uniform ethical teaching that can be easily applied to today's world. As has been said so often in this book, that is not so. Yet preachers are perhaps the people who most constantly imply that it is. Does the Bible, for example, denounce all polygamy and require the church to be rigorously monogamous? It was assumed by

generations of missionary preachers to be so, yet a careful reading of scripture raises very serious doubts indeed about this. The result is that one cannot after all draw an immediate inference from a presumed body of biblical teaching and from it formulate a marriage discipline on this matter; no preacher should suggest that one can, even in a society in which this is a very significant matter.[12]

3. Don't imply that Christian morality is always different from and superior to the morality of others. In many cases the general approach of Christians will overlap that of others and be almost undistinguishable from theirs (e.g. on human rights) and this is not a bad thing.

4. Don't imply that really all Christians ought to agree on major ethical stances, particularly that advocated by the preacher. Don't cast serious doubt on the moral positions of Christian minorities (e.g. pacifists, or the Greenham Common nuclear protesters). Often in Christian history the minorities have been the creative edge of the Christian witness, having a grasp of some vital matter which has been denied the majority in its moral complacency. Later, the majority has been proud of the minority, has espoused its cause, has recognized its Christian validity (as with the campaign to ban the slave trade).

5. Don't identify the 'Christian' attitude with that which happens to pertain within the social group within which one's own Christian life is located. The regular criticism of nineteenth-century missionaries is that they identified Christian morality all too easily with the norms of the English middle class at the time. But it is not a peculiar failing of those missionaries. Americans, too, readily identify Christian morality with some aspects of the American way of life; so do South Africans, so do Latin Americans, so do Scotsmen, so do Englishmen. I am always tempted to think that my judgments are somehow exempt from conditioning by my social class; but they never are. Of course not, or else the reverse side of the coin would not hold either – that I could not make a contribution to forming the general opinions and attitudes of the social groups within which I move. I can influence others; of course, they are always influencing me. But the others who influence me in current society are doing so in a great number of ways, and with a wide range of attitudes. I must never lightly assume that an attitude I hold is to be immediately identified with the area of views which can legitimately be regarded as 'Christian', or with the most responsible and

sensitive views of Christians. Preachers should note this because they are representatives of the whole church catholic, not just of a narrow spectrum of Christians within one narrow social stratum or grouping.

This all means that much of the substance of Christian ethics has to be taught and caught and then practised within the regular life of the church, and also perceived through the way it behaves. Here again are some simple guidelines for the teaching done within the considerable number of agencies encountered within normal church life, some having a specific educative role (e.g. Sunday Schools and adult classes), some being both educative and inspirational (e.g. fellowships), some being more recreational (e.g. Youth Clubs) and some evangelistic or healing (e.g. rallies, or counselling centres). They are parallel to John Stott's rules for preachers:

1. Set out the biblical traditions, showing how there is a place for 'law' but that it is always in need of correction and that, although useful, there are deeper challenges with which 'law' does not succeed in coping. It is fascinating and vital to see how experimental the early Christians were, how ready to borrow what was good from the culture that surrounded them, how shrewd to sense its weak points. It is essential to see how Jesus both conserved the past, purified it, and then fulfilled it with his dynamic radicalism. But he is not to be slavishly copied; what matters is the spirit in which he lived.

2. Outline the various Christian traditions, with their different ways and strengths and weaknesses, all of which merit our respect. The Protestant needs the Catholic, and to know why the Catholic differs; the Catholic needs the Protestant likewise.

3. Explain the teaching of your own tradition, for this is saying in effect, 'We Christians, who have been placed within our heritage, see the issue in this sort of way and want you to share this viewpoint with us. Where it needs improvement, help us.'

4. Respect those disciplines which help us with detailed information about the nature of an issue. Thus we do not dismiss all 'science' or technical expertise, but value the insights and knowledge of the experts; alas, experts often disagree. What then? One listens to them all with a certain critical detachment, trying to sift out the assumptions they are building upon, for some of those assumptions may not be legitimate as far as Christians are concerned (e.g. if a medical expert was talking

about persons as if they were sophisticated and cultured animals, but essentially animals nevertheless).

5. Leave people to make up their own minds. In Christian teaching each person is made in the image of God, able to choose for himself, not to be coerced or pressurized or dragooned, with a fundamental respect of the individual conscience.

But is there a place for rules or laws or some such plain teaching to guide Christians, especially the young? The distinction between 'law' and 'rule' or 'guideline' needs to be made again. Normally by 'law' one means an authoritative command which must be implicitly obeyed in all circumstances because in every situation it expresses Christian obligation. But there are only two (or three) laws of this nature set out for us in the New Testament in Mark 12.28–31 and parallels (and in John 15.12). Undoubtedly these should be taught and rehearsed, over and over again. But in addition, when these two or three fundamental laws are being made more precise in everyday practice, there emerges a useful place for 'rules', which are rough summaries of what is usually right in most circumstances. There may well be exceptions to them, but when in doubt the onus is always upon our conscience if we proceed to set them aside. They are a bit like the ropes sometimes put up in a field to keep spectators in one part; normally one stays behind them, unless there is particularly good reason for ducking under them and going on to the ground beyond. There may well be. Somebody over there may be injured or need help, but the fact of the rope being there makes one feel that to venture on to ground beyond is an act which must be justified somehow. It is noticeable that many Christians are now increasingly using the word 'rule' to express a whole series of obligations (or ropes giving clear guides to where they should go). In a sense, every Christian ought to be formulating his own personal 'rule of life', but all such rules should be plainly derived from the two basic and fundamental laws of Jesus. If it is a most tortuous business to derive a certain rule from the law of love, then that rule is probably a poor one and not worthy of much respect.

As devices to aid teaching and memory, rules are useful. But they can rarely do justice to the subtleties of many quite common situations, they cannot easily indicate attitudes or motives, and they almost always end up as a string of negatives. Thus in trying to provide guidance to Christians facing up to the ethical problems of our technological and complicated society Hugh Montefiore found himself utilizing the ten commandments in a delightful set of 'ten requirements' which included such shrewd items as: 'You shall not make to yourself any graven image or idol, such as GNP or possessions or riches . . . You shall not bear false witness against your overseas neighbours by lying to yourself about the extent of their need . . . You shall not covet an ever-increasing standard of living.'[13] They are useful as both general indicators of the pattern of one's life and as goads and proddings to one's conscience (rather like David Jenkins' description of human rights as 'disturbing notions'). Sometimes rules sound like simple little moral maxims, but should not necessarily be despised on that account. Thus the old maxim concerning sexual morality which said 'Chastity before marriage; faithfulness after' is a good general rule which derives from the laws of Jesus and makes good material for teaching, especially amongst the young. But it is not a law which admits of no exceptions, otherwise it would become a blunt and crude instrument. If applied woodenly it would, of course, rule out divorce and remarriage automatically in all circumstances. Again, as will be elaborated later, the rule 'Always tell the truth' cannot be regarded as an absolute statement (like a law) but, unlike the maxim about marriage and sexual behaviour, it probably cannot be sufficiently helpful to qualify as a rule either, so had better be relegated to a class of statements less useful still – perhaps an 'occasional moral guide'?

Probably the best teaching device is the story with a plain sting in it, challenging the listener to take up the ethics of someone in the story. Thus the parable of the Good Samaritan is intensely memorable; it plainly and attractively advocates a caring and compassionate response to all who are in need, including those divided from us by the human barriers of race, religion, social class, language, etc.; one cannot avoid the stinging conclusion: Go and do thou likewise. But there is a difference between the parable and what one can term the 'pious moral tale', which used to feature so largely in the edifying stories told in Sunday Schools and talks to children in church. The pious tales used to make out that if one were 'good' one would somehow prosper because good, nice behaviour always pays off in the end. That made morality into enlightened self-interest. Or the pious stories used to make their point too crudely: little boys who tell tales will get into trouble, those who are honest will become happy. The pious stories make life too simple; they imply that the world is an eminently fair sort of place with a fine system of virtue and reward running right through it. They tend to make 'good' people very obviously good, and 'bad' ones most despicably wicked. So life is over-simplified, virtue is over-simplified, tragedy is all ironed out and smoothed over, no mystery remains, morality is over-simplified. But worse still, the good people are often most dreadfully dull! The parable is not, however, so crass; the characters are not little puppets designed to serve some artificial moral purpose; they end up as a provocative disturbance.[14] To teach through parables is most effective, or else to utilize stories that do not have a wooden quality as simplistic versions of good and bad. Such stories become unbelievably unrealistic to anyone developing an awareness of the complexities and tragedies that make up life experience.

The church as a moral community

Ethics is mainly caught, not taught. The best way to help people to live better lives is to encourage them to share life in a community which has better moral standards; the heights of loving are best discovered within a circle of loving people. The implications of this are enormous. Consider, for example, the constantly perplexing questions of how to gain and how to spend one's money. If the Christian is to receive the best help, it involves the church not just in teaching about money, but in setting an example in the ways by which it earns and spends money. Its financial life must automatically inculcate responsible attitudes towards both gaining and giving. This is peculiarly difficult in a world in which the Western Christian is inevitably living in riches and a member of the most privileged sector of all mankind. The church in the West is inevitably tangled up in the financial and economic advantages which the West lives by and seeks to maintain. Thus Charles Elliott declares roundly that the present world economic order requires a massive reformation, but meanwhile: 'The Church can pronounce God's judgment and call for the thoroughgoing change, which is repentance, only if one of two conditions is met. Either the Church must be . . . wholly uncompromised by the injustices . . . or she must acknowledge her involvement in those injustices and seek ways to break out of them'.[15] The first alternative is impossible, for the church, like every individual member of it, is entangled in all the ambiguities of the world's economic structure. One cannot be detached from all that tangle of involvement, since one draws from it the necessary resources for maintaining ordinary physical existence. So the church must instead be seeking ways of breaking loose – by not directly profiting from those injustices (e.g. not investing capital in South Africa), and by never appearing to legitimize them (which a church with some sort of established status is most prone to do).

Or consider the sort of moral outrage one feels if one is told of a company which pays miserable wages or sacks employees ruthlessly and with no pretence even at some sort of justice. The church must be a people which feels deeply that all this is an outrage, and in many a case must say so. But in that event it must also be the sort of institution which will never knowingly pay its own employees miserable wages, or dismiss them without any attempt to act justly. If it owns property and is a landlord, then it must be an exemplary one, otherwise it is inviting its members to be bad landlords. If it has a controlling say in the disposition of some funds, it must be seen to be seeking honestly to perform the most useful ministry with them, or else by its example it is encouraging sloppy or selfish use of money. At the basic level of the local congregation it must teach a concern for the whole world by insisting that local money be used for needs far away overseas as well as those at home. Then there is a chance that its members will begin to learn what it is to be an international citizen simply by seeing the sort of priorities the local church is learning to live by and to spend with.

Or consider the ways in which humanity in its sinfulness erects firm barriers between people, putting asunder what God has joined, through snobbery, class consciousness, racism, flagrant nationalism, sexism, etc. One best learns to work to overcome these tragic barriers not by lectures or sermons, but by being part of a community which is all caught up in the struggle against them, and is dealing firmly with them when they occur within its own life. Discussing racism, Clifford Hill wrote, as long ago as 1968, that Christians 'have the opportunity of providing within the Christian Church a matrix of the new society where white and coloured are bonded together by love and mutual respect and engage in objective-based co-operative activities',[16] but the years that followed have hardly shown very convincing evidence of this 'matrix of the new society', so the teaching role of the church has been distorted by its own practice, from within. Nor is the teaching role assisted and validated and supported in the realm of sexism. The stereotypes of male superiority are maintained as much by church practice as by any other agency. So one could go on, constantly making the point that individuals are best helped to practise the moral life when the institutions in which they live are providing vision and stimulus and encouragement by setting themselves institutional goals for moral improvement, and struggling to attain them. To take another illustration, the Christian faith teaches our solidarity in both sin and redemption, the work of God being to draw all men to himself and to each other. The church is called to be a foretaste of that goal, a sign of all persons drawing together in mutual respect and interdependence. But the lumbering steps whereby the churches are trying to grope towards that goal – the ecumenical movement – hardly inspire people either inside or outside the churches to live for it. The progress is constantly cited as being considerable, but the degree of suspicion between the churches, compounded by ignorance and petty pride, is deeply chastening. A recent account of the movement ends up by suggesting that there are at least eight 'quite elementary things' which the churches, their leaders and members, must remember and act upon if progress is to continue.[17] All of these eight things would, as it happens, be regarded as commonplace if one were discussing relationships between one branch of a family and another (e.g. there must be no abatement of respect). No wonder the most prolific Roman Catholic moralist of our time – Bernard Häring – comments that 'in our time . . . moral theology would be absolutely unfaithful to its task if it did not give particular attention to ecumenism'.[18] Or again, consider styles of leadership and forms of government. It is all too easy for Christians (and especially Western ones) to criticize totalitarian or patriarchal régimes and to champion the democratic rights of all to participate properly in government, and then to argue that there is an essential Christian insight at the heart of such a position. But in that case the church communities must also be expressions of that right in the way they too are organized and controlled. They, too, must abhor styles of leadership that are patriarchal, domineering, or insensitive to the voices of those beneath them. They, too, must be governed by open and healthy justice, sweetened by much mercy. Their discipline must be noticeably more humane and sensitive than that of other secular or civil bodies. They must be an example of how one can structure human community so that decisions are taken responsibly and with the maximum participation by all involved.

Truth-telling

It has often been assumed that to be a Christian means having a meticulous concern for speaking the truth. The church should therefore be a community in which this happens – in two senses. The gospel is there proclaimed as the true and liberating Word of God, but also there the believers learn to speak truthfully to each other. As soon as one meditates carefully upon these obligations the problems appear yet again. When discussing the second obligation, to speak the truth, the different Christian traditions handle the matter quite differently.

The ninth commandment (Ex. 20.16) forbids one to bear false witness against a neighbour. This is a negative statement. It does not tell one positively what to do. Jesus teaches in Matt. 5.37, 'Let what you say be simply Yes or No; anything more than this comes from evil', but this is in a context talking about the swearing of oaths. In Eph. 5.37 we are enjoined: 'Putting away falsehood, let everyone speak the truth with his neighbour, for we are members one of another' in a passage which culminates in the injunction, 'Be imitators of God, as beloved children'. These passages are hardly sufficient to enable much to be offered by way of immediate rules or guidelines. Moreover the Old Testament patriarchs such as Abraham and Jacob were apparently great deceivers, and did not the Hebrew midwives have a strategy of gross deception? These instances caused the early fathers much distress; they struggled by all sorts of tortuous exegesis to escape from their unpalatable character. This led Augustine to propound a quite explicitly absolute law: Christians must always tell the truth and nothing but the truth.

However, the great classical tradition of Catholic ethics, developing through Thomas Aquinas, abandoned that absolute position of Augustine's. It was concerned to evaluate the intention behind each different act involving truth-telling, and came to a rather elaborate conclusion. There is a general obligation upon us all to see that nothing which we say with our lips contradicts what is in our minds. We must be as well acquainted with the facts of the matter as possible. But we are neither obligated nor permitted to speak all that is in the mind.

There is a legitimate place for the secret, and for the privilege of keeping to onself one's own point of view or perhaps information which pertains only to oneself. Then a whole range of types of lie was defined and evaluated. The 'malicious lie' in which one deliberately tells a falsehood with intent to deceive was reckoned as a grave sin. But the 'officious lie' (told to relieve one's neighbour from distress or misery without actually harming anyone), or the lie of the child (living in a carefree fantasy world), or the 'jocose lie' (part of a joke), are all venial and easily forgiven. Perhaps, too, the 'pathological lie' is not all that serious, since the liar can only be held to be partly responsible for it. These distinctions were still being maintained recently by moralists such as Häring, mainly because they are useful to priests handling confessions and needing to know the gravity of the various sins.[19]

Calvin remained true to the traditional Augustinian position, and condemned every lie as evil. Luther, sensing perhaps that loyalty to other principles might well take precedence over loyalty to the truth in the freedom Christ gives the Christian man, the freedom to love the neighbour, declared robustly that, 'A good hearty lie for the sake of the good and for the Christian Church, a lie in case of necessity, a useful lie, a serviceable lie would not be against God.' This position could be classed as 'creative love' – when love is in operation it will sometimes override basic moral obligations in the creative freedom of Christian love. One of the standard cases which the mediaeval moralists had debated had been that of the intending murderer who asks you where his victim may be found. If you know, do you tell him? Augustine presumably would have said yes. Luther would have said no. Calvin would have said yes. The classical answer would have been to define such an untruth as an 'officious lie' and regard it as a light sin easily pardoned.

However, in time significant Christian voices which were Protestant were raised against any such 'laxity.' Kant, stern in his moral and logical rigour, wrote a strong little essay claiming that the duty to tell the truth was an absolute one, apparently admitting of no exceptions. 'To be truthful in all declarations is a sacred and absolutely commanding decree of reason, limited by no expediency.' He referred especially to the case of the intending murderer and argued that one must tell him the truth of the victim's whereabouts if one knew it. If one told a falsehood the murderer might nevertheless come across the victim (who may, after all, have left the place where you thought him to be and have gone where you directed the murderer). If the murder is then committed, you share some of the blame. Now that is a decidedly odd sort of argument. The chances of the murderer coming across the victim in such a case are slender. If one had followed Luther's advice and told a good hearty lie, sending the murderer off on a wild goose chase, they would be even more slender. Whatever one does, one can be held to be slightly responsible if the murder occurs. But in any case reason could be held to tell one that a victim's life is more important than an emergency lie.[20]

But in our time Protestants are increasingly exploring the position called here 'creative love'. Thus Bonhoeffer's *Ethics* closes with a discussion of truth-telling in which he is deeply concerned to show two things – that 'telling the truth' must mean something different according to the situation or calling in which one stands (thus the obligations of parents to children regarding the truth are different from those of the children to the parents), but also that the whole discussion must be related much more immediately to the will of God, and the involvement of God. All speech has a special relationship to God, the fountain of all truth, who himself speaks to man. We owe truthfulness to God, but this means finding the 'right word' for each occasion. 'The lie is the denial, the negation and the conscious and deliberate destruction of the reality which is created by God.'[21] and is not simply to be equated with veracity towards data and information. The truth builds up a relationship of trusting reality before God: the lie corrupts it. There can even be a presumed 'truth' which is of Satan. So one seeks the 'truthful word', and Bonhoeffer (like Barth before him) appears to have a sublime confidence that one will be able to know what this truthful word is. In a similar way, but with a less powerful sense of God's immediacy in the situation, Paul Lehmann sees each occasion as subtly different and still requiring 'truth' in the sense of a holding upon the loving and gracious word of God which is always making life 'more human'. He discusses the case of a man selling a car. What does he say about it to intending purchasers? There is a difference between this question in the case of someone who already has two cars and wants to dispose of the spare one, and someone who desperately needs to sell his only car to pay for his wife's funeral. There is a difference in the cases of a high school adolescent and someone in middle life, and so on.[22]

This discussion obviously affects the reply one gives to the standard question raised frequently in pastoral practice – does not tell a dying person the truth about his condition? The absolutist case, as argued by Augustine or Kant, is that one does. The classical method is to give a general yes, but tempered by the need for other criteria to be involved, and the possibility that a 'lie of necessity' is called for. The more 'creative love' and usually Protestant position is more concerned to point to the truth of God, the 'living Word', the 'right word' in Bonhoeffer's terms. There is in that case no pat and standardized answer; it depends on various factors, including the patient's receptivity to the Word of God. This indicates how the discussion about truth-telling, which can easily acquire a somewhat abstract character, has nevertheless an immediate relevance to the life of the church and especially to pastoral care and practice. Thus the Congregational Church published a booklet in 1972 on *Morality and Christian Faith* and used truth-telling as an illustration of its approach. It remarked that, 'As a general rule complete truthfulness is obligatory', but then pointed out that, 'Christians should be concerned not so much with rigid adherence to canons of truthfulness as with using the gift (of speech) in every way for the benefit of their neighbours.'

This issue of truthfulness merges into that of confidentiality, a major concern in pastoral relationships. When one person confides deep secrets to another within the context of Christian caring, that confidence must be honoured. The confidant must not tell others, except with the express permission of the one whose secret it is. If the confidant feels that it is most important for others to be told (e.g. in illness requiring medical attention) the rule still applies. But suppose the confidant believes there to be serious danger to others? Suppose the 'secret' is that the teller is a compulsive child-molester or pathological murderer or rapist? Then the confidant must urge most strongly for the secret to be shared with others (e.g. psychiatrists) who ought to know it for the sake of the teller. But if the one with the secret categorically refuses for it to be divulged further? The absolutist moralists would say that the confidant still cannot divulge the secret further, but the other positions outlined here would have little hesitation in saying that the secret must be shared even against the teller's will. It is a last resort when all else has failed, not to be undertaken lightly but with due regard for possible victims of the murder/molesting/rape. One must lie – or disclose

– heartily, as Luther would say. Thus a report on Confidentiality and Pastoral Care presented to the Methodist Conference in 1980 stated that 'We are unable to assert that the pledge of confidentiality remains absolute in such difficult circumstances.'

What happens, however, if someone comes to another Christian, usually but not necessarily a minister or priest, to make a confession of sins? All Christian traditions have been in no doubt whatever that that communication is not just confidential but totally so. It may never be revealed in any circumstances whatever. Even if lawful authority requires the confessor to reveal it, he must never do so. He ought, of course, to urge the sinner to go to the police or to make appropriate reparation; he ought to point out that refusal to do so involves a further sin beyond the first one confessed; but he must never reveal a secret from the confessional relationship. A Roman Catholic priest doing so is liable to be unfrocked at once; a Protestant has committed a terrible sin against the sinner and the church. As the Methodist statement puts it: 'In such a situation the confidentiality required is absolute and unconditional.'

This can be misunderstood. It is sometimes believed that this absolute rule is based upon expediency, because if the rule were likely to be broken sinners would soon lose confidence in the practice of confession. That is not very convincing; burdened people will often confess the most intimate secrets to all sorts of others because of their desperate need to share their guilt somehow, and to get rid of some of the sting it seems to impart to them. Many of them would confess to a person who could not be wholly trusted, so the strong stand taken here by the various Christian traditions is not for this reason; it is not on grounds of mere expediency.

The absolute rule does still present moral problems though, because it appears to be a law permitting of no exceptions, and most Christian moralists are hesitant about admitting that any such laws exist. But this again is to misunderstand. The confessional is totally secret in all circumstances for different reasons than those we normally advance when handling other actions involving speech. When someone confesses sins, that person is baring his or her innermost spirit, that which is of the deepest self, part of the essential being, that which belongs in a unique sense to God and God alone. The confession can only belong to God alone and be expressed through someone who 'stands in for God', is in this matter God's representative. The secrets that are passed arc in no sense the confessor's to do what he feels right with; he is to ascertain whether or not there is genuine penitence, then to declare forgiveness on God's behalf and indicate appropriate ways for the sinner to put the situation right. Afterwards the secret has passed; it is no more. It belonged to another, and now has gone solely to God. As Bonhoeffer put it: '(My Christian brother) hears the confession of our sins in Christ's stead and he forgives our sins in Christ's name. He keeps the secret of our confession as God keeps it. When I go to my brother to confess, I am going to God.'[23]

In pastoral practice there is often much difficulty in knowing when a person is seeking counsel and general help, and when wanting to confess sin. The two tend to blur into each other in much pastoral conversation, making it necessary for the confidant to ask the other if the conversation has become a 'confession' and is to be treated as such. If later there is doulbt in the confidant's mind as to whether or not a conversation was a confession, always err on the side of the graver possibility. Assume that it was, and that its contents must remain quite inviolate. Thus the Christian community shows that it is indeed a place of truth, both because within it the truth of the gospel is shared, and because there is a truthful interchange of speech and concern between a caring people. But it is also the place where one can find the ultimate human blessing – forgiveness, the spring whence all the new life in Christ flows.

Questions for Discussion

(a) What would you include in a basic training programme in Christian ethics for young Christians in the 15–20 age range?

(b) Are there any moral laws for Christians? If so, what are they? Do they allow of any exceptions? If so, what?

Notes

Chapter 1   The Close Scrutiny of Christian Behaviour

1. *Situation Ethics*, SCM Press 1966.
2. See *Christian Freedom in a Permissive Society*, SCM Press 1970.
3. *A Survey of Christian Ethics*, Oxford University Press 1967.

Chapter 2   Ethics in the Bible

1. This consisted of 282 case laws dealing with civil, domestic and agricultural matters, dating from the eighteenth century BC.
2. G. von Rad, *Old Testament Theology* I, SCM Press 1975, 219.
3. Their usage is clearly described in Norman H. Snaith, *The Distinctive Ideas of the Old Testament*, Epworth Press 1944.
4. But it is untrue that the prophets opposed all organized worship. See H. H. Rowley, *The Faith of Israel*, SCM Press 1956, 136.
5. For much fascinating information about them see J. Jeremias, *Jerusalem in the Time of Jesus*, SCM Press 1969, 246ff.
6. A short introduction to this area of biblical criticism is provided by Norman Perrin, *What is Redaction Criticism?*, SPCK 1970.
7. So for example in John 13.34; 15.10, 12.
8. Possibly the parable of the Lost Sheep is one. In Luke 15.32 it appears as a defence of Jesus' love for sinners. In Matt. 18.12–14 it has become an exhortation to seek the lost member of the church.
9. See Luke 12.53–59, a warning about the imminent End. But in Matt. 5.25 this is a warning about court cases in general.
10. Thus the parable of the Ten Virgins, Matt. 25.1–13, was probably a general warning to everyone, but has been narrowed as though it were for church members only.
11. *The Parables of Jesus*, SCM Press [3]1972. Described as being like a 'skilful restorer of an Old Master, working with loving care to . . . make them shine out afresh'. See too T. W. Manson, *Ethics and the Gospel*, SCM Press 1960, last chapter.
12. C. F. D. Moule, *The Birth of the New Testament*, A. & C. Black 1962, 151.
13. Thus Matt. 22.34–39 and parallels.
14. Hence familiar passages like Matt. 6.25–53; Luke 9.57–62; Matt. 18.23–35.
15. As in Adolf von Harnack's *What is Christianity?*, ET Williams and Norgate 1901, reissued Harper Torchbooks, 1958.
16. Matt. 10.30.
17. See R. Bultmann, *Jesus and the Word*, reissued Fontana Books 1958, esp. ch. III.

18. The many positions are clarified in Norman Perrin, *The Kingdom of God in the Teaching of Jesus*, SCM Press 1963.
19. Matt. 5.43–48.
20. Matt. 7.12; 22.40; 23.2f.
21. E.g. Mark 3.16; Luke 12.16–21.
22. See e.g. Matt. 6.24; Luke 14.1–6.
23. Matt. 11.19.
24. See John A. Ziesler, *Christian Asceticism*, SPCK 1973.
25. *Ethics and the Gospel*, SCM Press 1960, 102.
26. Many of the responses are outlined in A. M. Hunter, *Design for Life*, SCM Press 1953, ch. 4, or more fully in Harvey McArthur, *Understanding the Sermon on the Mount*, Epworth Press 1961.
27. The classic statement of this position is in Reinhold Niebuhr, *An Interpretation of Christian Ethics*, SCM Press 1936.
28. Floyd V. Filson, *The Gospel according to St Matthew*, A. & C. Black 1960, 106.
29. P. S. Minear, *The Commands of Christ*, St Andrew Press 1976.
30. Ephesians was not actually written by St Paul. See C. L. Mitton, *Ephesians*, Marshall, Morgan and Scott 1973.
31. See e.g. V. P. Furnish, *Theology and Ethics in Paul*, Abingdon Press 1968.
32. See A. M. Hunter, *Paul and his Predecessors*, SCM Press 1940, ch. 6.
33. See C. H. Dodd, *Gospel and Law*, Cambridge University Press 1951, and C. E. B. Cranfield in *New Testament Issues for Today*, ed. Richard Batey, SCM Press 1970.
34. Hence I Cor. 3.17.
35. Henry Chadwick, *The Early Church*, Penguin Books 1968, 56.
36. See the discussion in D. E. Nineham, *St Mark*, Penguin Books 1963, 121–4.
37. See especially Oscar Cullmann, *The State in the New Testament*, SCM Press 1957.
38. Maurice Wiles, *The Christian Fathers*, SCM Press 1966, 175.

Chapter 3   *How can we Utilize the Bible?*

1. A brief, condensed introduction to these approaches is provided in J. L. Houlden, *Ethics and the New Testament*, Penguin Books 1973.
2. See e.g. Deut. 15.7–11; Ps. 41.1–3; Prov. 14.21.
3. E.g. Matt. 6.2–4. The biblical teaching is well summarized in Julio de Santa Ana, *Good News to the Poor*, WCC 1977.
4. It is posed in an extreme manner in D. E. Nineham, *The Use and Abuse of the Bible*, SPCK 1976.
5. Ex. 22.25; Deut. 23.19f.
6. See Martin Hengel, *Poverty and Riches in the Life of the Early Church*, SCM Press 1974, 41: 'The first Christians . . . cannot give us a practicable programme of social ethics to solve the question of possession which has become so acute today.'
7. James Barr, *The Bible in the Modern World*, SCM Press 1973, 119.
8. P. T. Forsyth, *The Principle of Authority*, Independent Press 1952, 24.
9. I Cor. 11.2–16.

10. I Tim. 2.11–14.

11. Thanks to the Women's Liberation Movement an immense literature has developed recently on the subject, but the case is pithily put by Don Cupitt, *The Crisis of Moral Authority*, Lutterworth 1972, 48–68.

12. R. E. O. White, *Biblical Ethics*, Paternoster 1979, 173, quotes Pauline teaching in the most favourably positive light, but is obliged to concede that, 'If he appeals to ancient ideas to press his counsel home, this does not lessen the expediency of what he advises.' He likewise calls I Peter 3.1–7 an 'adjustment ethic affecting an existing institution' (191).

13. *The Gospel of St Matthew*, Penguin Books 1963, 352.

14. *The Gospel of St Mark*, Penguin Books 1963, 316.

15. *The Gospel of St Luke*, Penguin Books 1963, 222. For further background to this passage see E. Stauffer, *Christ and the Caesars*, SCM Press 1955, 112–37.

16. See pp. 33f. above.

17. E.g. R. Schnackenburg, *The Moral Teaching of the New Testament*, Burns and Oates 1975, 50.

18. Ibid., 82.

19. E.g. Charles Villa-Vincencio, *The Theology of Apartheid*, Methodist Publishing House, Capetown 1977; Bishop Edmund Tutu, *On Trial*, John Paul Press 1982.

20. See Leo Pyle, *Pope and Pill*, Darton, Longman and Todd 1968.

21. Karl Barth, *Ethics*, T. & T. Clark 1981, 317.

22. Keith Ward, *Ethics and Christianity*, Allen & Unwin 1970, 199.

23. See Eric D'Arcy, *Conscience and its Right to Freedom*, Sheed & Ward 1961.

24. See James Gustafson, *Protestant and Roman Catholic Ethics*, SCM Press 1978, or, from the Catholic side, Charles Curran, *New Perspectives in Moral Theology*, Fides Press 1974.

25. A conservative work in ethics, purporting to be biblical, is F. E. Catherwood, *A Better Way*, Tyndale Press 1975. It is assessed by James Barr in *Fundamentalism*, SCM Press 1977, 117, as 'not very evangelical and not very Christian at all. Fundamentally it is a rational and prudential ethic of an eighteenth-century type to which a certain amount of Christian and biblical top dressing has been added.'

Chapter 4   The Development of Christian Social Teaching

1. Maurice Wiles, *The Christian Fathers*, SCM Press 1966, 167.

2. Ernst Troeltsch, *The Social Teaching of the Christian Churches* 1, Allen & Unwin 1931, 120.

3. Ibid., 159.

4. Thomas Cullinan, *Mine and Thine, Ours and Theirs*, Catholic Truth Society 1979, 3f.

5. G. E. Wright, *The Biblical Doctrine of Man in Society*, WCC 1954, 137.

6. Or possibly we moderns would agree with A. R. Vidler's thesis (in *Essays in Liberality*, 1957) that there is an essential rhythm in the Christian's attitude to the world: first of affirmation because it is created by God, second of negation because it is tainted by sin, and third of renewed

affirmation because it has been redeemed in principle by Christ.
7. Augustine, *City of God*, Penguin Books 1972, xvi.
8. Ibid., 593.
9. Except on one occasion, ibid., 524.
10. Stanley Evans, *The Social Hope of the Christian Church*, Hodder 1965, 99.
11. One of the major themes of D. Bonhoeffer, *Ethics*, SCM Press 1955.
12. Karl Barth, *The Church and the Political Problem of the Day*, Hodder 1939, 64.
13. E. G. Rupp, *The Righteousness of God*, Hodder 1953, 288.
14. A point which even Wolfhart Pannenberg has to concede: *Ethics*, Westminster Press 1981, 130.
15. Reinhold Niebuhr, *The Nature and Destiny of Man* II, Nisbet 1943, 204.
16. Troeltsch, op. cit., II, 577.
17. Calvin, *Institutes*, III, 10.
18. Max Weber, *The Protestant Ethic and the Spirit of Capitalism*, Scribner 1950.
19. R. H. Tawney, *Religion and the Rise of Capitalism*, Penguin Books 1938, 114.
20. G. M. Trevelyan, *English Social History*, Longmans Green 1944, 256.
21. Op. cit., 188.
22. Norman Sykes, *The English Religious Tradition*, SCM Press 1953, 59.
23. *Thoughts concerning the Origin of Power*, 1772, in Wesley's Works, fifth edition, John Mason, City Road, London 1863, XI, 46–53.
24. Thomas Madron, in Theodore Runyon (ed.), *Sanctification and Liberation*, Abingdon Press 1981. 115.
25. John Kent, in Runyon. op. cit., 84.
26. Sykes, op. cit., 91. See also Robert Wearmouth, *Methodism and Working Class Movements*, Epworth Press 1937; *Methodists and the Trade Unions*, 1959.
27. Hugh Price Hughes, *Social Christianity*, Hodder 1889, 8.
28. Henry Rack, *The Future of John Wesley's Methodism*, Lutterworth Press 1965, 30.
29. Sykes. op. cit., 89.
30. See A. R. Vidler, *The Theology of F. D. Maurice*, SCM Press 1948.
31. J. R. Moorman, *A History of the Church in England*, A. & C. Black 1953, 392.
32. Ibid., 393.
33. R. T. Handy, *A Handbook of Christian Theologians*, Meridian 1967, 211.
34. Reinhold Niebuhr, *Christian Realism and Political Problems*, Faber 1954, 107.
35. His thought is best outlined in Gordon Harland, *The Theology of Reinhold Niebuhr*, Oxford University Press 1960, but a larger assessment is available in R. W. Kegley and R. W. Brettall, *Reinhold Niebuhr. His Religious, Social and Political Thought*, Macmillan 1956.
36. *Religion and Change*, Hodder 1967, 187.

37. The strong thread linking him to Maurice is plain in M. Reckitt, *From Maurice to Temple*, Faber 1947.

38. W. Temple, *Christianity and the Social Order*, reprinted SPCK 1976, 65.

39. For this notion see R. H. Preston, *Explorations in Theology*, SCM Press 1981, ch. 3, and pp. 160f. below.

40. *Christ and Culture*, Harper and Row 1951.

Chapter 5   War and Violence

1. E.g. Matt. 5.38–48; 6.14f.; 18.21–35.

2. Luke 22.35–38; Matt. 26.50–54.

3. Matt. 22.15–21 and parallels; Matt. 17.24–27.

4. For this period especially see Roland Bainton, *Christian Attitudes towards War and Peace*, Abingdon 1960.

5. A competent recent example is John Ferguson, *The Politics of Love*, James Clarke 1973.

6. The most favourable view of them is expressed by G. M. Trevelyan, who calls them 'the first phase in that outward thrust of the restless and energetic races of the new Europe which was never to cease till it had overrun the globe, *History of England*, Longmans Green 1947, 163.

7. See Alan Wilkinson, *The Church of England and the First World War*, SPCK 1978.

8. *Christianity, Diplomacy and War*, Epworth Press 1953, 29, but see the whole chapter.

9. See Paul Ramsey, *The Just War*, Scribner 1968.

10. See Kenneth Slack, *George Bell*, SCM Press 1971. 94–6.

11. Alan Booth, *Not Only Peace*, SCM Press 1967, 70.

12. *Nevertheless: the Varieties of Religious Pacifism*, Herald Press 1971.

13. *The Liberated Zone*, SCM Press 1969.

14. Daniel Berrigan, *America is Hard to Find*, SPCK 1973, 104.

15. E.g. *Faith and Violence*, Notre Dame Press 1968.

16. An interesting instance is cited by Geoffrey Nuttall in *Christianity and Violence*, Priory Press 1972, 26f., the witness of a Czech named Chelcicky.

17. FOR. 9 Coombe Road, New Malden, Surrey.

18. His teaching is set out clearly in Satish Kumar, *Non-Violence or non-Existence*, Christian Action 1969.

19. Martin Luther King, *Strength to Love*, Fontana Books 1963. 52f.

20. Kenneth Slack, *Martin Luther King*, SCM Press 1970, 111, 115.

21. J. G. Davies, *Christians, Politics and Violent Revolution*, SCM Press 1976, is a thorough survey, but fails to give due weight to these distinctions.

22. *An Interpretation of Christian Ethics*, SCM Press 1936.

23. Niebuhr developed this more fully in *Moral Man and Immoral Society*, Scribner 1937 and SCM Press 1963.

24. Colin Morris, *Unyoung, Uncoloured, Unpoor*, Epworth Press 1969, 88.

25. Op. cit., 152.

26. Op. cit., 78.

27. Duke University Press 1961.

28. There is a useful summary in Sidney Bailey, *Christian Perspectives on Nuclear Weapons*, BCC 1981.

29. Alan Booth, *Christianity and Power Politics*, SCM Press 1961, 76.

30. Philip Toynbee (ed.), *The Fateful Choice*, Gollancz 1951.

31. *The Search for Security*, SCM Press 1972.

32. John Bennett (ed.), *Nuclear Weapons and the Conflict of Conscience*, Lutterworth Press 1962; John Bennett and H. Selfert (eds.), *US Foreign Policy and Christian Ethics*, Westminster Press 1977.

33. Richard Harries (ed.) *What Hope in an Armed World?*, Pickering and Inglis 1982, 108–11.

34. *The Church and the Bomb*, Hodder and Stoughton and CIO 1982.

35. *The Big Sin*, Marshall, Morgan and Scott 1982, 112–22.

36. *An Alternative to War or Surrender*, 1962.

37. Obtainable from the Division of Social Responsibility of the Methodist Church.

38. A favourite theme of theology in the 1960s, e.g. Hendrikus Berkhof, *Christ the Meaning of History*, SCM Press 1966, esp. ch. 5.

39. Andrew Kirk, *Theology encounters Revolution*, IVP 1980, is an admirable guide.

40. *Ethics*, SCM Press 1955, 314f. This was written between 1940 and 1943.

41. Quoted in J. G. Davies, op. cit., 57.

42. *Violence in Southern Africa*, SCM Press 1970, 77.

43. *Civil Strife*, General Synod Paper 28 May 1971.

44. Op. cit., 22.

45. M. Zeitlin (ed.), *Father Camilo Torres' Revolutionary Writings*, Harper Colophon 1972, 314f.

46. *World Conference on Church and Society*, WCC 1967, 200.

47. John Bennett (ed.) *Christian Ethics in a Changing World*, SCM Press 1966, 33.

48. *Theology Today*, April 1960, 27. See also his contribution to *When All Else Fails*, Pilgrim Press 1970.

49. S. G. F. Brandon, *Jesus and the Zealots*, Manchester University Press 1967.

50. Colin Morris, op. cit., 121.

51. *Was Jesus a Revolutionist?*, Fortress Press 1971; *Victory over Violence*, SPCK 1975; *Christians and Power*, Christian Journals 1977.

52. *Freedom Fighter or Prince of Peace?*, Study Encounter VIII, 4, 1972.

53. *Jesus across the Centuries*, SCM Press 1983, 53–66.

Chapter 6   Sexuality and Marriage

1. I Tim. 3.2; 3.12; Titus 1.6.

2. See N. P. Williams, *The Idea of the Fall and Original Sin*, Longmans 1927, lecture II.

3. Discussed in David Dungan, *The Sayings of Jesus in the Churches of Paul*, Blackwell 1971.

4. Work on these passages is conveniently summarized by Hugh Montefiore in Appendix 1 of *Marriage, Divorce and the Church*, rev. ed.

SPCK 1972.
5. There is a good brief outline in A. Kosnik (ed.), *Human Sexuality*, Search Press 1977.
6. E.g. Mark 10.7f.; I Cor. 7.14; I Peter 3.7.
7. For Augustine's position see N. P. Williams, op. cit., lectures V and VI.
8. The best two sources for this history are D. Sherwin Bailey, *The Man-Woman Relation in Christian Thought*, Longmans 1959; E. Schillebeeckx, *Marriage: Secular Reality and Saving Mystery*, Sheed and Ward 1965.
9. Interestingly Karl Barth's magisterial account of human sexuality is in *Church Dogmatics* III, 4, T. & T. Clark 1961, which is within his study of the doctrine of creation.
10. See *Marriage, Divorce and the Church*, appendix 3; Philip Sherrard, *Christianity and Eros*, SPCK 1976, is a modern Orthodox view.
11. See D. Sherwin Bailey, *Homosexuality in the Western Christian Tradition*, Longmans 1965.
12. The Reformers' handling of the Matthean exception is fully discussed in V. Olsen, *The New Testament Logia on Divorce*, J. C. B. Mohr 1971.
13. See A. R. Winnett, *Divorce and Remarriage in Anglicanism*, Macmillan 1958, and *The Church and Divorce*, Mowbray 1968.
14. Freud's wayward disciple Wilhelm Reich argued in *The Nature of the Orgasm* (1927) that failure to achieve orgasm caused a wide range of psychological disturbances.
15. A. Kinsey, *The Sexual Behaviour of the Human Male*, Saunders 1948; id., *The Sexual Behaviour of the Human Female*, Saunders 1953.
16. *Human Sexual Responses*, Churchill 1966.
17. E.g. Irving Singer, *The Goals of Human Sexuality*, Wildwood House 1973.
18. See Donald Goergen, *The Sexual Celibate*, SPCK 1976.
19. See A. E. Dyson, *Freedom in Love*, SPCK 1975.
20. As is obvious in Rachel Moss (ed.), *God's Yes to Sexuality*, Collins 1981, a BCC report.
21. Paras 50, 52.
22. Text in Leo Pyle, *Pope and Pill*, Darton, Longman and Todd 1968.
23. Charles Curran, *Issues in Sexual and Medical Ethics*, Notre Dame 1978, 189.
24. *The Family in Contemporary Society*, SPCK 1958, 122, 131.
25. *The Mystery of Love and Marriage*, SCM Press 1947.
26. *The Ethics of Sex*, James Clarke 1964.
27. Barth, op. cit., 268ff.
28. *Christian Uncertainties*, Hodder 1975, 118.
29. *Selected Essays*, Collins 1939, 259.
30. *Putting Asunder*, SPCK 1966.
31. Op. cit., 36.
32. Helen Oppenheimer, *The Marriage Bond*, Faith Press 1976.
33. *Marriage and the Church's Task*, CIO 1978.
34. E.g. Cheslyn Jones (ed.), *For Better for Worse*, Church Union ²1977.
35. E.g. Geoffrey Bromiley, *God and Marriage*, T. & T. Clark 1981.
36. *The Church and the Law of Nullity of Marriage*, SPCK 1955.

37. *The Feminine Mystique*, Gollancz 1963, Penguin Books 1965.

38. E.g. Rachel Moss, *God's Yes to Sexuality*.

39. See Walter Trobisch, *I married You*, IVP 1972, or Larry Christenson, *The Christian Family*, Fountain Trust 1973.

40. See the summary in D. J. West, *Homosexuality*, Duckworth 1977.

41. Fully described in Peter Coleman, *Christian Attitudes to Homosexuality*, SPCK 1980.

42. E.g. John McNeill, *The Church and the Homosexual*, Darton, Longman and Todd 1977.

43. E.g. Green, Holloway and Watson, *The Church and Homosexuality*, Hodder 1980.

44. Letha Scanzoni and Virginia Mollenkott, *Is the Homosexual my Neighbour?*, SCM Press 1978.

45. *Time for Consent*, SCM Press [3]1976.

46. *A Christian Understanding of Human Sexuality*, Division of Social Responsibility.

47. *Homosexual Relationships*, CIO 1979.

48. *The Lord is my Shepherd and He knows I'm Gay*, Bantam Books 1973.

49. Edward Shorter, *The Making of the Modern Family*, Collins 1976.

50. *Sex and Morality*, SCM Press 1966.

51. *Living with Sex*, SCM Press 1967, 132.

52. Op. cit., 139.

53. *Proposals for a New Sexual Ethics*, Darton, Longman and Todd 1977, 86.

Chapter 7   Theories Many

1. The most helpful introductory works in current moral philosophy are: J. L. Mackie, *Ethics: Inventing Right and Wrong*, Penguin Books 1977; G. J. Warnock, *Contemporary Moral Philosophy*, Macmillan 1967; Mary Warnock, *Ethics since 1900*, Oxford 1960; W. D. Hudson, *Modern Moral Philosophy*, Macmillan 1970; id., *A Century of Moral Philosophy*, Lutterworth Press 1980; B. Williams, *Morality: An Introduction to Ethics*, Cambridge 1972.

2. Mary Warnock, op. cit., 145.

3. Jose Miguez Bonino, *Christians and Marxists*, Hodder 1976, 115f.

4. *Rules, Roles and Relations*, Macmillan 1966, 147.

5. *Situation Ethics*, SCM Press.

6. SCM Press 1963, 1964. The latter was later included in *Christian Freedom in a Permissive Society*, SCM Press 1970.

7. Such criticism is powerfully argued in e.g. Paul Ramsey, *Deeds and Rules in Christian Ethics*, Oliver & Boyd 1965; J. Austin Baker, *The Foolishness of God*, Darton, Longman and Todd 1970, 94ff.

8. A criticism made especially by the Roman Catholic Bernard Häring.

9. Baker, op. cit., argues that 'love' alone is never an adequate guide.

10. Op. cit., 20.

11. *Three Issues in Ethics*, SCM Press 1970, 13.

12. *Situation Ethics*, 94.

13. *Honest to God*, 115.

14. *Ethics in a Christian Context*, Harper and Row 1963.
15. *Moral Decisions*, Darton, Longman and Todd 1980.
16. Op. cit., 44.
17. *A Christian Method of Moral Judgment*, SCM Press 1976.
18. Wogaman's work in the field of social ethics is valuable. See e.g. *Christians and the Great Economic Debate*, SCM Press 1977.

Chapter 8   Ethics and the Churches Today

1. *Built as a City*, Hodder 1974, 99.
2. John Stott, *I Believe in Preaching*, Hodder 1982, 36.
3. See Horton Davies, *Worship and Theology in England* IV, Oxford University Press 1962, 311–22.
4. See Roger Lloyd, *The Church of England 1900–1965*, SCM Press 1966, 306–8.
5. Charles West, in *A Dictionary of Christian Ethics*, ed. John Macquarrie, SCM Press 1967, 98.
6. See Chapter 4 above.
7. *Explorations in Theology* 9, SCM Press 1981, Chapter 3.
8. Op. cit., viii.
9. *The Churches Survey Their Task*, Allen and Unwin 1937, 94.
10. All published by SCM Press 1966.
11. Official Report, WCC 1967, 49.
12. *Who Speaks for the Church?*, St Andrew Press 1967.
13. See *Christian Noncomformity in International Affairs*, Epworth Press 1970, 29.
14. R. H. Preston (ed.) *Technology and Social Justice*, SCM Press 1971, 34.
15. See Richard Fagley, *The Population Explosion and Christian Responsibility*, Oxford 1960.
16. Theodore Roszak, *The Makings of a Counter Culture*, Faber 1970.
17. *The Limits to Growth*, Universe Books 1972.
18. Egbert de Vries, *Technology and Social Justice*, 53.
19. See Michael Taylor (ed.), *Christians and the Future of Social Democracy*, G. W. & A. Hesketh 1982, 103.
20. E. R. Norman, *Christianity and World Order*, Oxford University Press 1979, 2.
21. Op. cit., 19, 84.
22. Kenneth Wilson (ed.) *Christian Faith and Political Hopes*, Epworth Press 1980.
23. *Amsterdam to Nairobi*, Georgetown University Press 1979.
24. Kenneth Sansbury, *Combatting Racism*, BCC 1975.
25. A semi-official report, Elisabeth Adler, *A Small Beginning*, WCC 1974, showed few signs of such sensitivity.
26. Rodger Charles, *The Christian Social Conscience*, Mercier Press 1970, 88.
27. Trevor Beeson, *Discretion and Valour*, Fontana Books, rev. ed. 1982, 381.
28. A critique powerfully made by Charles Curran, *Catholic Moral Theology in Dialogue*, Fides 1972, 116–25. Recent Protestant reflection is

well put in G. R. Dunstan (ed.) *Duty and Discernment*, SCM Press 1973.

29. See Gibson Winter (ed.), *Social Ethics*, SCM Press 1968, 225–30.

30. E.g. *In Search of a Theology of Development*, WCC 1970.

31. Full text in Alain Gheerbrant, *The Rebel Church in Latin America*, Penguin Books 1974, 170–80.

32. Published by the Catholic Truth Society.

33. *The Challenge of Peace: God's Promise and Our Response*, CTS and SPCK.

34. On this point see Daniel Jenkins, *The British: Their Identity and their Religion*, SCM Press 1975, Chapter II.

35. Published by CIO.

36. Published by CIO.

37. Published by CIO.

38. Published by CIO.

39. Op. cit., 124, 128.

40. Published by SCM Press.

41. Gerald Burt in the Foreword to the 1981 collection of these statements, published by the Methodist Division of Social Responsibility.

42. A hint that a wider scope was needed came in 1937 when selections from John Wesley's teaching were published: E. C. Urwin and Douglas Wollen (eds.), *John Wesley, Christian Citizen*, Epworth Press 1937.

43. See John Atkinson (ed.), *Abortion Reconsidered*, Methodist Division of Social Responsibility 1977.

44. Reports published by SCM Press.

45. See John Vincent, *Christ in a Nuclear World*, Crux Press 1962.

46. Trevor Beeson, Fontana Books 1978.

47. James Gustafson, *Protestant and Roman Catholic Ethics*, SCM Press 1978, 29.

48. Ibid., 146.

49. Mark Santer (ed.), *Their Lord and Ours*, SPCK 1982, 75.

50. Published by Christian Journals 1976.

51. *Public Statement on Moral Issues*, BCC and Catholic Information Services 1978.

Chapter 9   Some Current Problems

1. O. Frederick Nolde, *Free and Equal*, WCC 1968, 7.

2. Maurice Cranston, *What are Human Rights?*, Bodley Head 1973, draws a distinction between judicial/legal rights and inalienable rights. Here the former are being considered.

3. 88A Islington High Street, London N1 8FG.

4. 10 Southampton Street, London WC2E 7HF.

5. See *Human Rights in a One-Party State*, Search Press 1978.

6. 36 Craven Street, London WC2N 5NG.

7. Para 9.

8. Paul Ramsey, *Basic Christian Ethics*, SCM Press 1950, 354.

9. *Study Encounter*, WCC, X.2, 1974.

10. *Study Encounter*, WCC XI.3, 1975.

11. *Human Rights. Our Understanding and our Responsibilities*, CIO 1977.

12. See A. F. Carrillo de Albernoz, *The Basis of Religious Liberty*, SCM Press 1963.

13. Thomas S. Derr, *Ecology and Human Liberation*, WSCF 1973, 34f.

14. See *Decisions about Life and Death*, CIO 1965, appendix 3.

15. Paul Ramsey, *The Patient as Person*, Yale University Press 1970.

16. See *Truthfulness and Tragedy*, University of Notre Dame Press 1977, 127ff.

17. Op. cit., 184ff.

18. See J. A. T. Robinson. *Christian Freedom in a Permissive Society*, SCM Press 1970, 54.

19. There are exceptions. Bernard Häring, *Medical Ethics*, St Paul Publications 1974, 82 comments: 'I think it can be said that at least before the twenty-fifth to fortieth day the embryo cannot yet (with certainty) be considered as a human person'.

20. G. R. Dunstan, *The Artifice of Ethics*, SCM Press 1974, 80.

21. *Abortion, An Ethical Discussion*, CIO 1965.

22. *Ethics*, SCM Press 1955, 144.

23. Hugh Trowell, *The Unfinished Debate on Euthanasia*, SCM Press 1973.

24. See the Anglican report *On Dying Well* (1975) or the Methodist Conference Statement (1974).

25. *Human Reproduction*, BCC 1962; Norman Anderson, *Issues of Life and Death*, Hodder 1976, 51; John Atkinson, *Doctors' Dilemmas*, Epworth Press 1976, 48.

26. D. Gareth Jones, *Genetic Engineering*, Grove Books 1978, 16.

27. A powerful exposition of this whole case is set out in Paul Ramsey, *Fabricated Man*, Yale University Press 1970.

28. Dunstan, op. cit., 66.

29. *Issues in Sexual and Medical Ethics*, University of Notre Dame Press 1978, 87.

30. E. F. Shotter (ed.), *Matters of Life and Death*, Darton, Longman and Todd 1970, 59.

31. See Herbert Butterfield, *The Origins of Modern Science*, Bell 1951.

32. *Technology, Faith and the Future of Man*, WCC, 30.

33. *A Working Faith*, Darton, Longman and Todd 1980, 80.

34. *Can Man Survive?*, Fontana Books 1970, 75.

35. Argued cogently in J. Austin Baker, *The Foolishness of God*, Darton, Longman and Todd 1970.

36. Roger Shinn, in *Facing up to Nuclear Power*, ed. John Francis and Paul Abrecht, St Andrew Press 1976, 148.

37. *Christian Life-Style*, Mowbray 1976, 18.

38. Oddly, one of the best statements on Christian traditions in this matter is by an agnostic, John Black, *The Dominion of Man*, St Andrew Press 1970.

39. Helmut Gollwitzer, *The Rich Christians and Poor Lazarus*, St Andrew Press 1970, 92.

40. *North-South. A Programme for Survival*, Pan 1980.

41. *Enough is Enough*, SCM Press 1975.

42. *Rich Christians in an Age of Hunger*, Hodder 1977, 99.

43. *Lifestyle in the Eighties*, Paternoster Press 1982, 16.

44. Details from the Dean, Bristol Cathedral.

Chapter 10   Ethics in Church Life

1. This is the central theme of Paul Lehmann, *Ethics in a Christian Context*, Harper and Row 1963. But it is rare to find much reference to worship (or evangelism) in books on Christian ethics. James Pike's *Doing the Truth*, Gollancz 1966, is an interesting exception (see Chapter 9), but the discussion is very superficial.

2. *Christ and the Moral Life*, Chicago University Press 1968, 268.

3. J. D. G. Dunn, *Unity and Diversity in the New Testament*, SCM Press 1977, 230.

4. Mervyn Wilshaw in *The Testing of the Churches*, ed. Rupert Davies, Epworth Press 1982, 187.

5. John Stott, *I Believe in Preaching*, Hodder 1982, 82.

6. Ibid., 138.

7. Ibid., 171.

8. *Preaching Reassessed*, Epworth Press 1980, 87.

9. Ibid., 125.

10. Jack Keiser, in *Industrial Conflicts*, ed. R. H. Preston, SCM Press 1974, 115.

11. *Perspectives on Strikes*, SCM Press 1975.

12. See Adrian Hastings, *Christian Marriage in Africa*, SPCK 1973.

13. *Doom or Deliverance*, Manchester University Press 1972, 25.

14. The parables of Jesus occasion such a vast scholarly literature that an introduction is needed to it all. An admirable one, which gives a clear account of the nature of the parable, is A. M. Hunter's article 'The Interpreter and the Parables', reprinted in Richard Batey (ed.), *New Testament Issues*, SCM Press 1970, 71–87.

15. *Inflation and the Compromised Church*, Christian Journals 1975, 117.

16. Clifford Hill and David Mathews (eds.), *Race: A Christian Symposium*, Gollancz 1968, 184.

17. Rupert Davies, *The Church in Our Times*, Epworth Press 1979, 123ff.

18. *Free and Faithful in Christ*, Vol. 2, St Paul Publications 1979, 3.

19. *The Law of Christ*, III, Newman Press 1966, 566–76.

20. The argument occurs in Immanuel Kant, *Critique of Pure Reason*, Beck edition, Chicago 1945, 346–50, in a section entitled 'On a supposed right to lie from altruistic motives'.

21. *Ethics*, SCM Press 1955, 332.

22. Op. cit., 129.

23. *Life Together*, SCM Press 1954, 102.

Index